800 Great Places to Stay

in Britain

The Best of British Holidays

Full range of family accommodation

Duddings Country Cottages, Dunster, Somerset

Bosinver Farm Cottages, Trelowth, St Austell, Cornwall

2013

www.holidayguides.com

Contents

England

Board

SOUTH WEST ENGLAND

LONDON & SOUTH EAST ENGLAND

EAST OF ENGLAND

EAST MIDLANDS

HEART OF ENGLAND

YORKSHIRE

NORTH EAST ENGLAND

NORTH WEST ENGLAND

Self-Catering

SOUTH WEST ENGLAND

SOUTH EAST ENGLAND

EAST OF ENGLAND

EAST MIDLANDS

HEART OF ENGLAND

YORKSHIRE

NORTH EAST ENGLAND

NORTH WEST ENGLAND

Caravans & Camping

Wales

Board

Self-Catering

Caravans & Camping

Scotland

Board

Self-Catering

Caravans & Camping

Ireland

Caravans & Camping

Pubs & Inns

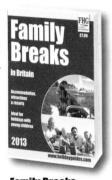
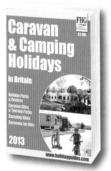

Cornwall

High Cross Farm　Lanivet, Near Bodmin PL30 5JR

Bed and Breakfast accommodation in either Victorian farmhouse or newly restored barn.
Two ground floor en suites in barn; two en suite rooms in farmhouse, plus one with private bathroom.
Surrounded by fields and ample off-road parking.
Lanivet is the geographical centre of Cornwall and thereby
excellent for touring the moor and North and South coasts.
Close to the Eden Project, Lanhydrock House,
Lost Gardens of Heligan. Full English breakfast –
special diets catered for. Non-smoking. Excellent facilities.

Tel: 01208 831341 • Mrs Joy Rackham

The Old Coach House

Relax in a 300 year old former coach house now tastefully equipped to meet
the needs of the new millennium with all rooms en suite, colour TVs,
refreshment trays and central heating. Good cooking. This picturesque village is
a haven for walkers with its dramatic coastal scenery, a photographer's dream,
and an ideal base to tour both the north and south coasts.
The area is famed for its sandy
beaches and surfing whilst
King Arthur's Tintagel is only
three miles away.
Come and enjoy a friendly
holiday with people who care.
Large garden and patio area.
- *Bed and Breakfast from £35-£39pp*
- *Non-smoking*
- *Accessible for disabled guests.*

**Geoff and Jackie Horwell, The Old Coach House,
Tintagel Road, Boscastle PL35 0AS
Tel: 01840 250398 • Fax: 01840 250346
e-mail: stay@old-coach.co.uk • www.old-coach.co.uk**

Bude

Fowey, Lostwithiel

Mawgan Porth

SB

Wi-Fi

Blue Bay
HOTEL, RESTAURANT & LODGES

**Trenance, Mawgan Porth,
Cornwall TR8 4DA
Tel: 01637 860324
e-mail: hotel@bluebaycornwall.co.uk
www.bluebaycornwall.co.uk**

Blue Bay offers two different styles of accommodation across two different sites, beautifully situated in a tranquil location between Padstow and Newquay, overlooking Mawgan Porth beach.

Blue Bay Lodges
Five individually designed Cornish lodges, open all year round. The lodges are located in the heart of Mawgan Porth, overlooking the Vale of Lanherne and beach. All fully equipped (sleep 4-8) with own balcony or patio area. Linen, towels, electricity incl. Laundry room. Dogs welcome.

Blue Bay Hotel
Located in Trenance on the cliff tops overlooking Mawgan Porth beach, the hotel has two garden rooms, two family suites, one family room and one double room, all en suite. Twin and single rooms available.

**Hotel prices
from £38pppn
Lodge prices from
£50 per Lodge per night.**

symbols ⚞🐴SB&♉Wi-Fi

🐕	Pets Welcome	🐴	Children Welcome
SB	Short Breaks	♿	Suitable for Disabled Guests
♉	Licensed	Wi-Fi	Wi-Fi available

Lynn & Les Cox

Bolankan Cottage stands on the main A30 trunk road approximately half way between Penzance and Land's End.

SB

Wi-Fi

The cottage has been fully modernised with double, twin and family rooms, all en suite with central heating, colour TV, hairdryer and tea/coffee making facilities. Off-road parking. Pets welcome.

B&B from £65 per room based on 2 sharing.

Crows-an-Wra, St Buryan, Penzance TR19 6HU • 01736 810168

bolankancottage@talktalk.net • www.bolankan-cottage.co.uk

We are sure you will enjoy your time in Cornwall while staying at Bolankan Cottage.

SB

Polgreen is a family-run dairy farm nestling
in the Pentewan Valley in an Area of
Outstanding Natural Beauty. One mile from
the coast and four miles from the
picturesque fishing village of Mevagissey, a
perfect location for a relaxing holiday in the
glorious Cornish countryside.
Centrally situated, Polgreen is ideally
placed for touring all of Cornwall's many attractions; Cornish
Way Leisure Trail adjoining farm. Within a few minutes' drive
of the spectacular Eden Project and Heligan Gardens.
All rooms with private facilities, colour TV, tea/coffee making
facilities. Guest lounge. Children welcome.
Terms from £30 per person per night.

Mrs Liz Berryman, Polgreen Farm, London Apprentice,
St Austell PL26 7AP • Tel: 01726 75151
e-mail: polgreen.farm@btinternet.com
www.polgreenfarm.co.uk

Dalswinton House

St. Mawgan-in-Pydar, Cornwall TR8 4EZ. Tel: 01637 860385
www.dalswinton.com • dalswintonhouse@btconnect.com

HOLIDAYS FOR DOGS AND THEIR OWNERS

Overlooking the village of St Mawgan, Dalswinton House stands in
10 acres of gardens and meadowland midway between Padstow and
Newquay with distant views to the sea at dog-friendly Mawgan Porth.

- Dogs free of charge and allowed everywhere except the restaurant
- 8 acre meadow for dog exercise. Nearby local walks. Beach 1.5 miles
- Heated outdoor pool (May-Sep). Off street car parking
- All rooms en suite with tea/coffee fac., digital TV and clock radios
- Wifi access in public rooms and all bedrooms (except the lodge)
- Residents' bar and restaurant serving breakfast and dinner
- Bed and breakfast from £46 per person per night
- Weekly rates available and special offers in Mar/Apr/May/Oct
- Self-catering lodge sleeps 3 adults
- Easy access to Padstow, Eden Project, Newquay Airport & Coastal Path

Regret no children under 16
Maximum 3 dogs per room at proprietor's discretion

Bampton

Devon

SB

Think of Devon, and wild moorland springs to mind, but this is a county of contrasts, with the wild moors of the Exmoor National Park to the north fringed by dramatic cliffs and combes, golden beaches and picturesque harbours, and busy market towns and sleepy villages near the coast. The award-winning resort of Woolacombe has everything to offer for a traditional family holiday, while Ilfracombe, originally a Victorian resort, provides all kinds of family entertainment including an annual Victorian festival. An experience not to be missed is the cliff railway between the pretty little port of Lynmouth and its twin village of Lynton high on the cliff, with a backdrop of dramatic gorges or combes.

Our breathtaking venues, in the heart of Devon, boast a range of craft, sport & leisure facilities that we believe are without equal anywhere in the UK!

The **Manor** House Hotel
&
The **Ashbury** Hotel

As Seen On TV!

Facilities FREE to residents of both hotels

Sports	Racket Sports	Family
Bowls	Tennis	Funhouse
Table Tennis	Badminton	Gamezone
5-A-Side	Squash	Waterslides
Basketball	Short Tennis	Play Area
Leisure	**Ranges**	**Golf**
Swimming	Archery	3 x 18 Hole Courses
Spa & Sauna	Air Pistols	3 x 9 Hole Courses
Snooker	Air Rifles	18 Hole Par 3 Course
Ten-Pin	Laser Clays	Practice Facilities

+ Unique Craft Centre with Pottery, Woodwork & Hot Press Printing.
(Minimal Costs Apply)

Spring Breaks - 3nts from £212   4nts from £251
Summer Breaks - 3nts from £253   4nts from £284
Autumn Breaks - 3nts from £205   4nts from £234
Winter Breaks - 3nts from £142   4nts from £168
(Prices - 3 nights weekend & 4 nights midweek)

All rooms en-suite · Full board · Child rates · Party discounts

0800 118 2674 sportsandleisurebreaks.co.uk

Barnstaple

Lee House is a secluded Elizabethan Manor House set in 8 acres of gardens, woods and paddocks. Approached by a long private drive, it is surrounded by rolling Devon countryside, and the gardens overlook Clovelly and Hartland Point in the far distance across Barnstaple Bay.

LEE HOUSE
Marwood, Barnstaple
EX31 4DZ
Tel: 01271 374345

Lee House is a small, friendly guesthouse, family-run for over 40 years. The three bedrooms are large and comfortable, and all face south overlooking the valley.

One four-poster, one double and one twin; all en suite, with bath, tea/coffee making facilities and central heating. A traditional English breakfast is served in the elegant south-facing dining room. There is ample safe parking for cars in front of the house.

Bed and Breakfast from £30pppn, two or more nights from £28pppn.

e-mail: michael.darling74@gmail.com

SB

Graham and Liz White, **Bulworthy Cottage**, Stony Cross, Alverdiscott, Near Bideford EX39 4PY

Tel: 01271 858441

Once three 17th century miner's cottages, Bulworthy has been sympathetically renovated to modern standards whilst retaining many original features. Our twin and double guest rooms both offer en suite accommodation, with central heating,colour TV, and many other extras. Relax in the garden with views across the countryside to Exmoor. Standing in quiet countryside, Bulworthy is within easy reach of the moors, Tarka Trail, South West Coastal Path, Rosemoor and numerous National Trust properties. We offer a choice of breakfasts and evening meals, using home grown and local produce. A selection of wines and beers to complement your evening meal is available.

B&B from £34pppn.

e-mail: bulworthy@aol.com • www.bulworthycottage.co.uk

FREE or **REDUCED RATE** entry to Holiday Visits and Attractions – see our **READERS' OFFER VOUCHERS** on pages 389-400

The FHG Directory of Website Addresses

on pages 381-387 is a useful quick reference guide for holiday accommodation with e-mail and/or website details

Please note...

All the information in this book is given in good faith in the belief that it is correct. However, the publishers cannot guarantee the facts given in these pages, neither are they responsible for changes in policy, ownership or terms that may take place after the date of going to press. Readers should always satisfy themselves that the facilities they require are available and that the terms, if quoted, still apply.

Bideford

Dartmouth, Dawlish

Cladda is Gold award-winning quality 4-Star B&B, with double and twin rooms plus two-room suites (bedroom and living room).

In Dartmouth town with on-site (off-road) parking, just a stroll to the waterfront, restaurants and shops.

Varied, quality breakfasts using locally sourced produce.

Wi-Fi

88-90 Victoria Road and Ford Valley, Dartmouth TQ6 9EF

Tel: 01803 835957 / 07967 060003

info@cladda-dartmouth.co.uk • www.cladda-dartmouth.co.uk

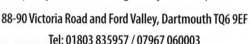

The South Devon Hotel with a Different Outlook...

- Family Friendly
- 66 En suite Bedrooms
- Indoor & Outdoor pools
- Magnificent Sea Views
- Relaxation Therapies
- Fitness Room
- Hairdresser • Tennis • Snooker
- Table Tennis
- Licensed Bars
- Extensive Lounges
- 19 Acres of Grounds

Langstone Cliff Hotel

AA ★★★ HOTEL

Dawlish • South • Devon • EX7 0NA

Telephone 01626 868000

www.langstone-hotel.co.uk

symbols

	Pets Welcome		Children Welcome
SB	Short Breaks		Suitable for Disabled Guests
♉	Licensed	Wi-Fi	Wi-Fi available

Exeter

DEVONCOURT HOTEL
& APARTMENTS

Standing in four acres of mature subtropical gardens, overlooking two miles of sandy beach, yet within easy reach of Dartmoor and Exeter, Devoncourt provides an ideal base for a family holiday at any time of year.

ACCOMMODATION: comprises luxury en suite bedrooms (single, double/twin and family), all with tea/coffee making and TV/DVD. In addition there are one and two bedroom self-catering apartments, with excellent furnishings and well-equipped kitchenettes; many with sea views/balconies.

AMENITIES: include swimming pool, sauna, steam room, whirlpool spa, solarium and fitness centre, snooker room, hair salon.

OUT OF DOORS: tennis court, croquet lawn, attractive outdoor heated pool, 18-hole putting green, all within the grounds.

OUTLOOK: palm trees and uninterrupted sea views of the Bay form a Continental landscape to this first-class hotel in the delightful Devon resort of Exmouth.

RESTAURANT: Brasserie 16, overlooking the gardens and coastline, offers a friendly welcome, good food and good service.

DEVONCOURT HOTEL
& APARTMENTS
Douglas Avenue, Exmouth, Devon EX8 2EX
Tel: 01395 272277
e-mail: enquiries@devoncourt.com • www.devoncourthotel.com

Kingsbridge, Lifton

Pittaford Farm Bed & Breakfast

Pittaford is a beautiful Devonshire 17th century farmhouse set in peaceful countryside on a family farm 1½ miles from the pretty village of Slapton, 2 miles from the coast and beaches. Guests have their own cosy sitting room with TV, DVD, books and games, and log fire for chilly evenings.

Wi-Fi One double and one twin en suite bedrooms with tea/coffee making facilities, hairdryer and TV; views over the garden to the fields and meadows.

Child's bed and cot available. Pets by prior arrangement.

£32 - £38 per person per night including breakfast.

Pittaford Farm B&B • Slapton • Kingsbridge • Devon TQ7 2QG
• Tel: 01548 580357 • Mob 07585 375069 • www.pittafordbandb.co.uk

The Lifton Hall Hotel and Village Inn

Lifton, Devon PL16 0DR

A family-run hotel where old-fashioned values of service, style and comfort can still be enjoyed. On the Devon/Cornwall border, ½ mile off the A30, it offers the perfect opportunity to explore the West Country.

The tastefully furnished bedrooms have en suite bath or shower and a full range of amenities; there is also a light and airy residents' lounge, a stylish dining room and a cosy bar with open fire.

Meals are an essential part of the Lifton Hall experience, with something to suit every taste and appetite, using only the best quality local produce. A carefully chosen and reasonably priced wine list provides the perfect accompaniment.

Tel: 01566 784863 Fax: 01566 784770

relax@liftonhall.co.uk www.liftonhall.co.uk

Visit the FHG website
www.holidayguides.com
for all kinds of holiday
accommodation in Britain

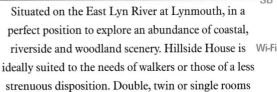

Pinn Barton, Peak Hill, Sidmouth EX10 0NN

Peace, comfort and a warm welcome where we offer the little extras that attract guests back time and time again. Two miles from Sidmouth seafront. Lovely coastal walks and views from the farm. Warm and comfortable en suite bedrooms with TV, fridge, beverage trays and access at all times.

SB

Wi-Fi

**Open all year • No smoking
Children welcome**

One twin, one double and
one family room available.
Terms from £34 to £36 per person.

**Mrs Betty S. Sage
Tel & Fax: 01395 514004
e-mail: betty@pinnbartonfarm.co.uk
www.pinnbartonfarm.co.uk**

The Glenorleigh

26 Cleveland Road
Torquay, Devon TQ2 5BE
Tel: 01803 292135
Fax: 01803 213717

As featured on BBC Holiday programme
David & Pam Skelly
AA ★★★★

SB

Wi-Fi

Situated in a quiet residential area, Glenorleigh is 10 minutes' walk from both the sea front and the town centre. • Delightful en suite rooms, with your comfort in mind. • Digital flat screen TVs and free Wi-Fi internet access. • Good home cooking, both English and Continental, plenty of choice, with vegetarian options available daily. • Bar leading onto terrace overlooking Mediterranean-style garden with feature palms and heated swimming pool.
• Brochures and menus available on request • Discounts for children and Senior Citizens. • B&B £35–£45pp; Dinner £16.

**e-mail: glenorleighhotel@btinternet.com
www.glenorleigh.co.uk**

Torquay

Lanscombe House

Cockington Village, South Devon TQ2 6XA

Five Star Lanscombe House is now completely refurbished and transformed into the kind of place we have enjoyed staying in over the years. Tucked away in a quiet spot amongst the famous thatches of Cockington Village in beautiful South Devon and not far from Torquay. Our emphasis has been on retaining the original Country House ambience with individually decorated rooms, period and reproduction furniture complemented by quality en suites. We are just a short stroll to the sea and central to Torbay – an enviable oasis of peace and tranquillity on the English Riviera.　　Leon & Paula Butler.

Tel: 01803 606938 · www.lanscombehouse.co.uk · e-mail: stay@lanscombehouse.co.uk

Dorset

Bournemouth

Bournemouth B&B
Southernhay
Hotel

42 Alum Chine Rd, Westbourne,
Bournemouth BH4 8DX
Tel & Fax: 01202 761251

The Southernhay Hotel provides warm, friendly, high standard accommodation with a large car park and a hearty breakfast. All rooms have central heating, colour TV with Freeview, tea/coffee making facilities and hairdryer. Six bedrooms, four en suite.

The hotel is ideally situated in Westbourne, within walking distance of many bars, restaurants and designer shops. Across the road a path leads through Alum Chine wood, down to miles of safe sandy beaches. The Bournemouth International Centre, cinemas, theatres, restaurants, clubs and pubs are all within easy reach; minutes by car or the frequent bus service. Open all year.

Details from Tom and Lynn Derby. 2 for 1 Golf deals available

**Bed and Breakfast from £20 to £30 per adult per night.
Contact Tom or Lynn for last minute offers.**

enquiries@southernhayhotel.co.uk · www.southernhayhotel.co.uk

Charmouth, Dorchester

SB

Wi-Fi

Cardsmill
Farm Holidays
**Whitchurch Canonicorum,
Charmouth, Bridport,
Dorset DT6 6RP
Tel & Fax: 01297 489375
e-mail: cardsmill@aol.com
www.farmhousedorset.com**

Stay on a real working family farm in the Marshwood Vale, an Area of Outstanding Natural Beauty. Enjoy country walks to the village, coast and around farm and woods. Watch the daily milking, see baby calves and lambs, and seasonal activities here on this 590-acre farm. En suite family, double and twin rooms available, with CTV, tea/coffee trays. *B&B £32-£40pppn.* ETC ★★★★

Also available,four large, rural, quiet farmhouses/barn conversions. Private gardens, conservatories and ample parking. Three-four miles from coast.
•TAPHOUSE has 6 bedrooms, 4 bathrooms. Sleeps 16. Games barn, lounge, 22'x15' kitchen/diner. Hot tub.
•COURTHOUSE DAIRY has 4 bedrooms,3 bathrooms. Sleeps 11. Games barn, large kitchen/lounge and dining room in conservatory. Hot tub.
•THE STABLE and HAYLOFT barn conversions 2010 and 2011, each has 3 bedrooms and 3 bathrooms, some en suite. Each will sleep 6 and 7.
Dogs welcome.Cots and high chairs in each house. Available all year for long or short stays. Check the website or telephone for more details.

Westwood House

SB

**29 High West Street, Dorchester DT1 1UP
01305 268018 • www.westwoodhouse.co.uk
reservations@westwoodhouse.co.uk**

Wi-Fi

Personally run by owners, Tom and Demelza Stevens, Westwood House offers comfortable, informal, non-smoking accommodation.
Each bedroom has digital TV, complimentary wi-fi, and tea/coffee making.
Breakfast is served in the light and airy conservatory.

*A variety of pubs, restaurants and cafes are just a short stroll away.
The lovely market town of Dorchester has many places of historical interest, and is an ideal base for exploring the Dorset coast and countryside.*

Nethercroft
Winterbourne Abbas, Dorchester DT2 9LU

SB

This country house with its friendly and homely atmosphere welcomes you to the heart of Hardy's Wessex. Central for touring the many places of interest that Dorset has to offer, including Corfe Castle, Lyme Regis, Dorchester, Weymouth, Lulworth Cove, etc. Lovely country walks and many local attractions.

Two double rooms, one single, en suite or separate bathroom. TV lounge, dining room. Large garden. Open all year. Central heating. Car essential, ample parking.

Bed and Breakfast from £30.

Take A35 from Dorchester, we are the last house at the western edge of the village.

Mrs V.A. Bradbeer • Tel: 01305 889337
e-mail: val.bradbeer@btconnnect.com
www.nethercroft.com

The Alessandria
71 Wakeham, Easton, Portland DT5 1HW

Highly recommended by our guests

Good old fashioned friendly service and good value

15 BEDROOMS • MOST EN SUITE. 2 on ground floor.
All with tea/coffee, colour television, some rooms with sea views
Spacious en suite family rooms.
Comfortable accommodation • Friendly atmosphere
Quiet location • Reasonable prices • Free Parking
Vegetarians catered for. • Under same management for 23 years

Tel: Giovanni 01305 822270 • Fax: 01305 820561• www.alessandriahotel.co.uk

SB

Wi-Fi

SB

Wi-Fi

A peaceful oasis and wonderful atmosphere
where families matter

~

Easy access to three miles of golden beach
Outdoor pool (level deck), golf and tennis for all ages
Health Spa with plunge pool and sauna

~

Connecting rooms for families with children
Separate younger children's restaurant
Playroom and fabulous Adventure Playground

~

Open Easter to January including Christmas and New Year. Dogs welcome.

STUDLAND BAY
DORSET
BH19 3AH
01929 · 450450
info@knollhouse.co.uk
www.knollhouse.co.uk

ONLY
2 HOURS
FROM
HEATHROW

In Dorset on the south coast, there are resorts to suit everyone, from traditional, busy Bournemouth with 10 kilometres of sandy beach and a wide choice of entertainment, shopping and dining, to the quieter seaside towns of Seatown, Mudeford and Barton-on-Sea, and Charmouth with its shingle beach. Lulworth Cove is one of several picturesque little harbours. Fossil hunters of all age groups are attracted by the spectacular cliffs of the Jurassic Coast, a World Heritage Site, and walkers can enjoy the wonderful views from the South West Coast Path at the top.

Cheltenham

Gloucestershire

Parkview Guest House
4 Pittville Crescent, Cheltenham GL52 2QZ

Parkview is a fine Regency guesthouse which stands in Cheltenham's nicest area, only 10 minutes' walk from the centre. The bedrooms are large and airy and have TV, tea, coffee and provide views onto Pittville Park. Cheltenham is famous for horse racing and festivals of music and literature, and two theatres provide a regular programme of entertainment.

Nearby Prestbury is the most haunted village in England, the Cotswold villages stand in the surrounding hills, and Stratford is one hour's drive.

Tel: 01242 575567
e-mail: stay@cheltenhamparkviewguesthouse.co.uk
www.cheltenhamparkviewguesthouse.co.uk

Just to the north of Bath, Gloucestershire forms the major part of the Cotswolds Area of Outstanding Natural Beauty, with gently rolling hills, sleepy villages and market towns full of character and wonderful local food to sample, altogether ideal for a relaxing break whatever the season. There are gardens to visit, country pubs, antiques, craft and farm shops, cathedrals and castles, as well as all kinds of outdoor activities, from horse riding and 4x4 off-road driving to all the watersports on offer at the Cotswold Water Park, in the south east corner of the county. Canoeing, kayaking, climbing and abseiling are all available in the Wye Valley, while the dedicated cycle routes in the Forest of Dean are ideal for families. There's a vast network of underground caves just waiting to be explored, or walk above ground on the local paths or long distance trails.

SB

A warm and friendly welcome awaits you at our completely
refurbished 15th century Grade ll Listed farmhouse,
in the heart of this beautiful village.

SB

Wi-Fi

Spacious beamed rooms, inglenook fireplace in the dining room
where a full English breakfast is served. Large private car park at rear.
All bedrooms are en suite, with coffee/tea making facilities, TV, radio and hairdryer.

Accommodation comprises two double, two twin and one family suite
consisting of a single and a double room en suite.

Sorry no pets allowed in the house • Non-smoking • No children under 12.

Terms per night*: from £65 per suite, 2 persons sharing.*
More than two nights from £60. Family room for 3 persons sharing £90.

Veronica Stanley,
Home Farm House,
Ebrington, Chipping Campden
GL55 6NL
Tel & Fax: 01386 593309
willstanley@farmersweekly.net
www.homefarminthecotswolds.co.uk

Corse Lawn House Hotel

SB

Wi-Fi

*There is a refreshing vitality about this
elegant Queen Anne Listed building
which lies in 12 enchanting acres
complete with large ornamental pond.
Seemingly remote yet only six miles
from the M5 and M50, it is also
wonderfully placed for the Cotswolds,
Malverns and numerous sporting locations. The atmosphere is relaxed and the
services of an enthusiastic young staff is an added bonus.*

*Superbly appointed guest rooms each have a private bathroom, Wi-Fi, satellite colour
television, radio, direct-dial telephone and tea and coffee-making facilities; some
rooms with four-poster beds are available. The noteworthy restaurant is another
reason for choosing to stay here, imaginative dishes being supported by expertly
chosen wines. There is also a popular bistro situated in the bar area.*

Corse Lawn, Gloucestershire GL19 4LZ
Tel: 01452 780771 • Fax: 01452 780840
e-mail: enquiries@corselawn.com • www.corselawn.com

The **Speech** House Hotel • Forest of Dean

SB

A friendly hotel set in the heart of the Forest of Dean, perfect for walking and cycling. Built by King Charles II as a Hunting Lodge and almost completely surrounded by trees, The Speech House Hotel offers 35 comfortably appointed bedrooms, which offer modern facilities whilst retaining their original charm, several with four-poster beds. Why not pay us a visit and get away from it all. Courtyard ground floor rooms are available. Pets are welcome.

The Speech House Hotel, Coleford, Forest of Dean GL16 7EL
Tel: 01594 822607 • relax@thespeechhouse.co.uk
www.thespeechhouse.co.uk

Tel : 01452 840224

Quality all ground floor accommodation. "Kilmorie" is Grade II Listed (c1848) within conservation area in a lovely part of Gloucestershire. En suite double, twin, family or single bedrooms, all having tea tray, colour digital TV, radio. Very comfortable guests' lounge, traditional home cooking is served in the separate diningroom overlooking large garden. Choice of golf nearby. Perhaps walk waymarked farmland footpaths which start here. We have ponies and "free range" hens. Rural yet perfectly situated to visit Cotswolds, Royal Forest of Dean, Wye Valley and Malvern Hills. Children over four years welcome. Hartpury College 3 miles. Ample parking.

Bed and full English Breakfast from £30 per person

S.J. Barnfield, "Kilmorie Smallholding", Gloucester Road, Corse, Staunton, Gloucester GL19 3RQ
mobile: 07966 532337 • e-mail: sheila-barnfield@supanet.com

FREE or **REDUCED RATE** entry to Holiday Visits and Attractions –
see our **READERS' OFFER VOUCHERS** on pages 389-400

While every effort is made to ensure accuracy, we regret that FHG Guides
cannot accept responsibility for errors, misrepresentations or omissions in our entries
or any consequences thereof. Prices in particular should be checked.
We will follow up complaints but cannot act as arbiters or agents for either party.

Somerset

Somerset shares in the wild, heather-covered moorland of Exmoor, along with the Quantock Hills to the east, ideal for walking, mountain biking, horse riding, fishing and wildlife holidays. The forty miles of coastline with cliffs, sheltered bays and sandy beaches includes family resorts like Weston-super-Mare, with its famous donkey rides and brand new pier with 21st century facilities and entertainment for everyone. More family fun can be found at Minehead and Burnham-on-Sea, or opt for the quiet charm of Clevedon. With theatres, festivals, museums, galleries, gardens, sporting events and of course, shopping, the city of Bath has everything for a short break or longer stay. Attracting visitors from all over the world, this designated World Heritage Site boasts wonderful examples of Georgian architecture and of course, the Roman Baths.

The Kennard

11 Henrietta Street,
Bath BA2 6LL
• Tel: 01225 310472 •

The Kennard is an original Georgian townhouse, carefully maintained and restored and offering all the modern features which are now expected: en suite rooms with showers, telephones with data port, wireless internet connection, flat screen TV and beverage trays.

The original Georgian kitchen, now a delightful breakfast room, is thesetting for a full choice of English or Continental breakfasts.

For those arriving by car, free residents' parking permits will be provided. No smoking. Children over 8 years of age are most welcome.

Terms on request.

e-mail: reception@kennard.co.uk • www.kennard.co.uk

Eden Vale Farm

SB

Wi-Fi

Eden Vale Farm nestles down in a valley by the River Frome. Enjoying a picturesque location, this old watermill offers a selection of rooms including en suite facilities, complemented by an excellent choice of full English or Continental breakfasts. Beckington is an ideal centre for visiting Bath, Longleat, Salisbury, Cheddar, Stourhead and many National Trust Houses including Lacock Village.

Only a ten minute walk to the village pub, three-quarters of a mile of river fishing. Local golf courses and lovely walks.

Very friendly animals. Dogs welcome.

Open all year.

Mrs Barbara Keevil, Eden Vale Farm, Mill Lane, Beckington, Near Frome BA11 6SN • Tel: 01373 830371
e-mail: bandb@edenvalefarm.co.uk • www.edenvalefarm.co.uk

Wi-Fi

The Old Red House

Welcome to our romantic Victorian "Gingerbread" house which is colourful, comfortable and warm; full of unexpected touches and intriguing little curiosities. The leaded and stained glass windows are now double glazed to ensure a peaceful night's stay.

All rooms have colour TV with Freeview, complimentary beverages, radio alarm clock, hairdryer and en suite shower.

Easy access to city centre, via road or river paths. The English breakfast and buffet will keep you going all day. We have private parking. Non-smoking.

Theresa Elly, The Old Red House,
37 Newbridge Road, Bath BA1 3HE
01225 330464
e-mail: theoldredhousebath@onebillinternet.co.uk
www.theoldredhousebath.co.uk

Walton Villa • Bath

◆ Our immaculate Victorian family-run B&B offers a relaxed and friendly atmosphere.

Wi-Fi

◆ Just a short bus journey or 25 minute stroll to town centre, via the beautiful gardens of the Royal Victoria Park.

◆ Our three en suite bedrooms are delightfully decorated and furnished for your comfort, with colour TV, hairdryer and hospitality tray.

◆ Enjoy a delicious Full English or Continental breakfast served in our gracious dining room.

• Off-street parking • Free Wi-Fi
• Non-smoking accommodation
• Sorry, no pets • Bed and Breakfast from £50.

Michael & Carole Bryson, Walton Villa, 3 Newbridge Hill, Bath BA1 3PW
Tel: 01225 482792 • Fax: 01225 313093
e-mail: walton.villa@virgin.net • www.waltonvilla.co.uk

Whitecroft Farm B&B

A friendly and informal welcome awaits at our recently refurbished family home, set in approximately four acres of beautiful Somerset countryside

Wi-Fi

We are a short drive from the Market town of Shepton Mallet and the City of Wells. A trip across the stunning Mendip Hills will take you to Bristol airport in about forty minutes. Or you can enjoy our beautiful scenery by choosing from a number of local walks

We offer single, twin or family en suite accommodation and a comfortable guest lounge. Delicious breakfasts feature eggs from our own hens and home-made jams and chutney.

Ample off road parking and outdoor storage is also available.

Single from £40, Twin from £70, Family Room from £85.

Pylle, Shepton Mallet, Somerset BA4 6ST
01749 838692 • whitecroftfarm@btinternet.com
www.whitecroft-bandb.co.uk

THATCHED COUNTRY COTTAGE & GARDEN B&B

SB

An old thatched country cottage halfway between Taunton and Honiton, set in the idyllic Blackdown Hills, a designated Area of Outstanding Natural Beauty. Picturesque countryside with plenty of flowers and wildlife. Central for north/south coasts of Somerset, Dorset and Devon. Double/single and family suite with own facilities, TV, tea/coffee.

Large Conservatory/Garden Room and a separate summer house available for guests' relaxation and al fresco meals if preferred.

Evening Meals also available.
Children and small
well behaved dogs welcome.
Open all year.
B&B from £24pppn.

Mrs Pam Parry, Pear Tree Cottage,
Stapley, Churchstanton, Taunton TA3 7QA
Tel: 01823 601224
e-mail: colvin.parry@virgin.net
www.SmoothHound.co.uk/hotels/thatch.html OR www.best-hotel.com/peartreecottage

Wells

SB

Wi-Fi

Weston-Super-Mare, Woodford (near Williton)

Wiltshire

SB

Longwater
Bed & Breakfast
Erlestoke, Devizes
SN10 5UE

Tel & Fax: 01380 830095

Welcome to Longwater. We offer good old-fashioned hospitality with all the comfort and facilities of a modern home. Explore the beautiful cities of Bath and Salisbury, play golf on the adjacent 18-hole course, or simply relax in our gardens or conservatory overlooking our picturesque lakes and parkland. Traditional farmhouse breakfast; local inns offer excellent dinners.

All rooms en suite with tea/coffee facilities, fridge, TV, radio.
Twin and double rooms and family room (children over 5 years).
Ground floor rooms. Brochure on request.

Terms: Single Rooms from £38, Double/twin from £55 and Family from £65.

For the greatest concentration of prehistoric sites in Europe, visit Wiltshire. Most famous is the UNESCO World Heritage Site, Stonehenge, on Salisbury Plain, dating back at least five thousand years, while the stone circle at Avebury is the largest in the world. Salisbury, as well as the famous medieval cathedral, has plenty to choose from in arts and entertainment, while, Swindon, with its railway heritage, is the place to go for shopping and a lively nightlife. In the countryside there are interesting old market towns to explore, stately homes and gardens, including the safari park at Longleat, to visit, and ample opportunities for walking and cycling

London
(Central & Greater)

London has it all - theatres, shopping, concerts, museums, art galleries, pageantry and sporting events, a magnet for visitors from all over the world. There's plenty to see and do, from all the hands on activities of the Science Museum and the Natural History Museum, the National Gallery with one of the largest art collections in the world, the thought-provoking artworks at the Tate Modern, the splendour of Buckingham Palace and the magnificent gardens at Kew, to a sumptuous afternoon tea at a top hotel. With a wide range of accommodation at prices to suit every pocket, it's easy to spend a weekend here or a take a longer break. Take a bird's eye view of the city on the London Eye, the world's highest observation wheel, or meet celebrities (or at least their wax doubles) at Madame Tussauds. There are fashion and designer shops to suit all ages and tastes, markets for all kinds of goods, entertainment for all tastes, with over 400 venues where you can listen to the music of your choice, or watch musicals and plays, and eating places of all kinds offering menus from all over the world.

The Athena

110-114 SUSSEX GARDENS, HYDE PARK, LONDON W2 1UA

Tel: 0207 706 3866; Fax: 0207 262 6143

e-mail: stay@athenahotellondon.co.uk • www.athenahotel.co.uk

TREAT YOURSELVES TO A QUALITY HOTEL AT AFFORDABLE PRICES

The Athena is a newly completed family run hotel in a restored Victorian building. Professionally designed, including a lift to all floors and exquisitely decorated, we offer our clientele the ambience and warm hospitality necessary for a relaxing and enjoyable stay. Ideally located in a beautiful tree-lined avenue, extremely well-positioned for sightseeing London's famous sights and shops; Hyde Park, Madame Tussaud's, Oxford Street, Marble Arch, Knightsbridge, Buckingham Palace and many more are all within walking distance.

Travel connections to all over London are excellent, with Paddington and Lancaster Gate Stations, Heathrow Express, A2 Airbus and buses minutes away.

Our tastefully decorated bedrooms have en suite bath/shower rooms, satellite colour TV, bedside telephones, tea/coffee making facilities. Hairdryers, trouser press, laundry and ironing facilities available on request. Car parking available.

We offer quality and convenience at affordable rates.

A VERY WARM WELCOME AWAITS YOU.

Single Rooms from £50-£89

Double/Twin Rooms from £64-£99

Triple & Family Rooms from £25 per person

All prices include full English breakfast plus VAT.

All major credit cards accepted, but some charges may apply.

Buckinghamshire

symbols ⚞ 🐴 SB & ♉ Wi-Fi

🐕	Pets Welcome	🐴	Children Welcome
SB	Short Breaks	&	Suitable for Disabled Guests
♉	Licensed	Wi-Fi	Wi-Fi available

Hampshire

SB

Wi-Fi

Bramble Hill Hotel

unpretentious and welcoming ....

...in the heart of the New Forest

Peacefully located in tranquil surroundings, this country house hotel, noted for its wonderful collection of rhododendrons and other flowering shrubs and trees, is set in ancient woodlands, with 15 acres of glades, lawns and shrubbery to enjoy.

Bramble Hill, a former Royal Hunting Lodge, looks out across a valley designated as a nature reserve, where deer, badgers and other wild life of the New Forest abound.

A short drive from Lyndhurst, the hotel is only three miles from Junction 1 of the M27, and is ideal for country walks and horse riding. All bedrooms have en suite bathrooms and some have antique four-poster beds. A warm, friendly welcome and a hearty home-cooked breakfast assured.

**Bramshaw, New Forest,
Hampshire SO43 7JG
Telephone: 023 80 813165
bramblehill@hotmail.co.uk
www.bramblehill.co.uk**

Kent

South Wootton House

**Capel Road, Petham,
Canterbury CT4 5RG**

A lovely farmhouse with conservatory set in extensive garden, surrounded by fields and woodland. Fully co-ordinated bedroom with private bathroom. Tea/coffee facilities, colour TV. Children welcome. Canterbury four miles. Non-smoking. Open all year. Bed and Breakfast from £35.

FARMHOUSE

Wi-Fi

**Contact: Frances Mount
Tel: 01227 700643 • Mobile: 07885 800843
e-mail: mountfrances@btconnect.com**

B&B accommodation, hostel-style • Quiet camping for tents only

SB

Wi-Fi

Relaxing and flexible hostel-style accommodation (duvets, freshly laundered linen and Continental breakfast included in price).
In converted farm buildings on working farm in Kent Downs.
Ten fully heated en suite rooms, fully fitted self-catering kitchen, comfortable lounge.
Quiet, tent-only campsite, with toilet and shower block.

HOSTEL

Green Tourism GOLD

Palace Farm Hostel & Campsite

**Doddington, Near Faversham ME9 0AU
Tel: 01795 886200 • e-mail: info@palacefarm.com
www.palacefarm.com**

In AONB, ideal for cycling and walking. Visit Canterbury and other historic sites. Convenient for day trips to France.

SB

Luxuriously converted Kentish oasthouse set in a quiet, picturesque hamlet of about 12 houses, off A274 south of Maidstone and close to Leeds Castle. Ideal touring base for all of Kent's attractions, and for London. Also makes a good stopover to or from Europe.

Stay in one of our two large Roundel rooms, one with Jacuzzi bath, or in a twin or double room with half-tester canopy.

B&B from £30 to £50 per person,

AA ★★★★

Langley Oast B&B

**Langley Park, Langley, Maidstone, Kent ME17 3NQ
Tel: 01622 863523
langleyoast@btinternet.com**

SB

Wi-Fi

LITTLE SILVER
COUNTRY HOTEL

Versatility combined with efficiency, friendliness and a personal regard for detail are the hallmarks offered by the management and staff. Each of the bedrooms is stamped with its own identity, including standard rooms, four-posters and suites with spa baths. Bespoke bedrooms are offered to those guests with mobility needs, and the hotel is totally accessible for wheelchair users.

The excellent Oaks Restaurant offers locally sourced foods with plenty of surprises to keep our menus exciting.

The wine list is varied and offers a selection of new world wines as well as wines from local vineyards. Pre-dinner drinks are served in the oak-beamed lounge, where log fires burn on those cold winter nights.

Morning coffee, light lunches and afternoon tea are served in the Orangery overlooking the landscaped gardens.

Licensed for wedding ceremonies and partnerships, the magnificent Kent Hall holds up to 120 guests. Al fresco weddings are held in the beautiful garden gazebo on those warm summer days.

The hotel is ideally suited for anyone wishing to explore the beautiful countryside, castles and gardens which abound in the area. The medieval town of Rye and the wonderful city of Canterbury are within easy reach, whilst Tenterden, one of the loveliest towns in the Weald and steeped in history, is just up the road.

Little Silver Country Hotel, the Jewel in the Weald
Ashford Road, St Michaels, Tenterden, Kent TN30 6SP
Tel: 01233 850321 • Fax: 01233 850647
e-mail: enquiries@little-silver.co.uk • www.little-silver.co.uk

Tenterden

Oxfordshire

Oxford

Surrey

——— Chase Lodge House———

Sky TV described Chase Lodge as "The best kept secret in West London". This small, romantic and independent hotel is just half an hour from Heathrow Airport and Central London. Hampton Court Palace, the River Thames and Bushy Park are just a stone's throw away. There are many excellent restaurants nearby, including Jamie's Italian, Carluccio's and Simply Thai, which won Best Local Thai on Gordon Ramsay's *F-Word*.

Each room at Chase Lodge is unique, and has a flatscreen TV and free Wi-Fi.

The hotel is dog-friendly, and we recently accommodated the dogs from the BBC TV series *"Over the Rainbow"*.

Parking is free between 4pm and 10am; there is an £8 charge during the day.

"A hidden gem".

Rates: Single room from £49, double from £69. Price includes VAT and Continental breakfast.

Chase Lodge House

10 Park Road, Hampton Wick, Kingston upon Thames KT1 4AS

Tel: 020 8943 1862 • Fax: 020 8943 9363

e-mail: info@chaselodgehotel.com • www.chaselodgehotel.com

Visit the FHG website
www.holidayguides.com
for all kinds of holiday
accommodation in Britain

Lingfield

Stantons Hall Farm

is an 18th century farmhouse, set in
18 acres of farmland and adjacent to
Blindley Heath Common. Family,
double and single rooms, most with
WC, shower and wash-hand basins
en suite. Separate bathroom.

All rooms have colour TV, tea/coffee facilities and are centrally heated.

Enjoy a traditional English breakfast in our large farmhouse kitchen.

Conveniently situated within easy reach of M25 (London Orbital), Gatwick Airport
(car parking for travellers) and Lingfield Park racecourse.

* Bed and Breakfast from £30 per person, reductions for children sharing
* Cot and high chair available • Well behaved dogs welcome by prior arrangement
* There are plenty of parking spaces.

Mrs V. Manwill, Stantons Hall Farm, Eastbourne Road,
Blindley Heath, Lingfield RH7 6LG Tel: •01342 832401
www.stantonshallfarm.co.uk • e-mail: vanessa@stantonshallfarm.co.uk

Alfriston

East Sussex

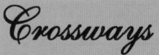

From the dramatic cliffs and sandy beaches of the Sussex coast to the quiet countryside of the Weald and the South Downs, there's an endless choice of the things to do and places to explore. Sailing, walking, cycling, horse riding, golf are all available for an active break, while the fascinating history of 1066 country, castles like Bodiam and the seaside ports will attract all the family. If you're looking for beaches, the 100 miles of coast offer something for everyone, whether your preference is for action-packed fun at a family resort or a quiet, remote spot. Best known for a combination of lively nightlife and all the attractions of the seaside, Brighton has everything from its pebble beach, classic pier, Royal Pavilion and Regency architecture, to shopping malls, art galleries, antique shops, and the specialist boutiques and coffee shops of The Lanes. There's so much to choose from!

Brighton

SB

Wi-Fi

Paskins
town house

Distinctive, different, comfortable

PASKINS is a small, green hotel that has found its own way. It's an eclectic, environmentally friendly hotel with nice and sometimes amusing rooms, with the bonus of brilliant breakfasts. You arrive at the Art Nouveau reception to be shown to one of the 19 slightly out of the ordinary rooms, each individual in design, perhaps a little quirky, but not at the expense of being comfortable. For example, one room has a genuine Victorian brass bed with several mattresses, just as Queen Victoria's did, which enabled her to sleep higher than all her subjects. Having been welcomed royally, you will sleep like a monarch, and come down to a regal spread at breakfast, prepared with mainly organic, fair trade or locally sourced produce. The Art Deco breakfast room continues the charming theme of the hotel, and has a menu of celebrated choice, including a variety of imaginative vegetarian and vegan dishes, some intriguing signature dishes, and a blackboard full of specials.

PASKINS TOWN HOUSE • 18/19 Charlotte Street, Brighton BN2 1AG
Tel: **01273 601203** • Fax: **01273 621973**
www.paskins.co.uk • welcome@paskins.co.uk

Eastbourne

EBOR LODGE

SB

71 Royal Parade, Eastbourne BN22 7AQ

Wi-Fi

Ebor Lodge has a warm, friendly atmosphere, offering accommodation at realistic prices.

Recently refurbished, all rooms are en suite and furnished to a high standard, fully centrally heated with hospitality trays, colour TVs, clock radios, bedside lights and hairdryers. A ground floor room is adjacent to the dining room and guest lounge. Front rooms boast sea views with one having a private balcony. Open all year. We offer off-peak reductions for Senior Citizens. Opposite the Redoubt and bowling greens, it is a short walk to Prince's Park, tennis courts, putting greens and children's amusements.

Tel: 01323 640792 • info@eborlodge.co.uk
www.eborlodge.co.uk

The Palm Court Hotel is ideally situated just off Eastbourne's seafront close to the Bandstand and Theatres.
All 38 rooms are en suite, colour TV, CD player, direct-dial telephone, hospitality tray.
Free Wi-Fi access in the Lounge and Bar.
Lift to all floors. Special diets catered for.
Licensed bar with comfortable lounges and a large plasma screen. A large permanent ramped entrance and a talking lift to all floors make the Hotel fully accessible to wheelchair users.
Traditional cuisine.
Christmas and New Year Programme.

T·H·E
PALM COURT
H·O·T·E·L

what a difference a stay makes....

15 Burlington Place,
Eastbourne, East Sussex BN21 4AR
Telephone: 01323 725811
Fax: 01323 430236
e-mail: thepalmcourt@btconnect.com
www.thepalmcourthotel.co.uk

Longleys Farm Cottage

SB

Situated in quiet private country lane one mile north of the market town of Hailsham with its excellent amenities including modern sports centre and leisure pool, surrounded by footpaths across open farmland. Ideal for country lovers. The coast at Eastbourne, South Downs, Ashdown Forest and 1066 country are all within easy access.

The non-smoking accommodation comprises one twin room, double room en suite; family room en suite and tea/coffee making facilities.

Bed and Breakfast from £30pp.

David and Jill Hook,
Harebeating Lane, Hailsham, East Sussex BN27 1ER

Tel & Fax: 01323 841227
www.longleysfarmcottage.co.uk

Grand Hotel

On the seafront, half-a-mile from Hastings Pier. Spacious lounge, licensed bar, central heating. En suite rooms with Freeview TV available. Disabled parking in front of hotel; ramp, fully accessible wet room.
In the heart of 1066 Country close to Battle, Bodiam and Hever Castles, Kipling's Batemans and Rye, plus Hastings Castle, Smugglers' Caves, Aquarium, local golf courses and leisure centres. Major credit cards accepted

SB
ⓠ
♿
Wi-Fi

- *Wi-Fi available*
- *Non-smoking throughout*
- *Children welcome,*
  – half price when sharing room
- *Open all year*

GRAND HOTEL, 1 GRAND PARADE,
ST LEONARDS, HASTINGS TN37 6AQ
Tel & Fax: 01424 428510
e-mail: info@grandhotelhastings.co.uk
www.grandhotelhastings.co.uk

Hastings & St. Leonards Hotels & Tourism Association

B& B from £25
Evening Meal from £15

Wi-Fi

RYE LODGE HOTEL

"A little gem of an Hotel"

The Stylish Place to Stay in Rye

From the moment you arrive at Rye Lodge you will enjoy the attentive service and attention to detail that only a small, family-run hotel can offer. The friendly reception staff will be pleased to greet you and help you to settle in. They have a wealth of information to offer you about Rye and the surrounding area and will be pleased to help you with any queries or special requirements you may have throughout your stay.

From spacious superior de luxe rooms with private balconies and family rooms to a cosy bedroom with shower en suite, all of the bedrooms at Rye Lodge offer luxury accommodation. Whatever standard of room you choose, you are assured of comfortable and stylish accommodation. Every room has remote-control TV with satellite channels, hospitality tray, radio and direct-dial telephone. De luxe rooms all have well stocked mini-bars and, in the bathroom you will find quality toiletries, bathrobes for your use and complimentary slippers. Standard rooms have en suite shower rooms or bathrooms.

Enjoy the luxury of breakfast in bed (or on your balcony if your room has one), without extra charge for room service. Terms can include dinner which can be taken at any one of three top restaurants.

A new **Champagne Bar** has opened recently and guests can enjoy a chilled glass of champagne at any time - there is also a menu of light dishes served throughout the day.

With a heated swimming pool, spa bath, and sauna you can relax or exercise in Rye Lodge's Venetian Leisure Centre. Rye Lodge is the only hotel with a swimming pool in Rye, and guests have exclusive and unlimited complimentary use of the centre throughout their stay.

"One of the finest small luxury hotels in the country"

Recommended by Signpost and designated a "Best Loved Hotel of the World"

RYE LODGE HOTEL

Hilder's Cliff, Rye, East Sussex TN31 7LD
Tel: 01797 223838 • Fax: 01797 223585
info@ryelodge.co.uk
www.ryelodge.co.uk

Polegate

West Sussex

Henfield

Cambridgeshire

THE MEADOW HOUSE

**2a High Street, Burwell,
Cambridge CB25 0HB**
Tel: 01638 741926
Fax: 01638 741861

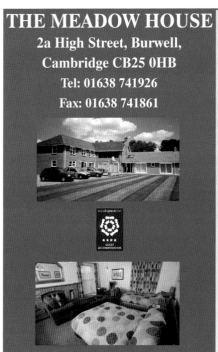

The Meadow House is a magnificent modern house set in two acres of wooded grounds offering superior Bed and Breakfast accommodation in spacious rooms, some with king-size beds. The variety of en suite accommodation endeavours to cater for all requirements; a suite of rooms sleeping six complete with south-facing balcony; a triple room on the ground floor with three single beds and the Coach House, a spacious annexe with one double and one single bed; also one double and two twins sharing a well equipped bathroom. All rooms have TV, central heating and tea/coffee facilities.
Car parking. No smoking
Family rate available on request.
**e-mail: hilary@themeadowhouse.co.uk
www.themeadowhouse.co.uk
www.hilaryscottage.co.uk**

SB

Cambridgeshire immediately brings to mind the ancient university city of Cambridge, lazy hours punting on the river past the imposing college buildings, students on bicycles, museums and bookshops. This cosmopolitan centre has so much to offer, with theatres, concerts varying from classical to jazz, an annual music festival, cinemas, botanic gardens, exciting shops and to round it all off, restaurants, pubs and cafes serving high quality food. In the surrounding countryside historic market towns, pretty villages and stately homes wait to be explored. Visit Ely with its magnificent cathedral and museum exhibiting the national collection of stained glass, antique shops and cafes. Shopping is one of the attractions of Peterborough, along with Bronze Age excavations and reconstructed dwelling, a ghost tour of the museum and an annual CAMRA Beer Festival.

Cambridge

Manor Farm

Landbeach, Cambridge CB25 9FD
Tel: 01223 860165

Wi-Fi

Manor Farm is a lovely Georgian house with large spacious bedrooms, all with en suite or private bathroom, and a light airy sitting room that guests may use. Wifi available. Guests are welcome to relax in the large walled garden or take a walk on the farm.

Landbeach is a small, pretty village about six miles north of Cambridge and ten miles south of Ely. There are many local pubs and restaurants, although none are within walking distance - why not bring a bicycle and cycle along the tow path into Cambridge? There is also a local bus service and a mainline train service from the next village.

Ample off road parking.

Terms from £50 per room single, £60 double and £75 triple.

e-mail: vhatley@btinternet.com • www.manorfarmcambridge.co.uk

- Within walking distance of city centre.
- Single, double/twin and family bedrooms, all en suite.
- All rooms with colour TV, hairdryer, tea/coffee making facilities, iron etc.
- Varied breakfast menu served in dining room overlooking picturesque garden.
- On-site parking; easy access to A14, M11, A10.

57 Arbury Road, Cambridge CB4 2JB
Tel: 01223 350086
www.victoria-guesthouse.co.uk
e-mail: victoriahouse@ntlworld.com

Victoria
Guest House

Essex

Earls Hall Farm

Clacton-on-Sea, Essex CO16 8BP

SB

Excellent base for the Essex Sunshine Coast.
Ideal for birdwatching, beaches, woodland walks and exploring East Anglia.
Non-smoking. Open all year. Pets welcome by arrangement.

Wi-Fi

Pond House Bed & Breakfast

Victorian farmhouse with one double (super king-size) and one twin room, both en suite. Guests' sitting room. Delicious breakfasts using local produce. Chilldren over 12 years welcome. Wi-Fi available.

Pond Cottage Self Catering Holidays

Cosy cottage annexe, very well equipped, with full central heating. Sleeps four in one king-size double and one twin room, both en suite. Children over 2 years. Pets by arrangement. Wi-Fi. Short breaks available - ring for details.

Contact Mrs Brenda Lord • Tel: 01255 820458
e-mail: brenda_lord@farming.co.uk • www.earlshallfarm.info

From the historic port of Harwich in the north to the Thames estuary in the south, the 300 miles of coastline and dry climate of maritime Essex have attracted holiday makers since early Victorian times. Nowadays there's plenty for everyone, from the fun family resorts with plenty of action like Clacton, on the Essex sunshine coast, and Southend-on-Sea, with over six miles of clean safe sand and the world's longest pleasure pier to quiet walks through country nature reserves. Along the coast there are quiet clifftop paths, sheltered coves, long beaches, mudflats, saltmarshes and creeks. Previously the haunt of smugglers, these are now a great attraction for birdwatchers, particularly for viewing winter wildfowl. At Maldon take a trip on a Thames barge to see the seal colonies or cross the Saxon causeway to Mersea Island to taste the oysters, washed down by wine produced on the vineyard there, but watch the tides!

Rye Farm

Wi-Fi

Rye Lane, Layer de la Haye, Colchester CO2 0JL
Tel: 01206 734350/07976 524276
e-mail: peterbunting@btconnect.com
www.ryefarm.org.uk

This 17thC moated farmhouse enjoys a quiet location adjacent to Abberton Reservoir, one of Europe's most important wildfowl havens. Ideal for a relaxing break and a good base for exploring Colchester with its castle and museums, Colchester Zoo, Mersea Island, Layer Marney Towers, Beth Chatto Gardens, Maldon and Constable Country. 30 mins from the coast; 50 mins from Stansted Airport/Harwich Port. London 50 minutes by train.

Three comfortable en suite rooms, with
central heating, colour TV/DVD, tea and
coffee making facilities, fridge and
hairdryer. Wi-Fi. Substantial farmhouse
breakfast. No smoking. No pets.
Children over 12 years only

Norfolk

Along the Norfolk coast from King's Lynn to Great Yarmouth the broad, sandy beaches, grassy dunes, nature reserves, windmills, and pretty little fishing villages are inviting at all times of year. Following the routes of the Norfolk Coastal Path and Norfolk Coast Cycle Way, walk or cycle between the picturesque villages, stopping to visit the interesting shops and galleries, or to enjoy the seafood at a traditional pub or a restaurant. Take lessons in surfing at Wells-next-the-Sea, then enjoy the challenge of the waves at East Runton or Cromer, or go sea fishing here, or at Sheringham or Mundesley. An important trade and fishing port from medieval times, the historic centre of King's Lynn is well worth a visit, and take a break at Great Yarmouth for family entertainment, 15 miles of sandy beaches, traditional piers, a sea life centre and nightlife with clubs and a casino.

THE OLD PUMP HOUSE

Wi-Fi

LUXURY BED & BREAKFAST ACCOMMODATION

This comfortable 1750s house, owned by Marc James and Charles Kirkman, faces the old thatched pump and is a minute from Aylsham's church and historic marketplace.

It offers five en suite bedrooms (including one four-poster and two family rooms) in a relaxed and elegant setting, with colour TV, tea/coffee making facilities, bath robes, hairdryers and CD radio alarm clocks in all rooms. Wireless internet access in all rooms.

English breakfast with free-range eggs and local produce (or vegetarian breakfast) is served in the pine-shuttered sitting room overlooking the peaceful garden.

Aylsham is central for Norwich, the coast, the Broads, National Trust houses, steam railways and unspoilt countryside.

• Well behaved children welcome. • Non-smoking.
• Off-road parking for six cars.
• *B&B: single £80-£98, double/twin £98-£120, family room £123-£145*

Holman Road, Aylsham, Norwich
NR11 6BY
Tel: 01263 733789
theoldpumphouse@btconnect.com
www.theoldpumphouse.com

King's Lynn, Long Stratton

SB
Wi-Fi

THE STUART HOUSE HOTEL
35 Goodwins Road, King's Lynn, Norfolk PE30 5QX
Tel: 01553 772169 • Fax: 01553 774788

It would be hard to find a more pleasant place to stay at any time of year than the Stuart House Hotel, which manages to be both quiet and restful in its own grounds, and very central. It has comfortable and well-equipped bedrooms, including a honeymoon suite which boasts a romantic four-poster bed and a spa bath. There are two pleasant reception areas, an excellent CAMRA *Good Beer Guide* Listed bar, and the Stuart House Restaurant where the emphasis is on superb quality and good value.

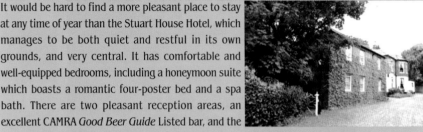

e-mail: reception@stuarthousehotel.co.uk • www.stuart-house-hotel.co.uk

The town of King's Lynn has many attractions, and Royal Sandringham, Burnham Thorpe (Nelson's birthplace) and the fine Norfolk beaches and countryside are all an easy drive away.

AA
★★★
HOTEL

Woodgreen, Long Stratton
SB
Norwich NR15 2RR

Wi-Fi

Period 17th century farmhouse on 30 acre common with ponds and natural wildlife, 10 miles south of Norwich (A140). The beamed sittingroom with inglenook fireplace invites you to relax. A large sunny dining room encourages you to enjoy a leisurely traditional breakfast. All en suite bedrooms (two double/twin) are tastefully furnished to complement the

Greenacres Farmhouse

oak beams and period furniture, with tea/coffee facilities and TV. Full size snooker table and all-weather tennis court for guests' use. Jo is trained in therapeutic massage, pilates and reflexology and is able to offer this to guests who feel it would be of benefit. Come and enjoy the peace and tranquillity of our home.

Bed and Breakfast from £30. Reductions for two nights or more. Non-smoking.

Tel: 01508 530261 • www.abreakwithtradition.co.uk

Norwich, Wymondham

SOUTH NORFOLK GUEST HOUSE

SB

♿

Wi-Fi

This former village school, set in the heart of Norfolk's unspoilt countryside, is an ideal location from which to explore East Anglia.

As a professionally run guest house, a comfortable stay is guaranteed, complemented by a delicious breakfast with locally sourced products.

FRITH WAY, GT. MOULTON, NORWICH, NR15 2HE

WWW.SOUTHNORFOLKGUESTHOUSE.CO.UK   (01379) 677359

Home Farm

Comfortable accommodation set in four acres, quiet location, secluded garden. Conveniently situated off A11 between Attleborough and Wymondham, an excellent location for Snetterton and only 20 minutes from Norwich and 45 minutes from the Norfolk Broads.

Accommodation comprises two double rooms and one single-bedded room, all with TV, tea/coffee facilities and central heating. Children over five years old welcome, but sorry no animals and no smoking. Fishing lakes only ½ mile away.

Bed and Breakfast from £30 pppn.

Mrs Joy Morter, Home Farm,
Morley, Wymondham **NR18 9US**
Tel: **01953 602581**

Suffolk

SB

A charming 17th century cottage in six-acres, situated in the centre of the village, just off the main Norwich to Bungay road.

Wonderful holiday area, ideal for touring Norfolk and Suffolk

Within 10 miles is historic Norwich, with its castle, cathedral, theatre and excellent shops. Coast 18 miles. Excellent pub meals available 100 yards.

George's House

Guest accommodation comprises three bedrooms – two double and one twin, all en suite. Dining room, lounge/TV, sun room. Ample parking.
B&B from £30pppn.

Mrs J. Read, George's House, The Nurseries, Woodton, Near Bungay NR35 2LZ • Tel: 01508 482214

e-mail: julietpeter@googlemail.com
www.rossmag.com/georges/

HIGH HOUSE FARM

Farmhouse Bed & Breakfast

High House Farm is a family-run farm in the heart of rural Suffolk, offering quality Bed & Breakfast in our 15th Century listed farmhouse.

Featuring: exposed oak beams • inglenook fireplaces • generous Full English Breakfast with locally sourced ingredients • tea and coffee making facilities • flat screen TVs • one double room, en suite and one large family room with double and twin beds and private adjacent bathroom

children's cots • high chairs • books • toys • outside play equipment • attractive semi-moated gardens • farm and woodland walks.

Explore the heart of rural Suffolk, local vineyard, Easton Farm Park, Framlingham and Orford Castles, Parham Air Museum, Saxtead Windmill, Minsmere, Snape Maltings, Woodland Trust.

High House Farm
Cransford, Framlingham, Woodbridge IP13 9PD
Tel: 01728 663461
e-mail: b&b@highhousefarm.co.uk • www.highhousefarm.co.uk

Suffolk's 40 miles of unspoilt World Heritage coastline is perfect for a seaside holiday. Whether you're looking for a quiet weekend break or an active family fortnight in a well established resort, a music festival - rock and pop or classical, farm parks and fun parks or just to indulge in the wonderful local food, it's all to be found here. Wander through the coastal forests or along the shingle and sandy beaches admiring the scenery, or hire bicycles for a family bike ride. Rent a gaily painted beach hut at Felixstowe, where the level esplanade and beaches are ideal both for small children and older family members, try crabs fresh from the sea at Walberswick, or enjoy the annual music and literature festivals at Aldeburgh. Eat oysters at Orford, and explore the Norman castle, or follow the Suffolk Coastal Churches Trail. At Woodbridge visit the Tide Mill and Buttrum's Mill, the tallest remaining windmill in Suffolk, and the nearby Anglo-Saxon burial site at Sutton Hoo. River yachting is another option, and of course right along the coast there are opportunities for all forms of boating, sailing, and diving holidays. Fishing is particularly popular on the Waveney and on many other rivers as well, and there are plenty of opportunities for still water angling or sea fishing too. Golfers are not neglected, with a choice between short local courses to some of championship standard, with luxury hotel accommodation on site. Horse racing enthusiasts can't miss Newmarket, whether for a fun day out, to visit the National Horseracing Museum or to take a guided tour round the National Stud.

Derbyshire

THROWLEY HALL FARM
ILAM, ASHBOURNE DE6 2BB
01538 308202/308243
Bed and Breakfast in farmhouse.
Near Alton Towers and stately homes.
4 double/twin rooms (3 en suite).
Dining/sitting room with TV.
Tea/coffee making • full central heating • open fire.
Terms from £32pppn • Reduced rates for children.
Cot and high chair available.
www.throwleyhallfarm.co.uk
e-mail: throwleyhall@btinternet.com

Self-catering accommodation in farmhouse for up to
12 and cottages for five and seven people
ETC ★★★★

For walking, climbing, cycling, horse riding, mountain biking and caving, visit Derbyshire. Visit Poole's Cavern to see the best stalagmites and stalactites in Derbyshire (and discover the difference!), and the Blue John Cave at Castleton where this rare mineral is mined, and perhaps buy a sample of jewellery in one of the local shops. Buxton was a spa from Roman times, but the main attractions now are concerts, theatre and the opera, music and literature festival held every year. Go to Wirksworth in spring for the annual well dressings or try out a wizard's wand at Hardwick Hall near Chesterfield, the market town with the church with the crooked spire. No stay in Derbyshire is complete without visiting Chatsworth, the best known of the stately homes, with impressive interiors and magnificent gardens and grounds, and for a contrasting step back in time go to Crich Tramway Village for a tram ride down a period street and on into the countryside.

Chesterfield, Chinley

🪀
🐎 **The Clarendon** Guest House
SB

Located near the town centre and within easy reach of the Peak District,
♿ this Victorian town house offers a warm and cheerful welcome, whether
Wi-Fi on business or pleasure.

Comfortable, cosy rooms, each with TV and tea/coffee facilities; free Wi-Fi. Two single rooms, one single en suite; one twin en suite, one double en suite.

The rear walled garden offers a peaceful summer retreat.

Full English breakfast; special diets catered for. Non-smoking throughout.

Bed and Breakfast from £25 single, from £50 double/twin room en suite.

Mr & Mrs A. Boardman • 01246 235004
The Clarendon Guest House,
32 Clarence Road, Chesterfield S40 1LN
www.clarendonguesthouse.com

Moseley House Farm
Maynestone Road, Chinley, High Peak SK23 6AH
Tel: 01663 750240

A stunning location in the Peak District is where you will find this quality farmhouse. Lovely bedrooms, en suite or with private bathrooms, charming ground floor suite with own entrance. Relax in the garden. Village half mile – good pubs and restaurants. Ideal spot for a holiday on a working farm.
Double or twin from £29 per person, single £30.
Also self-catering cottage. Farmhouse, sleeps six.

e-mail: goddardbromley@aol.com
www.visitderbyshire.co.uk

Glossop, Peak District National Park

symbols ⋔ 🐎 SB ♿ ♉ Wi-Fi

⋔	Pets Welcome	🐎	Children Welcome
SB	Short Breaks	♿	Suitable for Disabled Guests
♉	Licensed	Wi-Fi	Wi-Fi available

Winster

Mrs Jane Ball

Brae Cottage
East Bank, Winster DE4 2DT
Tel: 01629 650375

In one of the most picturesque villages in the Peak District National Park this 300-year-old cottage offers independent accommodation across the paved courtyard. Breakfast is served in the cottage. Rooms are furnished and equipped to a high standard; both having en suite shower rooms, tea/coffee making facilities, TV and heating.

The village has two traditional pubs which provide food.

Local attractions include village (National Trust) Market House, Chatsworth, Haddon Hall and many walks from the village in the hills and dales.

Ample private parking • Non-smoking throughout
Bed and Breakfast from £60 per double room

Belton-in-Rutland, Melton Mowbray

Leicestershire & Rutland

The county of Rutland is verdant, undulating, and largely unspoilt, making it an ideal place to spend a tranquil vacation. No better venue for such an excursion exists than this fine hotel, perched in the very centre of man-made Rutland Water.

The superb cuisine exhibits flair and refreshing originality, with the emphasis very much on seasonal, freshly sourced ingredients. Beautifully furnished in subtle shades, elegant and profoundly comfortable, with 17 individually and lavishly decorated bedrooms. Hambleton is within easy reach of numerous places of historic interest, wonderful gardens and antique shops. On-site tennis, outdoor heated swimming pool and croquet lawn, and within a short drive, horse riding, golf, sailing, fishing and boating.

Hambleton, Oakham, Rutland LE15 8TH

Tel: 01572 756991 • Fax: 01572 724721

hotel@hambletonhall.com • www.hambletonhall.com

Lincolnshire

Baumber Park

Bed & Breakfast on the farm

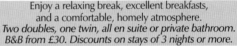

Spacious elegant farmhouse of character in quiet parkland setting, on a mixed farm. Large colourful and inspiring plantsman's garden with extensive vistas and wildlife pond. Fine bedrooms with lovely views, period furniture, log fires and books. Central in the county and close to the Lincolnshire Wolds, this rolling countryside is little known, quite unspoilt, and ideal for walking, cycling or riding. Championship golf courses at Woodhall Spa. Well located for historic Lincoln, interesting market towns and many antique shops.

Enjoy a relaxing break, excellent breakfasts, and a comfortable, homely atmosphere. Two doubles, one twin, all en suite or private bathroom. B&B from £30. Discounts on stays of 3 nights or more.

Mrs Clare Harrison, Baumber Park, Near Horncastle LN9 5NE
Tel: 01507 578235 • mobile: 07977 722776
e-mail: mail@baumberpark.com • www.baumberpark.com

Lea Holme

SB

A comfortable chalet-type home set in its own half-acre of peaceful garden. Central for Wolds, coast, fens, historic Lincoln. Market towns, Louth, Horncastle, Boston, Spilsby, Alford, Woodhall Spa.

Two double bedrooms. Washbasin, TV; bathroom, toilet adjoining; lounge with colour TV, separate dining room. Drinks provided. Children welcome at reduced rates. Car almost essential, parking. Numerous eating places nearby.

PETS WELCOME FREE
B&B from £30 per person (double/single let).
Open all year round offering a friendly service. Tourist Board Listed.

MISS JESSIE SKELLERN
LEA HOLME, LANGTON-BY-WRAGBY,
LINCOLN LN8 5PZ • Tel: 01673 858339

Northamptonshire

ENJOY A HOLIDAY in our comfortable 17th century farmhouse with oak beams and inglenook fireplaces. Four-poster bed now available. Peaceful surroundings, large garden containing ancient circular dovecote. Dairy Farm is a working farm situated in a beautiful Northamptonshire village just off the A14, within easy reach of many places of interest or ideal for a restful holiday. Good farmhouse food and friendly atmosphere. Open all year, except Christmas.

B&B from £27 to £38 (children under 10 half price); Evening Meal £18.

Mrs A. Clarke
Dairy Farm
Cranford St Andrew
Kettering NN14 4AQ
Tel: 01536 330273

symbols ♁⚘SB♿⛤Wi-Fi

♁	*Pets Welcome*		⚘	*Children Welcome*
SB	*Short Breaks*		♿	*Suitable for Disabled Guests*
⛤	*Licensed*		Wi-Fi	*Wi-Fi available*

Nottinghamshire

In Nottinghamshire the myths, legends and facts all play a part in the stories of Robin Hood, but visit Sherwood Forest, the hiding place of outlaws in medieval times, and make up your own mind from the evidence you find there. Watch cricket at Trent Bridge, horse racing at Nottingham and the all-weather course at Southwell, and ice hockey at Nottingham's National Ice Centre, or try ice skating yourself. There are golf courses from municipal and pay & play to championship standard, fishing in canals, lakes and fisheries, walking by rivers and canals and cycling in the woodland and country parks, and everyone is welcome to play at the Nottingham Tennis Centre. The city of Nottingham is a wonderful place to shop, with designer outlets, independent shops and department stores, and don't miss the traditional Lace Market.

SB

Willow House Bed and Breakfast

A period house (1857) in quiet village two minutes' walk from beautiful river bank, yet only five miles from City. Attractive, interesting accommodation with authentic Victorian ambience. En suite available. Bright, clean rooms with tea/coffee facilities, TV. Off-road parking. Porch for smokers.
Ideally situated for Holme Pierrepont International Watersports Centre; golf; National Ice Centre; Trent Bridge (cricket); Sherwood Forest; Nottingham Racecourse; and the unspoiled historic town of Southwell with its Minster and Racecourse. Good local eating. Please phone first for directions.
Rates: From £26 per person per night.

Mrs V. Baker, Willow House,
Burton Joyce NG14 5FD
Tel: 0115 931 2070; Mob: 07816 347706
www.willowhousebedandbreakfast.co.uk

SB

Wi-Fi

The Grange • Elton

The Grange offers traditional Farmhouse breakfast with mainly local produce used, served in a sunny conservatory looking out onto a beautiful garden.

Owned by ex Scottish International Footballer, Don Masson and his wife Brenda, The Grange is set in the scenic Vale of Belvoir, only 200 metres off the A52 between Nottingham and Grantham. There is an excellent pub and restaurant within a three minute walk away and a five minute drive to Bingham or Bottesford where there are many good eating places. The Grange is ideal for events at Belvoir Castle and also only a 20 minute drive to Trent Bridge cricket ground. Why not try The Grange where Don and Brenda will give you a very warm welcome. Please note that we do not accept credit/debit cards - cash and cheques only.

Terms from £45-£55 single, £60-£75 double/twin.

The Grange Bed & Breakfast, Sutton Lane, Elton NG13 9LA

Free wi-fi at The Grange

Mobile: 07887 952181
www.thegrangebedandbreakfastnotts.co.uk

Burghill

Herefordshire

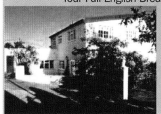

Outdoor activities, creative arts and crafts, wonderful food - Herefordshire, on the border with Wales, will appeal whatever your interest. With its rolling countryside and green meadows dotted with woodland and meandering streams, there are endless opportunities for all kinds of outdoor activities, from white water canoeing on the Yat Rapids through the steep-sided gorge at Symonds Yat, to longer, more gentle trips on the quieter sections of the River Wye. Footpaths, bridleways and traffic-free cycle trails through countryside rich in wildlife are perfect for families as well as the more experienced. The Black and White Village Trail takes visitors through beautiful countryside to pretty little villages, each with its own individual characteristics and shops, or follow the Cider Route in this county of apple orchards.

Lea House

SB

Wi-Fi

A 16th century former coaching inn, Lea House has been beautifully refurbished, with exposed oak beams, an inglenook fireplace, antiques and imaginative decor.

The spacious bedrooms have kingsize or twin beds and full en suite or private bathrooms. Free Wi-Fi, flat screen digital TV. AA award-winning breakfasts are a real treat, with home-made and local produce.

On the Hereford/Gloucester border, adjacent to the Royal Forest of Dean and the spectacular Wye Valley, there is a wealth of activities and wonderful walking.

We accept dogs and children
Bed and Breakfast from £34pppn.
See guests' comments on www.tripadvisor.com

AA
★★★★
Guest
Accommodation

Lea House, Lea, Ross-on-Wye HR9 7JZ • Tel: 01989 750652
enquiries@leahouse.co.uk • www.leahouse.co.uk

SB

Enjoy comfort and good food at this fully centrally heated 17th Century Inn. Situated near to Goodrich Castle in a beautiful part of the Wye Valley, it affords easy access to the Forest of Dean, rural Herefordshire and Wales; although in a quiet village it is only a mile from the A40. Dine in the elegant surroundings of the restaurant, or the cosy atmosphere of the bar choosing from our extensive menu of home made dishes.

THE HOSTELRIE
AT GOODRICH
Country Inn,
Restaurant & Rooms

A choice of real ales and fine wines, Morning Coffee and Afternoon Cream Tea is also available. Dogs are welcome in the bedrooms, main bar and garden.

Rates available for: B&B, Dinner, Bed & Breakfast for single occupancy or two or more sharing.

GOODRICH, ROSS ON WYE HR9 6HX • Tel: 01600 890241
e-mail: info@thehostelrieatgoodrich.com • www.thehostelrieatgoodrich.com

Church Stretton

Shropshire

If you're looking for a break from the pace of life today, but with plenty to do and see, Shropshire is the place to visit. For the active visitor the quiet countryside bordering on the Welsh Marches offers opportunities for walking, cycling, horse riding, kayaking, canoeing, and quad and mountain biking, while if the history of the region's turbulent past appeals, there are over 30 castles to visit, as well as stately homes and beautiful gardens. Visit the grass-roofed Shropshire Hills Discovery Centre at Craven Arms, where you can take a simulated balloon ride and meet the Shropshire mammoth, and Stokesay Castle, the finest 13th century fortified manor house in England. To find out about the more recent past visit the ten museums at the Ironbridge Gorge.

HAYNALL VILLA

Haynall Villa is set in a quiet position in the picturesque Teme Valley on the borders of Shropshire, Herefordshire and Worcestershire, near historic Ludlow, famed for its architecture, and food too. Ironbridge and mid-Wales are within easy reach. Nearby there are lots of attractive towns and villages, gardens and National Trust properties. There is a choice of good walks, stroll by the pretty brook running through the farm, or cycle around the quiet country lanes.

The farmhouse, built approx in the 1820s as a gentleman's residence, is set in large gardens. An oak staircase leads to the comfortable bedrooms, a double and twin en suite, and a family room with private bathroom, all with good views, TV and hot beverage facilities. Relax in the lounge, with a fire on cooler evenings. Enjoy a traditional English farmhouse breakfast using local produce.

In 2008 we were awarded Highly Commended by the AA Member Shropshire Nature Trust.

Mrs Rachel Edwards, Haynall Villa, Little Hereford, Near Ludlow SY8 4BA
Tel & Fax: 01584 711589
e-mail: rachelmedwards@hotmail.com
www.haynallvilla.co.uk

Henwick House
Gravel Hill, Ludlow SY8 1QU

A warm and friendly welcome awaits you in this privately owned former coach house Bed and Breakfast. Delightful en suite rooms, TV, tea/coffee making facilities, comfortable beds and good traditional English Breakfast. Private parking. Situated approximately half-a-mile from the castle and shops and local inns.
One double room, two twin, and one single room, all en suite. Terms from £28 per person.

Miss S.J. Cecil-Jones • 01584 873338
www.henwickhouse.co.uk • info@henwickhouse.co.uk

symbols 🐕🎠 SB ♿ ♉ Wi-Fi

🐕	Pets Welcome	🎠	Children Welcome
SB	Short Breaks	♿	Suitable for Disabled Guests
♉	Licensed	Wi-Fi	Wi-Fi available

AA

★★★
COUNTRY HOUSE
HOTEL

Wi-Fi

Food Award

Pen-y-Dyffryn COUNTRY HOTEL

RHYDYCROESAU, NEAR OSWESTRY, SHROPSHIRE SY10 7JD

This silver stone former Georgian Rectory, set almost a thousand feet up in the Shropshire/Welsh hills, is in a dream situation. Informal atmosphere, no traffic, just buzzards, badgers and beautiful country walks, yet Shrewsbury, Chester, Powis Castle & Lake Vyrnwy are all close by. The well-stocked bar and licensed restaurant are always welcoming at the end of another hard day's relaxing. All bedrooms en suite etc; four have private patios, ideal for pets; several have spa baths. Short breaks available from £88pppd, Dinner, B&B. Pets free.

Tel: 01691 653700
e-mail: stay@peny.co.uk • www.peny.co.uk

Staffordshire

Stratford-Upon-Avon

Warwickshire

Monks Barn Farm

SB

**Shipston Road,
Stratford-upon-Avon,
Warwickshire CV37 8NA
Tel: 01789 293714**

Wi-Fi

Monks Barn Farm is situated two miles south of Stratford on the A3400. Dating back to the 16th century, the farm lies along the banks of the River Stour. Now modernised, it still preserves the old character, and offers first-class amenities; some accommodation is separate from the main house. Ground floor rooms available. Pleasant riverside walks to the village of Clifford Chambers. Centrally situated for visiting Stratford, Warwick and the Cotswolds.

Double/twin/family/single rooms, all en suite.
Children of all ages welcome. Non-smoking.
B&B from £29-£32. Credit cards accepted.

ritameadows@btconnect.com • www.monksbarnfarm.co.uk

Warwickshire and Shakespeare's birthplace, Stratford-on-Avon, go hand in hand. A great way to view this interesting town of black and white, half-timbered buildings is from the tower of the newly rebuilt Royal Shakespeare Theatre next to the river. For a closer look take a guided walking tour, or for a more gentle approach to sightseeing cruise down the River Avon. Round off the day with a performance by the RSC of a favourite Shakespearian play. As well as Sir Basil Spence's Coventry Cathedral and two other churches designed by him, Coventry is home to Warwick Arts Centre, the largest in the Midlands, and of course, in the birthplace of the British motor transport industry, Coventry Transport Museum. .

Stratford-Upon-Avon

Forget-Me-Not Guest House

18 Evesham Place, Stratford-upon-Avon CV37 6HT
Tel & Fax: 01789 204907

Forget-Me-Not Guest House is a family-run establishment that offers immaculate en suite accommodation, delicious hearty breakfasts and a warm welcome right in the middle of Stratford upon Avon. A very enjoyable and unforgettable stay awaits you with Kate and John Morris. We are open all year round and are happy to accommodate you and your needs.

Forget-Me-Not offers 5 comfortable en suite rooms situated within 5 minutes' walking distance of the theatre and town centre - three double rooms, one twin, one luxury super king. Family rooms can be arranged. All bedrooms have colour television, tea and coffee making facilities. Iron and hair dryer are available on request. A babysitting service can be arranged if booked in advance. For your comfort, Forget-Me-Not is totally non-smoking.

AA ★★★ Guest Accommodation

Kate was 1st Runner-Up
"AA Friendliest Landlady in the UK" 2010

www.forgetmenotguesthouse.co.uk

Looking for Holiday Accommodation in the UK?
then visit our website:
www.holidayguides.com

Search for holiday accommodation by region, location or type; (B&B, Self-Catering, Hotel, Caravan & Camping, etc)

Special requirements, are you looking for accommodation where families or pets are welcome?, a short break, or maybe you want to be close to a golf course...

for details of hundreds of properties throughout the UK

Birmingham, Wolverhampton

West Midlands

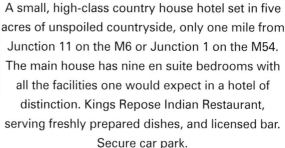

Droitwich Spa

Worcestershire

SB

Wi-Fi

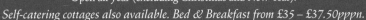

Worcestershire, stretching south-east from the fringes of Birmingham, is a county of Georgian towns, Cotswold stone villages and a Victorian spa, all centred on the cathedral city of Worcester. To the north canals were cut to satisfy the need for transport that grew with industrialisation, and now provide a wonderful opportunity for a leisurely break on a narrowboat, or take a restful look at the countryside from the Severn Valley Railway between Bromsgrove and Kidderminster. Long distance trails like the 100-mile Millenium Way cross the countryside in all directions, or follow one of the many shorter local circular walks. In the Malvern Hills choose between gentle and more strenuous exercise to appreciate the wonderful views of the surrounding countryside, or for a different kind of challenge, try mountain boarding in the hills near Malvern.

Great Malvern

Copper Beech
HOUSE

Great Malvern is renowned for its annual music festivals, prestigious theatres, garden shows, mineral water, and Morgan Cars. The area is a haven of elegant landscapes, open spaces, and fantastic walks. **Copper Beech House** is conveniently located a few minutes' walk from Great Malvern Station, a short distance from the theatres and town centre, and a few minutes by car to the Three Counties Showground.

SB

Wi-Fi

Family-owned and run late Victorian property with 7 en suite guest rooms. All rooms have flat-screen TVs, tea/coffee making facilities, hairdryer, radio alarm, and free Wi-Fi access. A large guest lounge with writing desk, widescreen Freesat television, and a wide range of books, overlooks the south-facing garden. The breakfast room comfortably seats a full house, and an extensive menu with vegetarian and other options is always available. There is ample on and off-road parking and a good choice of restaurants and pubs within walking distance. Non-smoking throughout and open all year. Our website shows availability and allows on-line bookings to be made 24 hours a day.

Copper Beech House
32 Avenue Road, Malvern WR14 3BJ • 01684 565013
www.copperbeechhouse.co.uk • enquiries@copperbeechhouse.co.uk

tHE COTFORD HOTEL
L'amuse-BOUCHE
restauRant

SB

We think of our hotel as our home and that's why we treat our guests as our friends. We invite you to take in the original features of our fully refurbished hotel, relax in our beautiful gardens and indulge with fine French-style cuisine in our award winning L'amuse-Bouche restaurant. And all of this is just a short stroll from the centre of historic Malvern. You can rest assured that from the moment you arrive at The Cotford Hotel, you'll have our complete attention and we'll take care of everything.

★★★

51 Graham Road · Malvern · Worcestershire · WR14 2HU
reservations@cotfordhotel.co.uk · www.cotfordhotel.co.uk

Tel 01684 57 24 27

Malvern Wells, Pirton

Cadmore Lodge Hotel & Country Club

Berrington Green, Tenbury Wells, Worcs WR15 8TQ
Telephone & Fax: 01584 810044
e-mail: reception.cadmore@cadmorelodge.com • www.cadmorelodge.co.uk

A friendly, family-managed Hotel & Country Club, set in a private estate and nature reserve in rural Worcestershire, just a few minutes' drive from Tenbury Wells. Facilities include a picturesque but challenging 9-hole golf course, indoor swimming pool and leisure facilities, bowls and two fishing lakes (trout and coarse). The hotel provides a warm welcome with a homely atmosphere, an excellent choice of daily menus and 15 en suite bedrooms.
In addition, self-catering accommodation is available in the Water Mill cottage, Millenium Tower and a number of Nordic log cabins.

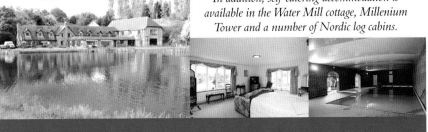

The FHG Directory of Website Addresses

on pages 381-387 is a useful quick reference guide for holiday accommodation with e-mail and/or website details

East Yorkshire

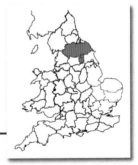
North Yorkshire

Dominated by the magnificent York Minster, the largest medieval Gothic cathedral in northern Europe, the city of York in North Yorkshire is full of attractions for the visitor. Have fun finding your way through the Snickelways, the maze of hidden alleyways, and enjoy a morning – or longer – in the array of independent shops and boutiques as well as all the top high street stores. Explore York's past at Jorvik, the recreation of the original Viking city from 1000 years ago or become an archaeologist for the day at Dig! and excavate for yourself items from Viking, Roman, medieval and Victorian times. Outside the city the vast open stretches of the North York Moors and Yorkshire Dales National Parks and the golden sandy beaches of the coast are perfect for an active holiday.

Glaisdale

Red House Farm

Listed Georgian farmhouse featured in "Houses of the North York Moors". Completely refurbished to the highest standards, retaining all original features. Bedrooms have bath/shower/toilet, central heating, TV and tea making facilities. Excellent walks straight from the doorstep. Friendly farm animals – a few cows, geese and pretty free-roaming hens. 1½ acres of gardens, sitting-out areas. Magnificent views. Interesting buildings – Listed barns now converted to 3 holiday cottages. Adult games room with snooker table. Eight miles from seaside/Whitby. Village pub within walking distance. Stabling available for horses/dogs. Non-smoking.

Tom and Sandra Spashett, Red House Farm, Glaisdale, Near Whitby YO21 2PZ • Tel & Fax: 01947 897242
e-mail: spashettredhouse@aol.com
www.redhousefarm.com

EGTON BANKS FARM

Glaisdale, Whitby
YO21 2QP
Tel: 01947 897289

Beautiful old farmhouse (pre 1750) situated in a lovely valley close to quiet roadside. Working farm set in 120 acres of pastureland and woods. Centre of National Park. Warm and friendly atmosphere. Diningroom/Lounge for guests with TV and books. Close to river, one mile from Glaisdale village and mainline railway, eight miles to Whitby, four miles steam railway and Heartbeat country. Both bedrooms have pretty decor and TV. One double and one family/twin room, both en suite. Full Yorkshire Breakfast. Packed lunches. All diets catered for. B&B from £28. No pets, no smoking.

e-mail: egtonbanksfarm@btconnect.com
www.egtonbanksfarm.agriplus.net

Barn Close Farm

Rievaulx, Helmsley, North Yorkshire YO62 5LH

01439 798321

Mrs J. Milburn

BARN CLOSE FARM is nicely situated in the North York Moors National Park. This family farm in beautiful surroundings offers homely accommodation to holidaymakers all year round. Within easy reach of Rievaulx Abbey and many other places of interest, it is an ideal centre for tourists.

Pony trekking nearby • Good walking terrain!
Highly commended for good food.

One double en suite and one double king-size four-poster with private bathroom; sitting room and dining room.

Bed and Breakfast from £28 to £40, Evening Dinner £20.
"WHICH?" RECOMMENDED. "DAILY TELEGRAPH" RECOMMENDED.

Laskill Grange
Near Helmsley

Delightful country house is set in a one-acre garden which has a lake with ducks, swans, peacock and a visiting otter.

Guests can walk in the garden, fish the River Seph which runs through the grounds, or visit nearby Rievaulx Abbey.

All rooms lovingly cared for and well equipped. Four bedrooms are in beamed outbuildings and open onto a lawn. All rooms en suite. Open all year.

Generous cuisine using local fresh produce, and vegetarians catered for.

B&B from £28.50-£50.

Also 7 luxury self-catering cottages.
Newly installed hot tubs.

Laskill Grange, Hawnby,
Near Helmsley YO62 5NB
(Contact Sue Smith)
01439 798268
e-mail: laskillgrange@tiscali.co.uk
www.laskillgrange.co.uk

Pickering

Banavie

is a large semi-detached house set in a quiet part of the picturesque village of Thornton-le-Dale, one of the prettiest villages in Yorkshire with its famous thatched cottage and bubbling stream flowing through the centre. We offer our guests a quiet night's sleep and rest away from the main road, yet only four minutes' walk from the village centre. One large double or twin bedroom and two double bedrooms, all tastefully decorated with en suite facilities, colour TV, hairdryer, shaver point etc. and tea/coffee making facilities. There is a large guest lounge, tea tray on arrival. A real Yorkshire breakfast is served in the dining room. Places to visit include Castle Howard, Eden Camp, North Yorkshire Moors Railway, Goathland ("Heartbeat"), York etc. There are three pubs, a bistro and a fish and chip shop for meals. Children and dogs welcome. Own keys. Car parking at back of house.

B&B from £30pppn • No Smoking
Welcome To Excellence
SAE please for brochure
Mrs Ella Bowes

BANAVIE, ROXBY ROAD, THORNTON-LE-DALE, PICKERING YO18 7SX
Tel: 01751 474616 • e-mail: info@banavie.uk.com • www.banavie.uk.com

Farfields Farm

Peacefully situated working farm overlooking beautiful Newton Dale. Four comfortable ground floor rooms in a lovely old converted character barn just opposite the farmhouse. All rooms are en suite, either twin or super-king, and have digital/DVD TV, beverage tray, fridge and microwave. Delicious farmhouse breakfast using locally sourced produce. Ideal central location for exploring moors, coast and York. Dalby Forest only one mile away. Marvellous walking and bird watching from the farm. Fantastic views of the steam train in the valley below. Inn serving excellent meals only a short stroll away.
Tariff £38-£45pppn. Single £50-£60.
Special weekly rates.

Mrs E. Stead, Farfields Farm, Lockton,
Pickering YO18 7NQ • Tel: 01751 460239
e-mail: stay@farfieldsfarm.co.uk
www.farfieldsfarm.co.uk

Scarborough, Skipton

A warm welcome awaits on a 180- acre mixed farm in beautiful Boltby village, nestling in the valley below the Hambleton Hills, in the midst of Herriot country and on the edge of the North York Moors National Park. An 18th century stone-built farmhouse with full central heating, comfortable en suite bedrooms (one family, one twin) with original old oak beams, and tea/coffee facilities; spacious guests' lounge with colour TV. Good English breakfast. Walks right from the farm. Central for touring the Dales, York and East Coast. Pony trekking in village.

Children welcome • Pets welcome
B&B from £35 - £45

Mrs M. Fountain, Town Pasture Farm,
Boltby, Thirsk YO7 2DY
Tel: 01845 537298
www.townpasturefarm.co.uk

Golden Fleece Hotel
Market Place - Thirsk - York YO7 1LL
Tel: 01845 523108   Fax: 01845 523996

The Golden Fleece Hotel is a 400-year-old Coaching Inn overlooking the cobbled market place in Thirsk, situated between two outstanding areas of natural beauty, the Yorkshire Moors and Dales National Parks. The hotel has a range of 25 individually designed en suite rooms equipped with all the amenities that make today's traveller feel completely at home.

Food is home cooked using local produce and the service is relaxed and friendly.

For information about our Shortbreaks please contact the reception team at the hotel.

www.goldenfleecehotel.com • reservations@goldenfleecehotel.com

Whitby

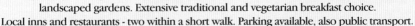

York

Blossoms York

Set in a Georgian townhouse on a leafy avenue, a warm welcome awaits at our friendly, family-run guest house. Located only minutes' walk from the historic Bar Walls and York Minster, restaurants, bars and shopping, we are in an ideal location for exploring York.

We pride ourselves on offering a good service combined with value-for-money prices. All rooms are recently decorated and en suite with WC and shower; TV, tea tray and phone. Family rooms for up to 6 people. Bar and lounge.

Free internet access and wi-fi • Free car park.
Local information available.

Sun-Thurs from £22.50pp • Fri and Sat from £30pp.
3-night midweek spring and autumn specials from £20pp
See our website for latest prices and offers

www.blossomsyork.co.uk

Tel: 01904 652391   Fax: 01904 652392
e-mail: fhg@blossomsyork.co.uk

SB

Wi-Fi

Alder Carr HOUSE

A country house, set in its own extensive grounds, offering spacious and comfortable accommodation.

- All bedrooms look towards the rolling hills of the Yorkshire Wolds.
- Only a 10 minute drive to York's Park & Ride enables you to combine city sightseeing with quiet country relaxation.
- A wide range of restaurants and country pubs in a three mile radius gives excellent choice for evening meals.
- An ideal base for exploring the many aspects of Yorkshire.
- Twin/double/family rooms - all en suite or private bathroom.
- Price £30-£32.50 per person. Single occupancy in double room £40.

Mr and Mrs G. Steel, Alder Carr House, York Road, Barmby Moor,
York YO42 4HT • Tel: 01759 380566 • mobile: 07885 277740
e-mail: chris.steel@aldercarrhouse.plus.com
www.aldercarrhouse.com

South Yorkshire

Not only does South Yorkshire have a considerable industrial heritage to offer, but the twin attractions of the southern Pennines and the Peak District National Park makes it an ideal destination for an outdoor break, whether for walking, climbing, biking or horse riding across the wild, wide open moors. Adults and children can have fun and learn at the same time at the Magna Science Adventure at Rotherham, where the interactive displays are based on the four elements, air, earth, fire and water, or at the Weston Park Museum in Sheffield. The beautiful grounds of the historic Roche Abbey at Maltby are a perfect picnic spot, while children will love getting really close to wild and farm animals from all over the world at the Yorkshire Wildlife Park near Doncaster. If the weather isn't so good, brush up your mountaineering skills at a choice of indoor climbing walls, and there's swimming and ice skating and for relaxation, a tropical spa, at Doncaster Dome.

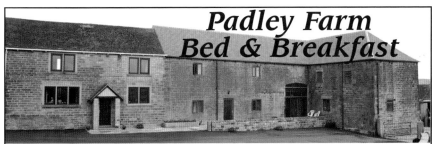

Bingley

West Yorkshire

Large Victorian house tucked away in tranquil area, but close main roads, tourist sites, cities. Good views, individual decor, informal style. Comfy sofas, interesting artworks. Antidote to chain hotels. Historic canal locks and excellent walking (dogs and humans) close by.

THE FIVE RISE LOCKS HOTEL & RESTAURANT,
BECK LANE, BINGLEY, YORKSHIRE BD16 4DD
Tel: 01274 565296 • e-mail: info@five-rise-locks.co.uk
www.five-rise-locks.co.uk

West Yorkshire is a mix of wild moorland and towns and cities with an historic industrial heritage. Spend some time in one of the many fascinating museums of past working life, then stride out over the moors, taking in the dramatic scenery, before a shopping spree or a wonderful afternoon tea. Visit the Rhubarb Triangle near Wakefield early in the year to see the crop being harvested by candlelight. At the model Victorian village for mill workers at Saltaire UNESCO World Heritage Site, Salts Mill has been transformed into the Hockney Gallery, with a restaurant and everything from musical instruments to carpets for shoppers to browse and buy. From there, wander along the banks of the Leeds-Liverpool Canal, so vital for trade in a past age, and watch the Five Rise Locks in action. Leeds is the destination for a lively city break. Theatres, ballet, opera, festivals, restaurants, clubs, and of course, one of the best shopping experiences in the country.

Cullingworth

If you are looking for a warm and comfortable environment in which to relax and enjoy your stay whilst visiting Yorkshire then The Manor will be perfect for you. This luxurious 5 Star Gold Award retreat offers a relaxing and refreshing base from which to explore some of the most beautiful countryside in Yorkshire. Lovingly restored, this 18th Century Manor House is enhanced by many original features. Ideally situated for exploring the rugged Pennine moorland or Bronte Country, the Yorkshire Dales and beyond.

- Ample off-road car parking
- Centrally heated en suite rooms
- Welcome tray with homemade biscuits
- Top quality beds and linen
- Satellite TV with DVD player
- Wi-Fi Internet access
- Extensive DVD library
- Hairdryer, CD player & radio alarm clock
- Easy access to all major attractions
- Debit & credit cards accepted
- Private guest lounge
- Thick fluffy towels
- Extensive complimentary toiletries
- Iron & ironing board available
- Packed lunches available on request
- Hearty Yorkshire breakfast menu

The Manor Guest House
Sutton Drive, Cullingworth, Bradford BD13 5BQ
Tel: 01535 274374
e-mail: info@cullingworthmanor.co.uk
www.cullingworthmanor.co.uk

Beamish

Durham

Bushblades Farm

Harperley, Stanley, Co. Durham DH9 9UA

Comfortable Georgian farmhouse set in large garden. Twin ground floor en suite, and double first floor en suite bedrooms.

All rooms have tea/coffee making facilities, colour TV and easy chairs.
Ample parking.
Children over 12 years welcome. Sorry, no pets.

Bed and Breakfast from £35-£40 single, £60-£65 double.
Self-catering accommodation also available.

Tel: 01207 232722

bushbladesfarm@hotmail.com
www.bushbladesfarm.co.uk

**Near Durham, Metro Centre, Beamish Museum;
Hadrian's Wall, Northumberland Coast under an hour.**

If you're looking for a few days' break somewhere different, why not go to the city of Durham? Set between the North Pennines and the Durham Heritage Coast, the old medieval heart with its cobbled streets is dominated by the cathedral and castle, a World Heritage Site, and a must for visitors. On the way back to the modern shopping centre, browse through individual boutiques and galleries in the alleys and vennels, then enjoy a stroll along the riverside walks. Stay for longer in County Durham, tour all the heritage sites and enjoy invigorating walks and hikes through the dramatic Pennines countryside and along the clifftop path at the coast. There are paths, trails and tracks for all standards of fitness, whether a family ramble and picnic or a hike along the Pennine Way. High Force, the highest waterfall in England, on the Raby Castle estate, is easily accessible. Include it in a long distance hike or a gentle wander from the car park.

Northumberland

The Saddle Bed & Breakfast

24/25 Northumberland Street, Alnmouth NE66 2RA • 01665 830476

This friendly family run B&B is situated in Alnmouth on the Northumberland coast with miles of white sandy beaches and unspoilt countryside

SB

Wi-Fi

- Residents' lounge
- Private car park
- Children welcome
- Pets welcome

All rooms are en suite with flat-screen TV, DVD player and iPod connectivity, tea/ coffee making facilities and full central heating.

e-mail: thesaddlebedandbreakfast@hotmail.com
www.thesaddlebedandbreakfast.co.uk

14 Blakelaw Road, Alnwick NE66 1AZ

A friendly welcome awaits you at this award-winning Bed and Breakfast. The spacious en suite room has a double and single bed so can be let as double or twin; table and chairs and settee so you can relax and enjoy panoramic views over Alnwick, with the coast in the distance. The en suite bathrom is large, with bath and shower cubicle etc. Hospitality tray, basket of fruit and home-baked treats. *Alnwick is the perfect base to explore many attractions, castles and the spectacular coastline. From £31 pppn.*

SB

Tel: 01665 604201
www.visitalnwick.org.uk/accommodation/bb_rooftops.htm

SB

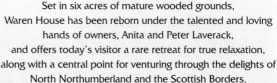

Set in six acres of mature wooded grounds,
Waren House has been reborn under the talented and loving
hands of owners, Anita and Peter Laverack,
and offers today's visitor a rare retreat for true relaxation,
along with a central point for venturing through the delights of
North Northumberland and the Scottish Borders.

Breakfast and dinner are served in the beautiful and romantic
dining room where food is presented with the utmost care.
Our cellar is stocked with a huge choice of reasonably priced
fine wines. All public rooms and bedrooms are non-smoking.

Relax in the gardens or in the comfortable lounge and adjacent library. For those seeking the
simple pleasures of walking - the sandy shore offers mile upon mile of beautiful scenery.

From this tranquil setting it is easy to find the treasures of the Heritage Coast, including the
magnificent castle at Bamburgh, just two miles away.

Waren Mill, Belford, Near Bamburgh, Northumberland NE70 7EE
Tel: 01668 214581 • Fax: 01668 214484
e-mail: enquiries@warenhousehotel.co.uk
www.warenhousehotel.co.uk

❖ Struthers Farm ❖

Catton, Allendale, Hexham NE47 9LP

Struthers Farm offers a warm welcome in the heart of England, with many splendid local walks from the farm itself. Panoramic views. Situated in an area of outstanding beauty. Double/twin rooms, en suite bathrooms, central heating. Good farmhouse cooking. Ample safe parking. Come and share our home and enjoy beautiful countryside. Near Hadrian's Wall (½ hour's drive).

Children welcome, pets by prior arrangement. Open all year.

Bed and Breakfast from £30; Optional Evening Meal from £12.50.

Contact Mrs Ruby Keenleyside
01434 683580
www.struthersfarmbandb.com

PETH HEAD •COTTAGE•

Bed & Breakfast in Hadrian's Wall Country

SB

Wi-Fi

AA
Highly Commended
★★★★
Bed & Breakfast

Welcome to our pretty rose-covered cottage dating from 1825 and located in the quiet hamlet of Juniper, 4 miles south of Hexham market town, Northumberland. An ideal base for visiting Hadrian's Wall, Durham Cathedral, Beamish Museum, Northumberland's Coast and Castles and the heather covered North Pennines.

We have 2 double en suite rooms with sunny south-facing aspects. Both rooms can be either double (super king-size) or twin-bedded rooms. Aga-cooked breakfasts. Private off-road parking available for your vehicle. Very quiet and peaceful countryside location. Non-smoking, sorry no pets.

Contact Joan Liddle, Peth Head Cottage, Bed and Breakfast,
Juniper, Hexham, Northumberland NE47 0LA
Tel 01434 673 286 • E-mail info@peth-head-cottage.co.uk
www.peth-head-cottage.co.uk

Katerina's Guest House

High Street, Rothbury NE65 7TQ • 01669 620691

Wi-Fi

Charming old guest house, ideally situated for the amenities of pretty Rothbury village, and to explore Northumberland's hills, coast, Alnwick Castle and gardens. Beautiful bedrooms, each decorated and colour co-ordinated to enhance its individual character; some with original stone fireplaces/beamed ceilings, all en suite, with four-poster beds, TV, and superbly stocked tea tray. Free Wi-Fi. Wide, interesting choice of breakfasts; licensed evening meals also available – sample Cath's bread, 'whisky porridge', vegetarian nutballs, or Steak Katerina.

Bed and Breakfast from £68-£78 per room per night, depending on number of nights booked.

e-mail: ian.mills6@btopenworld.com
www.katerinasguesthouse.co.uk

Wi-Fi

Glimpse the red squirrel from our splendid 18th century Georgian farmhouse on this 1100 acre livestock farm. Relax in beautifully appointed, spacious en suite bedrooms with superb views over open countryside. Elegant, comfortable lounge with log fire. Delicious Aga cooked breakfasts using local produce, with home-made bread and preserves.

Ideally located for visiting Northumberland's many attractions including Alnwick Castle and Gardens and National Trust Cragside.

• *'Pride of Northumbria' Best B&B Award Winner*
• *Open March-November*
• *Children welcome*
• *Terms from £40 twin/double, £55 single.*

**Lee Farm, Near Rothbury,
Longframlington, Morpeth NE65 8JQ**
Contact: Mrs Susan Aynsley
Tel & Fax: 01665 570257
e-mail: enqs@leefarm.co.uk
www.leefarm.co.uk

Seahouses, Wooler

Wyndgrove House

Bed & Breakfast Accommodation on
the Northumberland coast

Wi-Fi

Welcome to Wyndgrove House in the pretty North Northumberland village of Seahouses.
10 minutes' walk from the beaches and the harbour, in a quiet leafy conservation area.
Light large rooms are perfect for relaxing; the spacious bedrooms feature king-size beds
with pure Egyptian cotton bed linen and generous bath sheets. Hospitality trays are well
stocked with quality Fair Trade products and biscuits. Breakfast is served in our light,
sunny, south-facing dining room where a freshly cooked breakfast of the best local
produce will set you up for the day. Ideal base for exploring this scenic area.

**156 Main Street, Seahouses,
Northumberland NE68 7UA
Telephone: 01665 720 767
e-mail: wyndgrovehouse@gmail.com
www.wyndgrovehouse.co.uk**

East Horton Farmhouse

BED & BREAKFAST

East Horton is situated between the market town of Wooler and the coastal village of
Belford in the most historic and beautiful corner of Northumberland. It has stunning
views south down the valley towards Alnwick and west to the Cheviot Hills.

Recently refurbished to a very high standard, our three en suite guest bedrooms are
south facing, spacious and well appointed with TVs, hospitality trays, hairdryers etc.

All food is sourced locally and we use free range and organic produce
whenever possible.

**East Horton, Wooler, Northumberland NE71 6EZ • Tel: 01668 215 216
e-mail: sed@hazelrigg.fsnet.co.uk • www.farmhousebandb.co.uk**

Cheshire

Ambleside

Cumbria

The stunning scenery of the region now known as Cumbria, in England's north west, from the Solway Firth in the north to the coasts of Morecambe Bay in the south, the ports and seaside villages in the west to the Pennines in the east, and including the Lake District National Park, has been attracting tourists since the end of the 17th century, and the number of visitors has been increasing ever since. All kinds of outdoor activities are available, from gorge walking and ghyll scrambling to a trek through the countryside on horseback or a quiet afternoon rowing on a tranquil lake. The area is a walkers' paradise, and whether on foot, in a wheelchair or a pushchair there's a path and trail for everyone. Whether you're following one of the 'Miles without Stiles' on relatively level, well laid tracks around the towns and villages, climbing in the Langdales or tackling Scafell Pike, the highest mountain in England, you won't miss out on all the Lake District has to offer.

Ambleside

Dower House

SB   Lovely old house, quiet and peaceful, stands on an elevation overlooking Lake Windermere, with one of the most beautiful views in all Lakeland. Its setting within the 100-acre Wray Castle estate (National Trust), with direct access to the Lake, makes it an ideal base for walking and touring. Hawkshead and Ambleside are about ten minutes' drive and have numerous old inns and restaurants. Ample car parking; prefer dogs to sleep in the car. Children over five years welcome. Open all year.

Bed and Breakfast from £39.00pp
Dinner, Bed & Breakfast from £59.00pp
e-mail: margaret@rigg5.orangehome.co.uk
www.dowerhouselakes.co.uk

SB

A relaxing hotel break in the Lake District

ROTHAY MANOR
HOTEL & RESTAURANT

The Rothay Manor Hotel & Restaurant offers a relaxed, warm and friendly atmosphere in a luxury country house setting, with large, individually designed en suite bedrooms, spacious comfortable lounges, delicious fresh food and outstanding service. Free use of nearby Leisure Club with sauna and jacuzzi.

Special offers, packages and a wide range of special interest breaks available.

ROTHAY MANOR HOTEL & RESTAURANT
Rothay Bridge, Ambleside, Cumbria LA22 0EH • Tel: 015394 33605
e-mail: hotel@rothaymanor.co.uk • www.rothaymanor.co.uk

Ees Wyke

• COUNTRY HOUSE •

Near Sawrey, Ambleside, Cumbria LA22 0JZ

Ees Wyke is an elegant and comfortable Georgian Country House overlooking Esthwaite Water in the centre of the Lake District. Once a holiday home of Beatrix Potter, Ees Wyke offers superb bed and breakfast, and dinner. Just a short walk away is Hill Top, where she made her home and wrote many of her Peter Rabbit books.

Many bedrooms, the lounge and the restaurant have stunning lake views and fells, from Coniston Old Man to the Langdale Pikes and Grizedale Forest. There are excellent walks nearby, from the easy and relaxing to the more challenging. Lavish Lakeland breakfasts and a daily five-course dinner menu offer dishes featuring local produce.

Tel: 015394 36393 • www.eeswyke.co.uk
e-mail: mail@eeswyke.co.uk

Good Food Guide • Good Hotel Guide Recommended

Ambleside, Appleby-in-Westmorland

Bowness-on-Windermere, Broughton-in-Furness

GRAHAM ARMS HOTEL

Longtown, Near Carlisle, Cumbria CA6 5SE

A warm welcome awaits at this 250-year-old former Coaching Inn. Situated six miles from the M6 (J44) and Gretna Green, The Graham Arms makes an ideal overnight stop or perfect touring base for the Scottish Borders, English Lakes, Hadrian's Wall and much more. 16 comfortable en suite bedrooms, including four-poster and family rooms with TV, radio etc. Meals and snacks served throughout the day. Friendly 'local's bar' and new 'Sports bar' serving real ale, extra cold lagers and a fine selection of malt whiskies. Secure courtyard parking for cars, cycles and motorcycles. Beautiful woodland and riverside walks. Pets welcome with well behaved owners!

• **Tel: 01228 791213** • **Fax: 01228 794110** •
• **e-mail: office@grahamarms.com** • **www.grahamarms.com** •

Bed and full traditional breakfast £35– £40.
Special rates for weekend and midweek breaks.

The Rook Guesthouse
9 Castlegate Cockermouth
Cumbria CA13 9EU

Interesting 17th century town house, adjacent to historic castle. We offer comfortable accommodation with full English, vegetarian or Continental breakfast.

All rooms are en suite with colour TV, beverage tray and central heating.

Cockermouth is an unspoilt market town located at the North Western edge of the Lake District within easy reach of the Lakes, Cumbrian Coast and Border country.

We are ideally situated as a base for walkers, cyclists and holidaymakers.
Open all year, except Christmas.

B&B from £50 Double,
£30 Single.

Mrs V. A. Waters • Tel: 01900 828496
e-mail: sarahwaters1848@btinternet.com
www.therookguesthouse.gbr.cc/

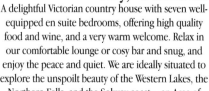

Children of all ages will want to visit The Beatrix Potter Attraction at Bowness-on-Windermere and Hilltop, the author's home on the other side of the lake. Find out all about the area at Brockhole, the National Park Visitor Centre overlooking Windermere, with an adventure playground and lovely gardens. For the central Lakes stay at Ambleside or one of the many traditional Lakeland villages, like Grasmere, the home of Wordsworth. The busy market town of Keswick is the ideal centre for exploring the north Lakes, including the historic port of Whitehaven, the former centre for the rum trade. Stay in Penrith, Appleby-in-Westmorland or Kirkby Lonsdale to explore the western Pennines or Silloth-on-Solway to discover the Solway Firth coast. Finally don't miss out Carlisle and its cathedral and castle, the stronghold involved in so many battles with the Scots, the Jacobite rebellions and the Civil War.

Ullswater, Windermere

Windermere

LANGDALE CHASE HOTEL

Windermere, Cumbria LA23 1LW
Tel: 015394 32201

Magnificent country house hotel with over six acres
of beautifully landscaped grounds sloping to the
edge of Lake Windermere. Panoramic views of lake
and fells, log fires, excellent food, and friendly,
professional staff all ensure a memorable stay.

e-mail: sales@langdalechase.co.uk • www.langdalechase.co.uk

Cumbria Tourist Board - Hotel of the Year 2005 Silver Award
Website of the Year Award 2005 • Taste of England Award 2005

Guest House, Prince's Road, Windermere LA23 2DD

KIRKWOOD occupies a quiet spot between Windermere
and Bowness, offering guests a warm and friendly
atmosphere with an individual personal service. Rooms
are large and all en suite with TV and tea/coffee making
facilities; some have four-poster beds. Your hosts will be
pleased to help plan tours or walks with maps provided.
Three-night Special Breaks available. B&B £33–£45.

SB

Wi-Fi

Tel: 015394 43907
e-mail: info@kirkwoodguesthouse.co.uk
www.kirkwoodguesthouse.co.uk

Luxury in the Lakes –
The Queen's Head Hotel

Tucked away in the Troutbeck Valley near Windermere, this warm
and welcoming accommodation awaits your arrival, where you'll
experience first hand the luxurious rooms on offer, as well as an
array of tantalising dishes. Plus, you'll have no trouble discovering
all the area has to offer, with a maze of footpaths linking ancient
hamlets, as well as luring you into some beautiful gardens.

The Queen's Head Hotel, Townhead, Troutbeck
Near Windermere, Cumbria LA23 1PW
Tel 015394 32174 • reservations@queensheadtroutbeck.co.uk
www.queensheadtroutbeck.co.uk

SB

Wi-Fi

symbols

🐕	Pets Welcome	🪀	Children Welcome
SB	Short Breaks	♿	Suitable for Disabled Guests
🍷	Licensed	Wi-Fi	Wi-Fi available

Boscastle

Cornwall

Forget-Me-Not Farm Holidays

Situated on Trefranck, our 340-acre family-run beef and sheep farm, in North Cornwall, on the edge of enchanting Bodmin Moor and six miles from the spectacular North Cornwall Heritage Coast. We offer all year round luxury, 4-star, self-catering acccommodation.

SB

Forget-Me-Not Cottage can comfortably sleep 6 and is tastefully decorated and superbly equipped, with a real log fire and central heating. **The Old Wagon House** is a stylish barn conversion and sleeps 2, with a 4-poster bed – ideal for romantic breaks. Mobility rating. **The Stable** is an en suite twin annexe to the Old Wagon House. **Honeysuckle Cottage** sleeps 5. Lovely views of the moor; beautiful garden. Well equipped.
Meadowsweet Cottage (Okehampton, Devon) - barn conversion, sleeps 4, surrounded by own woodlands. Abundance of wildlife. Excellent for cycling and walking holidays.
Trefranck is within easy reach of the Eden Project, the Lost Gardens of Heligan, Padstow and the Camel Trail.

Visit Bude, Crackington Haven, Padstow, Tintagel & The Eden Project.

Trefranck Farm, St Clether, Launceston PL15 8QN
Mobile: 07790 453229
Tel: 01566 86284
e-mail: holidays@Trefranck.co.uk
www.meadowsweetcottage.co.uk OR
www.forget-me-not-farm-holidays.co.uk

Renowned for its wonderful coastline, the longest in the UK, Cornwall has everything to offer for lovers of watersports, whether sailing, surfing, windsurfing, water-skiing, scuba diving or simply enjoying a family holiday on the beach. In busy fishing towns like Looe and Padstow, and traditional villages such as Polperro, there are plenty of inns and restaurants where you can sample the fresh catch. The best-known centre for the arts is St Ives, with the Tate St Ives, and artists and galleries are also to be found in Fowey, St Agnes and Penzance. In summer, when the seaside towns are at their busiest, visit the Rame Peninsula in the south east of the county for a quieter break, or take a trip to the Isles of Scilly for a traditional and relaxing stay. The magnificent coast is ideal for birdwatchers, artists and photographers, golfers of every standard will find a wide choice of courses.

Coombe Cottages

Crackington Haven is a small unspoilt cove overlooked by 400 foot cliffs, with rock pools and a sandy beach at low tide – ideal for swimming or surfing.

Coombe Cottages are situated within this Area of Outstanding Natural Beauty, only 300 yards from the beach, coastal path or pub.

Little Coombe sleeps two, **Rivercoombe** sleeps four and both cottages have their own fenced gardens with picnic table and BBQ. Inside, they are well equipped and have open fires for those more chilly evenings.

Along the private drive there is a laundry room, and easy off-road parking is available outside each cottage.

**Paul & Helen Seez, Coombe Cottages,
Crackington Haven, Bude EX23 0JG
Tel: 01840 230664**

Fowey Harbour Cottages

Brochure and details from W. J. B. Hill & Son, 3 Fore Street, Fowey PL23 1AH

We are a small Agency offering a selection of cottages and flats situated around the beautiful Fowey Harbour on the South Cornish Coast. Different properties accommodate from two to six persons and vary in their decor and facilities so that hopefully there will be something we can offer to suit anyone. All properties are registered with VisitBritain and are personally vetted by us.

Short Breaks and weekend bookings accepted subject to availability (mainly out of peak season but sometimes available at "last minute" in season).

Tel: 01726 832211 • Fax: 01726 832901
e-mail: hillandson@talk21.com • www.foweyharbourcottages.co.uk

Penquite Farm

Golant, Fowey PL23 1LB

A stunning location in spectacular scenic countryside offering wonderful river views over the Fowey Valley. A perfect rural retreat for a relaxing, enjoyable holiday on a working farm, nestling beside a beautiful 13th century church on the edge of a peaceful riverside village.

A spacious, three-bedroom, split-level house with two bathrooms, and two beautifully restored barn conversions, all rooms en suite and tastefully furnished to a very high standard. Sleep four (wheelchair-friendly), six and ten persons. All have own large gardens, patio area, BBQs and ample parking. Ideal for touring, walking, beaches, National Trust properties, gardens, and the Eden Project close by.

Ruth Varco • Tel & Fax: 01726 833319

ruth@penquitefarm.co.uk
www.penquitefarm.co.uk

❖ Hollyvagg Farmhouse ❖

Part of cosy 17th century Listed Farmhouse in 80 acres of fields and woods. Working farm with sheep, geese, dogs and cats. Central to North and South coasts, Bodmin Moor, and the fabulous Eden Project. Golf and riding nearby. All modern conveniences. Sleeps 4.

Also available, LAKEVIEW, luxury mobile home with large verandah set in a secluded position overlooking a wooded valley and ponds with views of Dartmoor in the distance. There is a large parking area and enclosed garden suitable for large dogs only. Sleeps 4.

Hollyvagg Farm, Lewannick, Launceston, Cornwall PL15 7QH • Mrs Anne Moore
01566 782309 • www.hollyvaggfarm.co.uk

FREE COARSE FISHING FOR GUESTS ONLY (BOTH PROPERTIES)

Liskeard

Away from it all, yet close to everything

SB

Get away from it all at Rosecraddoc Lodge, Liskeard, a well maintained, purpose-built holiday retreat on the edge of Bodmin Moor. Pub/restaurant on site, but NOT 'holiday camp' style. Ideally located for visiting attractions, including the Eden Project.

Liskeard 2 miles • Looe 9 miles • Plymouth 20 miles

Several well equipped and comfortable bungalows available, sleeping 4, 5 or 6.
Everything you need including bed linen, etc.
Available March-December. Weekly rates £130-£480. Discounts available.

Visit our website at **www.gotocornwall.info** or **Freephone 0800 458 3886**
or **e-mail: rosecraddoc@uwclub.net**

CUTKIVE WOOD HOLIDAY LODGES

Nestling in the heart of a peaceful family-owned country estate are six well-equipped comfortable cedar-clad lodges. Set on the edge of ancient bluebell woods with lovely rural views, you can relax and enjoy yourself in this tranquil and idyllic setting. Help with the animals, explore the woods and fields, fun play area. So much for everyone to see and do – memorable beaches, wonderful coasts, walk the moors, inspiring gardens and Eden, theme attractions, historic gems. Dogs welcome. Ideally situated to enjoy coast and country holidays whatever the time of year.

St Ive, Liskeard, Cornwall PL14 3ND • Tel: 01579 362216
www.cutkivewood.co.uk • e-mail: holidays@cutkivewood.co.uk

Liskeard, Looe

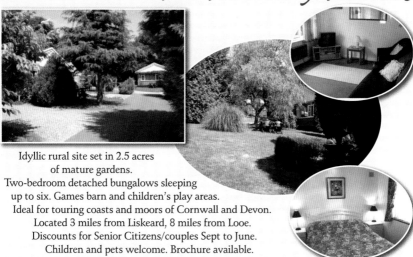

Looe, Perranporth

- All accommodation dog friendly - 2 dogs maximum
- Individual fenced gardens
- Dog walk and off-lead paddock on site
- Many dog friendly beaches
- Dog friendly local pubs
- Day kennelling nearby
- Open all year
- Short breaks available

Valleybrook

Villas & Cottages

Nestling in a tranquil country valley in the heart of Cornish farmlands, bordered by a sparkling stream, the 6 superb villas and 2 delightful cottages are located between Fowey, Polperro and Looe and just 2½ miles from the SW Coastal path. At Valleybrook you can enjoy the space and freedom of luxury self-catering accommodation, with all of life's little luxuries and everyday convenience at your fingertips. Internet ordered food from Waitrose, Tesco, Sainsbury's or Asda can be delivered to your accommodation.

Valleybrook   Peakswater   Lansallos
Looe   Cornwall   PL13 2QE

Tel: 01503 220493
www.valleybrookholidays.com

SB

Wi-Fi

TREMAINE GREEN
for MEMORABLE HOLIDAYS

"A beautiful private hamlet" of 12 traditional cosy Cornish craftsmen's cottages between **Looe** and **Polperro.** Clean, comfortable and well equipped, with a warm friendly atmosphere, for 2 to 8 people. Set in award-winning grounds, only 12 miles from the **Eden Project** with country and coastal walks nearby. Pets £20 pw; Breaks from only £129.

• Towels, Linen, Electric & Hot Water included • Dishwashers in larger cottages • Launderette • Kid's Play Area • Games Room • Tennis Court • TV/DVDs • Cots & Highchairs • Pubs & Restaurants in easy walking distance • Activities Area

Mr & Mrs J Spreckley, Tremaine Green Country Cottages, Pelynt, Near Looe, Cornwall PL13 2LT
www.tremaine-green.co.uk • e-mail: stay@tremaine-green.co.uk • Tel: (01503) 220333

The bungalow is in the centre of Perranporth and yet is secluded, with a garden and parking. It is near the park, shops, pubs, restaurants and the magnificent sandy beach.

Sleeps 6-8 (three bedrooms. only one bathroom).

From £295-£695 per week. Pets by arrangement.

Dorothy Gill-Carey, Penkerris,
Penwinnick Road, St Agnes TR5 0PA
Tel & Fax: 01872 552262 • e-mail: penkerris@gmail.com • www.penkerris.co.uk

The Links
Lelant, St Ives Cornwall TR26 3HY

If it's views, golf or walking you want, this is the place for you!

- Magnificent location alongside and overlooking West Cornwall Golf Course, Hayle Estuary and St Ives Bay.

- Both flats have lovely views. Wonderful spot for walking.

- Five minutes from the beach and dogs are allowed there all year round.

- Two well-equipped flats, open all year. Pets welcome.

Your hosts are Bob and Jacky Pontefract
Phone 01736 753326
e-mail: bobandjackyp@btinternet.com

St Tudy, Wadebridge

SB

CHAPEL COTTAGES • ST TUDY

Four traditional cottages, sleeping 2 to 5, in a quiet farming area. Ideal for the spectacular north coast, Bodmin Moor, and the Eden Project. Comfortable and well-equipped. Garden and private parking. Rental £205 to £485 per week. Also two cottages for couples at Hockadays, near Blisland - converted from a 17th century barn in a quiet farming hamlet. Rental £205 to £380 per week. Shop and pub/restaurant within walking distance. Regretfully, no pets. Brochure available.

**Mrs M. Pestell, 'Hockadays',
Tregenna, Blisland PL30 4QJ
Tel: 01208 850146
www.hockadays.co.uk**
Please quote FHG when enquiring

SB

&
Wi-Fi

Great Bodieve Farm Barns
Luxury Cottages in beautiful North Cornwall

Four spacious, luxury barns close to the Camel Estuary.

Furnished and equipped to a very high standard. Wi-Fi.

Most bedrooms en suite (king-size beds). Sleep 2-8.

Excellent area for sandy beaches, spectacular cliff walks, golf, Camel Trail and surfing. One mile from Wadebridge towards Rock, Daymer and Polzeath.

**Contact: Thelma Riddle or Nancy Phillips,
Great Bodieve Farm Barns, Molesworth House,
Wadebridge, Cornwall PL27 7JE
enquiries@great-bodieve.co.uk
www.great-bodieve.co.uk
Tel: 01208 814916 • Fax: 01208 812713**

Barnstaple

Devon

Think of Devon, and wild moorland springs to mind, but this is a county of contrasts, with the wild moors of the Exmoor National Park to the north fringed by dramatic cliffs and combes, golden beaches and picturesque harbours, and busy market towns and sleepy villages near the coast. An experience not to be missed is the cliff railway between the pretty little port of Lynmouth and its twin village of Lynton high on the cliff, with a backdrop of dramatic gorges or combes. In the centre of the county lies Dartmoor, with its vast open spaces, granite tors and spectacular moorland, rich in wildlife and ideal for walking, pony trekking and cycling. The Channel coast to the south, with its gentle climate and scenery, is an attractive destination at any time of year.

Little Bray House · North Devon

SB

Situated 9 miles east of Barnstaple, Little Bray House is off the beaten track, but ideally placed for day trips to North and East Devon, the lovely sandy surfing beaches at Saunton Sands and Woolacombe, and many places of interest both coastal and inland. Exmoor also has great charm. Come and share the pace of life and fresh air straight from the open Atlantic.

THE BARN COTTAGE • This cottage is built in the south end of one of the old barns, and enjoys beautiful views across to Exmoor. Kitchen, with microwave, cooker and fridge. Large living room with dining area and colour TV. Main double bedroom, a bunk room and a single bedroom.

THE ORCHARD COTTAGE • A pretty cottage. Kitchen, with microwave, cooker, washing machine and fridge. Large sitting room with dining area and stairs. Three bedrooms (sleeps up to 5) and a bathroom.

FLATLET FOR TWO • Self catering accommodation located within the oldest part of the main house, with access through the main front door. Twin beds. The kitchen/dining room is well equipped and the traditional-style bathroom is private to the flatlet.

Brayford, near Barnstaple EX32 7QG
Tel: 01598 710295
e-mail: holidays@littlebray.co.uk
www.littlebray.co.uk

BONEHAYNE FARM   COTTAGE: CARAVAN: BOARD
COLYTON, DEVON EX24 6SG

- Family 250 acre working farm • Competitive prices • Spectacular views
- Our two self-catering caravans are located on an exclusive site. Each on its own special area with stunning views over the enclosed garden and the Devon countryside.
- The 4-star farm cottage is full of character and adjoins Bonehayne farmhouse. South-facing with glorious views over the garden and the Devon countryside.
- Rooms are available for Bed and Breakfast in part of the farmhouse.
- Relax in the deckchairs provided.
- Four miles to the beach • Five minutes from Colyton
- Spacious lawns/gardens • Laundry room, BBQ, picnic tables
- Good trout fishing, woods to roam, walks
- Spacious enclosed lawn where children can play. Table tennis also.

Mrs Gould • Tel: 01404 871396/871416
www.bonehayne.co.uk • e-mail: gould@bonehayne.co.uk

SB

&

Pound Farm Fishing Holidays

Caravan & Fishing Holidays in Devon

A warm welcome awaits our visitors at Pound Farm. The static caravan is situated on its own grounds and has a double bedroom, the second room has 2 single beds with a bunk above, lounge, dining room (seating can be converted to a double bed), kitchen and bathroom. It is fully equipped including a fridge, hob, oven, TV and electric fire.

Adjacent outbuilding/ utility room ideal for storage of fishing gear and bait. Free shower and toilet area. Fish as many times a day as you wish in our pond heavily stocked with a variety of fish. *No closed season.*

Butterleigh, Cullompton EX16 1PH• Tel/Fax: 01884 855208
info@poundfarmfishingholidays.co.uk
www.poundfarmfishingholidays.co.uk

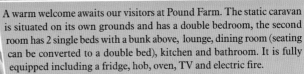

As far away from stress as it is possible to be!

SB

High on a hillside with magnificent views of the lovely Otter Valley, Odle Farm is peacefully set within 10 acres of grounds in the Blackdown Hills, an Area of Outstanding Natural Beauty on the Devon/Somerset border. Clustered around a pretty courtyard, the farmhouse and barns have been sympathetically converted to create five supremely comfortable and beautifully furnished cottages, fully equipped to make your holiday a stress-free break away from the rest of the world ! *Wireless internet access is available on site.*

Wi-Fi

Odle Farm, New Road, Upottery, Near Honiton EX14 9QE
Tel: 01404 861105 • www.odlefarm.co.uk
e-mail: info@odlefarm.co.uk

- *All cottage residents have free use of the Hydrotherapy Spa/hot tub (Honeysuckle and Willow Cottages have their own private hot tubs).*
- *Wisteria and Jasmine Cottages contain the following:*
- Woodburner • 1st log basket free • DVD and video player • Washer/dryer
- 2nd TV in main bedroom • Fridge/freezer • Mini hi-fi • Microwave • Hairdryer
- Dishwasher • Underfloor heating • Linen and towels (except beach towels and cot linen)
- LCD TV in main lounge and Freeview • Cots and highchairs available • Double oven
- Barbecue and garden furniture
- Complimentary homemade cake, pint of milk and tea tray on arrival.

HOPE BARTON BARNS

Nestling in its own valley close to the sandy cove, Hope Barton Barns is an exclusive group of 17 stone barns in two courtyards and 3 luxury apartments in the converted farmhouse. Superbly furnished and fully equipped, each cottage is unique, and vary from a studio to four bedrooms, sleeping 2 to 10.

Farmhouse meals • Ample parking • Golf, sailing and coastal walking nearby
• A perfect setting for family summer holidays, walking in Spring/Autumn or just a "get away from it all" break.
• Free-range children and well behaved dogs welcome • Open all year.
• Heated indoor pool, sauna, gym, lounge bar, tennis court, trout lake and a children's play barn. We have 35 acres of pastures and streams with sheep, goats, ferrets, chickens, ducks and rabbits.

For full colour brochure please contact:

Mrs M. Pope,
Hope Cove, Near Salcombe, South Devon TQ7 3HT
Tel: 01548 561393 • www.hopebarton.co.uk

MILL COTTAGE

Situated in the heart of beautiful South Hams countryside, 4 miles from Kingsbridge, 17 miles east of Plymouth, at end of a quiet lane, just off the A379. Spacious, single-storey accommodation, with private south-facing sun terrace, overlooking the mill pond and gardens.

Bedroom with double and single beds, en suite bathroom with separate WC. Lounge/dining room with sofa bed, satellite TV, DVD and video players. Large fitted kitchen with electric cooker, microwave, refrigerator and freezer.

Bedding, towels, linen, electricity and central heating included in price. (Sorry, no children under 13).

Sleeps 2 - 3 • Prices £350- £370.

Mrs M. Newsham, Marsh Mills, Aveton Gifford, Kingsbridge, South Devon TQ7 4JW
Tel: 01548 550549
e-mail: Newsham@Marshmills.co.uk
jrm@Newsham.eclipse.co.uk
www.Marshmills.co.uk

LOCATION, LOCATION!

The wild and beautiful Exmoor National Park coast.

Not only all village facilities, but spectacular walks are just yards from your door. Solitude is easy to find, even in high summer.

SB

Our 3★ and 4★ Quality Assured cottages in Combe Martin, Lynton and Lynmouth are in prime spots, with off-road parking, and are available all year, weekly or for cosy winter breaks. Phone us for brochure or see our website. A warm welcome awaits.

Tel: 01271 882449 • www.primespotcottages.co.uk

"West Ridge" bungalow stands on elevated ground above the small coastal town of Seaton. It has one-and-a-half-acres of lawns and gardens and enjoys wide panoramic views of the beautiful Axe Estuary and the sea. Close by are Lyme Regis, Beer and Branscombe.

Wi-Fi

The Lyme Bay area is an excellent centre for touring, walking, sailing, fishing and golf. This comfortably furnished accommodation is ideally suited for up to four persons. A cot can be provided. Available March to October, £215 to £550 weekly (fuel charges included). Full gas central heating. Digital TV. SAE for brochure.

Mrs E.P. Fox, "West Ridge"
Harepath Hill, Seaton
Devon EX12 2TA
Tel: 01297 22398
e-mail: fox@foxwestridge.co.uk
www.cottageguide.co.uk/westridge

enjoyEngland.com
★★★
SELF CATERING

SB

WEST PUSEHILL FARM COTTAGES

Resident proprietors, The Violet Family have been welcoming visitors to West Pusehill Farm for over twenty years, and many return time and time again.

Ideal for family summer holidays, restful spring/winter breaks, or a perfect base to explore Devon's outstanding coast and countryside and many outdoor activities.

West Pusehill Farm Cottages not only give you the freedom and independence of a self-catering holiday, but the local area offers a wide range of excellent restaurants and cafes, so your holiday can be enjoyed by every member of the family.

❖ Located in an Area of Outstanding Natural Beauty
❖ Eleven sympathetically converted cottages
❖ BBQ area
❖ Children's playground
❖ On-site heated outdoor pool
❖ Laundry room
❖ Golf, fishing, walking, exploring, shopping
❖ Family attractions

West Pusehill Farm
Westward Ho!
North Devon EX39 5AH
Tel: 01237 475638/474622
e-mail: info@wpfcottages.co.uk
www.wpfcottages.co.uk

Wi-Fi

Resthaven
Holiday Flats

On the sea front overlooking the beautiful Combesgate beach. Fantastic views of Morte Point and the coastline. Contact Brian Watts for details and brochure.
Tel: 01271 870248

★ Two self contained flats, sleeping 5 & 9 ★ Family, double and bunk bedrooms all with washbasins ★ All-electric kitchens. Electricity on £1 meter ★ Bathrooms with bath & shower ★ Colour TVs with DVD players ★ Free parking, lighting, hot water, laundry and Wi-Fi ★ Terms £220 to £1200 per week

The Esplanade, Woolacombe, Devon EX34 7DJ
e-mail: bwatts0248@btinternet.com • www.resthavenflats.co.uk

Woolacombe

CHICHESTER HOUSE HOLIDAY APARTMENTS

SB

Quiet, relaxing, fully furnished apartments.
Opposite Barricane Shell Beach – central seafront
position with outstanding sea and coastal views.
Open all year

FLATLETS • **Lundy Lights and Bay
Views** • both situated on the first floor, with
balconies with magnificent views over the Bay.
SLEEP 2.

SELF CONTAINED APARTMENTS • all with sea views.
The Retreat • on the first floor with bathroom, bedroom with double bed, sitting room and
combined kitchen, split level apartment. **SLEEPS TWO**
Shell Bay • on the second floor with double bedroom, bathroom, living room/kitchen overlooking
the sea. **SLEEPS TWO PLUS**
Hartland View • very large apartment on second floor with lounge overlooking the sea, two
bedrooms, each with a double and single bed. Kitchen diner. Bathroom. **SLEEPS UP TO SIX**
Morte View • on the first floor, with bathroom, sitting room/kitchen opening onto a balcony,
double bedroom. **SLEEPS TWO**
Sea Spray • on the ground floor, with bathroom, dining/bed-sitting room with foldaway double
bed, large bedroom with double and single beds. Kitchen. **SLEEPS FOUR.**

Well behaved dogs are welcome by prior arrangement • *Resident Proprietor: Joyce Bagnall*

**The Esplanade, Woolacombe EX34 7DJ • Tel: 01271 870761
www.chichesterhouse.co.uk**

Dorset

Orchard End & The Old Coach House
Hooke, Beaminster, Dorset

Orchard End is a stone-built bungalow, with electric central heating and double glazing. Four bedrooms, two bathrooms; sleeps 8. Well-equipped and comfortable. Enclosed garden and off-road parking.

For details contact: Mrs Pauline M. Wallbridge, Watermeadow House, Hooke, Beaminster, Dorset DT8 3PD • Tel: 01308 862619

Hooke is a quiet village nine miles from the coast. Good walking country and near Hooke Working Woodland with lovely woodland walks. Coarse fishing nearby.
Terms from £350 to £770 inclusive of VAT, electricity, bed linen and towels.

enquiries@watermeadowhouse.co.uk • www.watermeadowhouse.co.uk

Both properties ETC ★★★★ • Wi-Fi available

The Old Coach House, a cottage sleeping 9, is also finished to a high standard. Four bedrooms, two bathrooms; central heating. Large garden; off-road parking. Both properties (on a working dairy farm) are equipped with washing machine, dryer, dishwasher, fridge/freezers, microwaves and payphones.

Grace Cottage
Sydling St Nicholas • Dorset

Charming cottage with enclosed flint walled garden in peaceful village. Lounge/dining room, study/bedroom, two bedrooms, sleeps 4/5. Well-equipped kitchen, two bathrooms. Pub nearby serving lunch and evening meals. Non-smokers only. Excellent touring centre.

Contact Nicky Willis • Tel: 01308 863868

e-mail: veronicawillis@tiscali.co.uk • www.grace-cottage.com

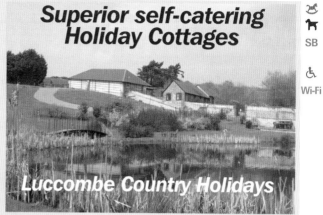

Superior self-catering Holiday Cottages

SB

Wi-Fi

Luccombe Country Holidays

Six stunning cottages in a private hidden valley, surrounded by extensive gardens, grounds and ponds. Situated at Dorset's very centre, close to Milton Abbas, with a fine pub and restaurant (01258 880233), we make a great touring base not too far from anywhere.

Try our indoor pool, jacuzzi, swim jet and sauna, or gymnasium and games room on wet days. Play tennis, explore our farm on foot or bike, followed by a lakeside barbecue on dry ones. Go riding (01258 880057), shoot a clay, fish or just relax in a very peaceful setting.

enjoyEngland.com

★★★★
SELF CATERING

There is something for everyone here at Luccombe

• Terms from £305 to £1550.

Online booking: please check our availability at www.luccombeholidays.co.uk or telephone 01258 880558

• Dogs welcomed by arrangement.

Luccombe, Milton Abbas, Blandford Forum, Dorset DT11 OBE

e-mail: luccombeh@gmail.com
www.luccombeholidays.co.uk

Sherborne

SB

White Horse Farm

★ Self-Catering Holidays in Rural Dorset ★

Four self-catering barn conversion cottages, a 4-star converted farmhouse annexe "The Willows", and a luxury 4-star 3 bedroom lodge "Otter's Holt".

Our holiday cottages were formerly part of the old courtyard. Tastefully converted with exposed stone walls and beams, providing comfortable accommodation.

- **Toad Hall** sleeps 4 • **Ratty's** sleeps 2/4
- **Moley's** and **Badger's** sleep 2

The Willows, converted 4 star 3 bedroom self-catering annexe for up to six people. Each en suite bedroom has lovely views over the surroundings fields and gardens. Surrounded by willow trees with a patio and private entrance to the duck pond.

Otter's Holt, 4 star luxury Wessex-built Milbourne lodge for 6 people in 3 bedrooms, with master bedroom en suite, a family bathroom and a large lounge diner with a vaulted ceiling, exposed beams and a rustic hearth with wood burner-style electric fire.

Surrounded by 2 acres of gardens and paddock with a large duck pond.
Fully equipped recreation room with table football, videos, books, indoor/outdoor games and much more.
Delightful walks in the surrounding area and many tourist attractions locally.
Fishing, walking, horse-riding and golfing facilities within a short drive.
Within easy travelling distance is the lovely Dorset coast including Lulworth Cove, Weymouth and Lyme Regis.

White Horse Farm, Middlemarsh, Sherborne, Dorset DT9 5QN

e-mail: enquiries@whitehorsefarm.co.uk

Tel: 01963 210222

www.whitehorsefarm.co.uk

enjoyEngland.com
3★ - 4★
SELF CATERING

PETS WELCOME

Weymouth

Holiday Cottages Weymouth

SB

Quality Accommodation on the Dorset Coast

Wi-Fi

Dorset's famous Jurassic Coast is very easy to explore from **Crescent Cottage** and **Broadmead Bungalow** and is well worth a visit to appreciate the county's rich heritage.

Weymouth has a lovely sandy beach and picturesque harbour with pavement cafes. There is plenty to do all year round.

Crescent Cottage   VisitBritain ★★★

Sleeps 6 guests in 3 bedrooms. One minute's walk to the main sandy beach, less than five minutes' walk to the town and railway station, bus station and harbour.
Ideal base for touring the Jurassic Coast. Decking area on the first floor with table and chairs. Sitting room and fully fitted kitchen. No pets. Parking permit.
£175 to £695 per week. Short breaks available.

Broadmead Bungalow

Sleeps 7 in 3 bedrooms. Detached chalet bungalow, close to town, main sandy beach, and harbour. Parking for up to three cars. Garden with patio seating area. Quiet location. Wireless broadband. Pets by arrangement only. £195 to £795 per week

For details contact:
Phone: 01305 836495 • Mobile: 07971 256160
e-mail: postmaster@buckwells.plus.com
www.holidaycottagesweymouth.co.uk

Dursley, Longhope

Gloucestershire

South Cerney

SB

A great place to come back to

Our 4 & 5 star holiday lodges and second homes are located in the Cotswold Water Park, an area of outstanding natural beauty. Surrounded by picturesque villages, historic market towns and an area of lakes larger than the Norfolk Broads.

The combination of this beautiful and unique setting, first-class accommodation, activities to suit everyone and our commitment to service makes us a great place to come back to.

Our guests do that, year after year.

Visit us at the Gateway Centre, Lake 6, Spine Road, South Cerney GL7 5TL

Or email us at contact@orionholidays.com

Or call us on
01285 861839

Orion Holidays
& Homes
Lakeside life in The Cotswolds

contact@orionholidays.com   www.orionholidays.com

Blue Anchor, Chard

Somerset

Primrose Hill

Primrose Hill offers spacious, comfortable accommodation in a terrace of four bungalows with private enclosed gardens and panoramic views over Blue Anchor Bay. The games room and boule pitch are popular with both adults and children. In walking distance of picturesque Blue Anchor Bay with its sandy beach, pubs, beachside cafes and indoor swimming pool. Within sight and sound of the West Somerset Railway.

Wheelchair-friendly • Dogs welcome • Internet connection

**Winner Accessible Somerset 2008, 2009 & 2010
and Exmoor Excellence Awards, 2006/2007**

**Primrose Hill Holidays, Wood Lane, Blue Anchor TA24 6LA
Tel: 01643 821200 • info@primrosehillholidays.co.uk
www.primrosehillholidays.co.uk**

TAMARACK LODGE, CHARD

SB

This luxurious, traditionally styled, ranch house-type log cabin enjoys extensive views of the delightful Yarty Valley. It was purpose-built to provide self-catering holiday accommodation for both able-bodied and disabled people, and sleeps up to eight. It is very wheelchair-friendly, and has two of the three double bedrooms on the ground floor, and a large ground floor wc/shower room. Tamarack Lodge is situated on a family-run beef and sheep farm in the beautiful Blackdown Hills, an Area of Outstanding Natural Beauty near the Somerset/Devon border.

NATIONAL ACCESSIBLE SCHEME LEVEL 1.

**Matthew Sparks, Fyfett Farm, Otterford, Chard TA20 3QP • 01823 601270
e-mail: matthew.sparks@tamaracklodge.co.uk • www.tamaracklodge.co.uk**

CHEDDAR • *SUNGATE HOLIDAY APARTMENTS*
Church Street, Cheddar, Somerset BS27 3RA

SB

Delightful apartments in Cheddar village, each fully equipped. Sleep 2/4. Laundry facilities. Private parking. Family, disabled and pet friendly.

Wi-Fi

The apartments are within easy walking distance of shops, swimming pool, leisure centre, and the stunning Cheddar Gorge and Caves.
The bus stop is only a few paces away.
The Mendip Hills offer open countryside and great views for cyclists, walkers and those wishing to walk along the Mendip Way to Wells or Weston-Super-Mare. Other facilities close to Cheddar include golf, fishing, sailing and an artificial ski slope with ski lift. There is so much to see and do in the area, as well as many local events, pubs and restaurants making this an ideal venue for a short break holiday.
Assistance and therapy dogs welcome FREE

Contact: Mrs. M.M. Fieldhouse for brochure.

Tel: 01934 842273/742264 • enquiries@sungateholidayapartments.co.uk
www.sungateholidayapartments.co.uk

West Withy Farm

SB

Situated on Exmoor, between Wimbleball Lake and Clatworthy Reservoir, West Withy Farm Holiday Cottages are a haven of peace and tranquillity. Set in a 23-acre small-holding, the two self-catering cottages have panoramic views across green pastures to the hills on the horizon.
Two local stone barns have been skillfully converted to create spacious, character holiday cottages offering centrally heated comfort, private, enclosed gardens and modern conveniences. Cottages sleep 4 and 5.
Fully inclusive prices • From £200-£595 per week • Short breaks available

UPTON, NEAR DULVERTON, TAUNTON TA4 2JH • Tel: 01398 371 322
e-mail: westwithyfarm@exmoor-cottages.com • www.exmoor-cottages.com

Dunster

SB

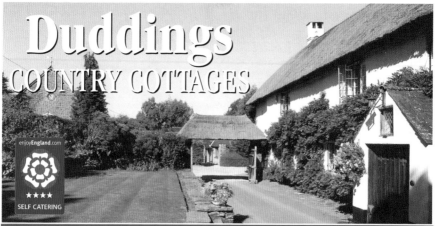

Duddings
COUNTRY COTTAGES

★★★★
SELF CATERING

As resident owners, we personally guarantee immaculate presentation of cottages on arrival. Each cottage has tasteful decor with matching, highest quality fabrics and is fully central heated. Amenities include comfortable lounges with colour TV/video/DVD, fully fitted modern kitchens with fridge-freezer, cooker and microwave. Our facilities include heated indoor pool, hard tennis court, putting green, pool and table tennis, trampoline, football net and play centre. Trout stream in 8.5 acres for fishing or picnics. Families and pets welcome, walking, riding, beaches nearby. Short breaks available off season, open all year. Full details and plans of the cottages together with up to date prices and availablity can be found on our website, or please call for brochure.

Thatched longhouse and 12 cottages for 2-16 persons, beautifully converted from old stone barns and stables. Original beams and exposed stonework retain the character of the buildings. Two miles from the picturesque village of Dunster in the Exmoor National Park.

Luxury Cottages
•
Indoor Heated Pool
•
Tennis Court

Duddings Country Cottages
Timberscombe Dunster, Somerset TA24 7TB

Telephone: 01643 841123
www.duddings.co.uk
e-mail: richard@duddings.co.uk

Weston-Super-Mare

Wiltshire

SB

The self-contained accommodation is part of a farmhouse, dating from the 16th century, on the edge of the village of Holt with views across open farmland. Within 10 miles of Bath, Bradford-on-Avon two miles, Lacock eight miles. Private fishing on River Avon available.

The apartment consists of a large lounge/dining room with open fire and sofa which converts into a double bed; two generously proportioned bedrooms upstairs, one twin-bedded, one with a double bed, both with washbasins; a separate toilet (downstairs); a large kitchen in the single storey wing, fitted with light oak finish units, electric cooker, microwave, refrigerator and automatic washing machine; shower room which opens off the kitchen. Electricity extra.

Sleeps 2-6

**Off-road parking. Choice of pubs in village.
Terms £200 to £225. Brochure and further details available.**

John and Elizabeth Moody • Tel: 01225 782203
Gaston Farm, Holt, Trowbridge BA14 6QA

For the greatest concentration of prehistoric sites in Europe, visit Wiltshire. Most famous is the UNESCO World Heritage Site, Stonehenge, on Salisbury Plain, dating back at least five thousand years, while the stone circle at Avebury is the largest in the world.Salisbury, as well as the famous medieval cathedral, has plenty to choose from in arts and entertainment, while, Swindon, with its railway heritage, is the place to go for shopping and a lively nightlife. In the countryside there are interesting old market towns to explore, stately homes and gardens, including the safari park at Longleat, to visit, and ample opportunities for walking and cycling.

Pangbourne

Berkshire

Brambly Thatch

Merricroft, Goring Heath RG8 7TA
Tel: 01189 843121 • e-mail: merricroft@yahoo.co.uk
www.easisites.co.uk/BramblyCottages

An attractive 17thC thatched cottage within easy reach of
Oxford and London. The acccommodation comprises living room,
dining room, fully equipped kitchen, 3 bedrooms (one downstairs), and bathroom.
TV and DVD. Wi-Fi. Parking available. Sleeps 5. A variety of local attractions include
National Trust properties and the Childe-Beale Wildlife Trust and further afield,
Windsor Castle and Legoland Windsor and more. Open all year.

Wi-Fi

Whatever your interests, whether in the countryside or the town, Berkshire has much to offer.
In the east of the county, just a short train ride away from central London, is Windsor Castle, the
largest inhabited castle in the world. Racegoers will find plenty of action in Berkshire, with
both Ascot and Royal Windsor in the east, and Newbury to the west, where you can also take a
tour of the stables at Lambourn and watch the early morning gallops.

symbols 🐕🐎SB♿♀Wi-Fi

🐕	Pets Welcome	🐎	Children Welcome
SB	Short Breaks	♿	Suitable for Disabled Guests
♀	Licensed	Wi-Fi	Wi-Fi available

FHG Guides publish a large range of well-known
accommodation guides. We will be happy to send you details or
you can use the order form at the back of this book.

Olney

Buckinghamshire

The Old Stone Barn • Olney •

SB

Wi-Fi

The Old Stone Barn is peacefully positioned on an arable farm 1½ miles from the beautiful market town of Olney where there is a wide variety of shops, cafes, bars and restaurants.

The accommodation is a charming combination of old character and modern facilities, and consists of seven spacious self-contained apartments (sleep 1-6), centrally heated and equipped with colour TV and payphone. Linen and towels are provided, and there is a laundry room with washing machines and a tumble dryer. Computer room and Wi-Fi available.

Guests can relax in the gardens, make use of the outdoor heated swimming pool, or take day trips to Oxford, Cambridge, London or the Cotswolds. Terms from £270 to £590 per week.

**Mr & Mrs Garry Pibworth, Home Farm,
Warrington, Olney MK46 4HN
Tel: 01234 711655
e-mail: info@oldstonebarn.co.uk
www.oldstonebarn.co.uk**

Only half an hour from London, the rolling hills and wooded valleys of the Buckinghamshire countryside provide a wonderful contrast to city life. Enjoy the bluebells in spring and the autumn colours of the woodland while following the innumerable footpaths, cycle paths, bridleways and two National Trails that cross the county and follow the meandering River Thames. Watch the red kites above the Chilterns, follow the Roald Dahl Trail or relax with a picnic in a country park. Fascinating historic towns and villages include West Wycombe, owned by the National Trust, just one of many interesting properties in the area, while Milton Keynes is the destination for an all-round shopping experience.

Milford-on-Sea, New Forest

Hampshire

Isle of Wight

SB

TOTLAND BAY – ISLE OF WIGHT

Modernised coastguard cottage c 1840; lovely walking; 500 yards from the sea; 6 walks start from the cottage; village shops; small town 1 mile; on regular bus route. Lounge opens onto patio and small secluded garden overlooking village bowling green and open space beyond. Family accommodation up to 5: lounge/dining kitchen area, 2 bedrooms; bathroom - separate shower and under-floor heating; heated throughout the year. **4 days' winter rent from £60**

**Mrs C Pitts, 11 York Ave
New Milton BH25 6BT
Tel 01425 615215**
Email: Christine@gcpitts.force9.co.uk

Non-smokers only

■ Indicates the approximate position of the cottage

The ultimate sailing destination is of course the Isle of Wight, only a short ferry ride away from the mainland, with marinas, golden, sandy beaches, water sports centres, seakayaking, diving, sailing and windsurfing. On land there are over 500 miles of interconnected footpaths, cycleways, historic castles, dinosaur museums, theme parks and activity centres, or view it all from the skies on a paragliding adventure. To the north and east the well-known resorts of Sandown, Shanklin, Ryde and Ventnor provide all the traditional seaside activities, as well as the sailing centre, Cowes, while West Wight, an Area of Outstanding Natural Beauty will appeal to nature lovers and birdwatchers. With a thriving arts community, and of course two internationally renowned music festivals held every year, there is something for everyone!.

Ashford

Kent

Ashby Farms - Holiday Cottages

Country cottages and detached pine lodges set in bluebell woods overlooking four acres of water, with a panoramic view of fields, woods and the nearby unspoilt village.

Eight detached PINE LODGES beautifully situated by the water's edge, with views across the water to the village of Woodchurch a mile or so away. Sleep up to 6.

attractive living/dining areas • lakeside terrace • sun decks • fully equipped pine kitchens • one double bedroom, two twin bedrooms • bathroom

ROUGHLANDS BUNGALOW, with its own large garden, set well back from the quiet country road between Appledore and Woodchurch. Sleeps up to 5.

attractive kitchen/dining area • fully equipped pine kitchen • one bedroom with double and single bed, one twin bedroom • large garden • off-road parking

Three terraced COTTAGES with views across the fields to the church. Sleep up to 5.

attractive kitchen/dining areas • fully equipped pine kitchens • one double bedroom, one twin bedroom, one single bedroom • off-road parking

**ASHBY FARMS LTD, PLACE FARM,
KENARDINGTON, ASHFORD TN26 2LZ
Tel: 01233 733332 • Fax: 01233 733326
e-mail: info@ashbyfarms.com
www.ashbyfarms.com**

Kent, the 'Garden of England', yet with such easy access to London, is a county of gentle, rolling downlands, edged by the famous White Cliffs and miles of sands and shingle beaches along the Channel coast. Walk along the North Downs Way through an Area of Outstanding Natural Beauty stretching from Kent through Sussex to Surrey, including the historic Pilgrim's Way, or enjoy the stunning scenery from the Saxon Shore Way with views to the coast of France, and the wildlife of the Medway Estuary and Romney Marsh. The resorts of the Isle of Thanet and the south-east coast, like Ramsgate, Margate, Herne Bay and Deal have plenty to offer for a traditional family seaside holiday, and there are steam trains, animal parks and castles full of history to explore too.

SB

Wi-Fi

Sunset Lodge at Great Field Farm
Stelling Minnis, Canterbury, Kent CT4 6DE
Tel: 01227 709223

Ground floor Lodge in lovely private position with panoramic views over beautiful countryside and magnificent sunsets. Light, spacious and modern with open-plan living, dining and kitchen area, spiral staircase to snug/kid's room. Two en suite bedrooms, 1 double with wet room with shower, 1 twin-bedded room with bath.
Free internet access. Open all year.
Also available in the main farmhouse on the SE corner is a cosy flat with a double bedroom, sitting room, kitchen and bathroom. Free internet access.
Both properties are also available for B & B, and we have 2 more en suite rooms for B & B, if required.
ETC ★★★★ and Breakfast Award
Lovely and quiet, yet easily accessible position, approximately 15 minute drive to Canterbury, Folkestone, Ashford and Eurotunnel.
Ample off-road parking, flexible start and finish days.
Please phone or Email for prices and availability.

Self-Catering • Bed & Breakfast
greatfieldfarm@aol.com • www.great-field-farm.co.uk

Apple Pye Self-Catering Cottage

Wi-Fi

Cottage on farm set in 45 acres, surrounded by beautiful rolling Kentish countryside. Well away from the road and next to the farmhouse B&B, it is only 10 minutes' drive from M20, J8. Central location for visiting Kent's many attractions, 6 miles from Leeds Castle, Canterbury half-hour drive, Dover one hour's drive, London one and a quarter hours by train. Sleeps four.
One double room en suite, one twin with own shower room; living room/kitchen/dining room with washer/dryer, fridge/freezer, electric cooker, microwave, TV, DVD, wireless broadband. Full Central heating. Garden and patio. Suitable for disabled. Rent £295-£495 per week. B&B also available.

Mr & Mrs Leat, Apple Pye Cottage, Bramley Knowle Farm, Eastwood Road, Ulcombe, Maidstone, Kent ME17 1ET
Tel: 01622 858878 • E-mail: diane@bramleyknowlefarm.co.uk • www.bramleyknowlefarm.co.uk

---

FREE or **REDUCED RATE** entry to Holiday Visits and Attractions –
see our **READERS' OFFER VOUCHERS** on pages 389-400

The FHG Directory of Website Addresses
on pages 381-387 is a useful quick reference guide for
holiday accommodation with e-mail and/or website details

Bicester

Oxfordshire

GRANGE FARM
COUNTRY COTTAGES
SB

A warm welcome from the Oakey family awaits you at Grange Farm, a working farm set in the small village of Godington.
This lovely location offers all the delights of the English countryside. Converted from Victorian barns, all cottages are equipped to the highest standards. Their style reflects beautiful country charm combined with outstanding levels of comfort. Conveniently located for major airports and motorways.
A perfect base for exploring the many delights of North Oxfordshire and the Cotswolds. Complimentary Wi-Fi access in every cottage, and meeting room facilities. Open all year.
　　Private fishing lake • Guests' gardens • Horses and dogs welcome
Lovely walks in peaceful, rural surroundings.

**Contact: Nigel & Penelope Oakey
Grange Farm Estates, Godington,
Bicester OX27 9AF
Tel: 01869 278778
Mobile: 07919 002132
e-mail: info@grangefarmcottages.co.uk
www.grangefarmcottages.co.uk**

enjoyEngland.com
★★★★
SELF CATERING

Oxfordshire, with the lively, historic university city of Oxford, the 'city of dreaming spires', at its centre, is ideal for a relaxing break. Quiet countryside is dotted with picturesque villages and busy market towns, while the open downland to the south is covered by a network of footpaths connecting up with the ancient Ridgeway Trail and the riverside walks of the Thames Path. Hire a rowing boat or a punt for a leisurely afternoon on the River Thames or explore the Cotswold villages to the west. Stretching from Oxford to the Cotswolds, the mysterious Vale of the White Horse is named after the oldest chalk figure in Britain, dating back over 3000 years. The historic market towns like Abingdon and Wantage make good shopping destinations, and all the family will enjoy the history, activities and beautiful gardens at Blenheim Palace.

Surrey

Shepherd's Hut Shortbreaks

Heath Hall Farm

Heath Hall Farm, Bowlhead Green, Godalming, Surrey GU8 6NW

Outdoor living without roughing it – ideal for a relaxing weekend or longer break.
A beautifully kitted-out shepherd's hut with living/sleeping accommodationand sole use of another
converted shepherd's hut into a wood-lined, warm bathroom with hot/cold water and modern
drainage. Exclusive use of hot tub/jacuzzi in its own hut, tennis court and use of 2 bicycles.
Set in the Surrey countryside, the perfect place to relax and unwind.
Excellent walking country and cycle routes nearby.

Tel: 01428 682808 • e-mail: reservations@heathhallfarm.co.uk
www.heathhallfarm.co.uk/shepherds-hut

Heathfield

East Sussex

Cannon Barn

Tel: 01435 812285

Cannon Barn, a Sussex wheat barn built in 1824, has been sympathetically converted to provide modern comforts. Boring House is a small working farm with sheep. There are ponds and a stream on the farm, and plenty of footpaths in the area, including one which crosses the farm, giving plenty of choice for walkers.

Wi-Fi

Locally, there is a good selection of pubs for meals, and also a great variety of things to do and places to visit for all the family. Wireless broadband available.

Please visit our website for photographs and further information. Short Breaks available out of season. Sleeps 8-10. Prices £725-£925

Contact: Mrs A. Reed, Boring House Farm, Nettlesworth Lane, Vines Cross, Heathfield TN21 9AS
e-mail: info@boringhousefarm.co.uk
www.boringhousefarm.co.uk

From the dramatic cliffs and sandy beaches of the Sussex coast to the quiet countryside of the Weald and the South Downs, there's an endless choice of the things to do and places to explore. Sailing, walking, cycling, horse riding, golf are all available for an active break, while the fascinating history of 1066 country, castles like Bodiam and the seaside ports will attract all the family. If you're looking for beaches, the 100 miles of coast offer something for everyone, whether your preference is for action-packed fun at a family resort or a quiet, remote spot. Best known for a combination of lively nightlife and all the attractions of the seaside, Brighton has everything from its pebble beach, classic pier, Royal Pavilion and Regency architecture, to shopping malls, art galleries, antique shops, and the specialist boutiques and coffee shops of The Lanes. There's so much to choose from!

SB

Distinctly different...

Pekes
Chiddingly
East Sussex

www.pekesmanor.com

In the grounds of a Tudor manor house, up a 350-yard drive, with unspoilt views of the Sussex countryside, Pekes offers a unique self-catering holiday. Peaceful, yet close to London, and with exceptional freedom to use the facilities: exotic indoor heated swimming pool, sauna, jacuzzi, lawn badminton, and tarmac tennis court.

**Fabulous large oast house
for 7 to 11
Four period cottages
for 4 to 10**

All very well equipped, with colour TV, full central heating, washing machine, tumble dryer, fridge freezer, microwave and dishwasher. Children and obedient dogs welcome. Open all year.

Contact Eva Morris
Tel: 020 7352 8088
e-mail: pekes.afa@virgin.net

*Short Breaks: 3 nights weekends or 4 nights midweek
Large Oasthouse £1024-£1262 • Mounts View Cottage £1000-£1500
Cottages £280-£586. Excludes main school holidays.*

Ely

Cambridgeshire

Cathedral House

SB

17 St Mary's Street, Ely
Cambridgeshire CB7 4ER

Tel: 01353 662124

The Coach House has been imaginatively converted into a delightful abode full of character and charm, situated close to Ely Cathedral.

Arranged on two floors, the accommodation downstairs comprises a sitting room and country-style kitchen. Upstairs there are two charming double rooms (one has a view of the Cathedral), and a cosy single room. All have an en suite bathroom, with a toilet, wash hand basin and a half-size bath with shower taps.

Gas central heating. Linen, towels, toilet soap, cleaning materials and some basic provisions are provided.

Prices range from £300 to £750 depending on season and length of stay. Special rates for two people.

www.cathedralhouse.co.uk
farndale@cathedralhouse.co.uk

Cambridgeshire immediately brings to mind the ancient university city of Cambridge, lazy hours punting on the river past the imposing college buildings, students on bicycles, museums and bookshops. This cosmopolitan centre has so much to offer, with theatres, concerts varying from classical to jazz, an annual music festival, cinemas, botanic gardens, exciting shops and to round it all off, restaurants, pubs and cafes serving high quality food. In the surrounding countryside historic market towns, pretty villages and stately homes wait to be explored. Visit Ely with its magnificent cathedral and museum exhibiting the national collection of stained glass, antique shops and cafes. Shopping is one of the attractions of Peterborough, along with Bronze Age excavations and reconstructed dwelling, a ghost tour of the museum and an annual CAMRA Beer Festival.

Norfolk

Red House Chalet & Caravan Park is a peaceful, family-run park set in two acres with beautiful sea views and private access to a tranquil sandy beach.

SB
Wi-Fi

• 15 Luxury Chalets
• De luxe caravan holiday homes
• Holiday Flats
• Licensed Bar with pool table
• Shop • Laundry
• Central heating in all accommodation

Situated on the unspoilt North Norfolk coast, Red House provides an ideal setting for days out to the seaside, and the peace and tranquillity of the Norfolk Broads, offering the whole family a relaxing and enjoyable experience. Open March to January. Sales and hire.

Red House Chalet and Caravan Park, Paston Road, Bacton-on-Sea, Norfolk NR12 0JB • 01692 650815 redhousechalets@tiscali.co.uk • www.redhousechalets.co.uk

The many RSPB and other nature reserves always attract birdwatchers to the region, whether for the migrating birds on the coastal sandspits and marshes, or inland on the low-lying Fens, the Norfolk Broads or the ancient pine forests and heathland of The Breck. Follow the walking, cycling and horse riding trails, or explore interesting market towns and villages from the calm waterways of the Broads to see the Norman churches, take part in the fun of a village fete, watch traditional morris dancing, or visit the one of the few remaining windmills, at Denver, Letheringsett or Great Bircham. In contrast, in the medieval city of Norwich with its historic streets and half-timbered houses, cathedral, Norman castle and museums you'll find not only history, but opera, ballet, theatre, music and restaurants as well as all kinds of shopping.

Dereham, Foxley

Scarning Dale

Six self-catering cottages, sleeping 2 to 6 people, in the grounds of Scarning Dale, a 16th century house set in 25 acres of landscaped gardens, paddocks and woodland. New log cabin, sleeps four. All with patio area. Guests have use of the indoor heated swimming pool, snooker table or table tennis. Good access Norfolk and Suffolk. The surrounding area is ideal for bird watchers and an inspiration to painters.
Dogs welcome by arrangement.
Grazing and stables available.
A warm welcome awaits you.
Dale Road, Scarning, East Dereham NR19 2QN
Tel: 01362 687269
e-mail: jean@scarningdale.co.uk • www.scarningdale.co.uk

SB

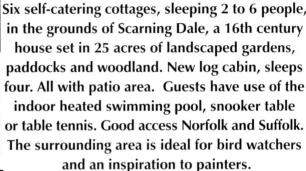

Located on a working farm, a courtyard of 2/3/4 bedroomed converted stables, 3 converted barns and 2 cottages, all fully equipped. Sleeps up to 10. Ideally situated for the beautiful North Norfolk coast, Sandringham, Norwich, and The Broads. 365 acres of mature woodland adjoining farm – private fishing in owners' lake. Indoor heated swimming Pool. Pets welcome at a charge of £15.

SB

Wi-Fi

MOOR FARM STABLE COTTAGES
FOXLEY, NORFOLK NR20 4QP

Heated Indoor Swimming Pool, with Spa

Well Stocked Fishing lake

Tel or Fax: 01362 688523
e-mail: mail@moorfarmstablecottages.co.uk
www.moorfarmstablecottages.co.uk

SB

The Holiday Estate with a difference

A selection of modern superior fully appointed holiday chalets in a choice of locations near Great Yarmouth.

No straight lines of identical chalets on this delightfully landscaped 35 acre estate of holiday homes. It has private access to Winterton's fine sandy beaches, with no main roads for children to cross. A wonderful place for a real away from it all holiday, very quiet and yet only 8 miles from Great Yarmouth. Both the beach and valley are ideal for dog walking, and pets are very welcome.

There are no shops, amusements or clubs on the site. The village of Winterton is a short distance away, with its well stocked stores and 300 year old pub which serves excellent food and drink at the bar or in the family room and garden.

Chalets are privately owned, sleep up to 6 people and each is of individual style. All have open plan lounge and dining areas adjoining the kitchens. Electric heating and TV. Kitchens are all equipped with an electric cooker, microwave and fridge. Bathrooms have a full size bath, wash basin and WC. Most chalets have a shower over the bath.

All chalets have two bedrooms which have a double bed in one room and either twin beds or bunk beds in the second bedroom. You are asked to supply your own bed linen: duvet covers, bottom sheets, pillow cases, towels and tea towels, but these can be supplied for hire if required. Pets are very welcome in most chalets at a small additional fee.

For those wanting a livelier holiday we also have chalets at nearby **California Sands.**

For colour brochure please ring 01493 377175 or write to 15 Kingston Avenue, Caister-on-Sea, Norfolk NR30 5ET

www.wintertonvalleyholidays.co.uk

Norwich

Spixworth Hall Cottages

These delightful quality cottages (sleep 3-12) are ideal for exploring historic buildings, exciting shops and restaurants in Norwich, the tranquillity of the Norfolk Broads and the marvellous beaches of the Norfolk Coast. Relax and unwind on the farm, enjoy walking secluded footpaths surrounded by pastures, ponds and woods, fishing, tennis, swimming and cosy log fires. We offer a warm and friendly welcome.

National Accessibility Scheme, Level 4. CLA Farm Buildings Award, Broadland Enhancement Award.

Grange Farm, Buxton Road, Spixworth NR10 3PR • Tel: 01603 898190
hallcottages@btinternet.com • www.hallcottages.co.uk

Terms from £300 to £1350 per week.
Short breaks and midweek breaks available Autumn to Spring.

Suffolk

Kessingland

Kessingland Cottage Kessingland Beach
• Sleeps 6 • Children and disabled persons welcome • Available 1st March to 7th January •

An exciting three-bedroomed semi-detached cottage situated on the beach, three miles south of sandy beach at Lowestoft. Fully and attractively furnished with Freesat TV and DVD. Delightful sea and lawn views from floor-to-ceiling windows of lounge. Accommodation for up to six people. Well-equipped kitchen with electric cooker, fridge, hot and cold water; electric immersion heater. Electricity by £1 coin meter. Bathroom with bath and shower. No linen or towels provided. Only a few yards to beach and sea fishing. One mile to wildlife country park with mini-train. Buses quarter-of-a-mile and shopping centre half-a-mile. Parking, but car not essential.

SAE to Mr. S. Mahmood, 156 Bromley Road, Beckenham, Kent BR3 6PG (Tel & Fax: 020 8650 0539) e-mail: jeeptrek@kjti.co.uk • www.k-cottage.co.uk

Weekly terms from £95 in early March and early December to £375 in high season.

Ashbourne

Derbyshire

Paddock House Farm
Holiday Cottages

SB

★★★★ **Luxury Holiday Cottage Accommodation**

Wi-Fi

Surrounded by 5 acres of delightful grounds and reached along its own long drive, Paddock House nestles peacefully in a secluded spot between the famous villages of Alstonefield and Hartington, renowned for its cheese shop. Arranged around a courtyard, these charming cottages enjoy uninterrupted views. Wi-Fi.

The area is a walker's paradise, and there are excellent cycle trails along Dovedale, Tissington and the Manifold Valley.

An ideal base for families, the surrounding area boasts a wealth of attractions to suit all tastes. Nearby the attractive market town of Ashbourne offers shops, restaurants and other town amenities. Slightly further afield, the magnificent Chatsworth House is an impressive sight to behold. The spa towns of Matlock and Buxton are as popular as their 'magical' waters have ever been. Alton Towers 20 minutes.

Peak District National Park, Alstonefield, Ashbourne, Derbyshire DE6 2FT
Tel: 01335 310282 • Mobile: 07977 569618
e-mail: info@paddockhousefarm.co.uk • www.paddockhousefarm.co.uk

For walking, climbing, cycling, horse riding, mountain biking and caving, visit Derbyshire. Visit Poole's Cavern to see the best stalagmites and stalactites in Derbyshire (and discover the difference!), and the Blue John Cave at Castleton where this rare mineral is mined, and perhaps buy a sample of jewellery in one of the local shops. Buxton was a spa from Roman times, but the main attractions now are concerts, theatre and the opera, music and literature festival held every year. Go to Wirksworth in spring for the annual well dressings or try out a wizard's wand at Hardwick Hall near Chesterfield, the market town with the church with the crooked spire. No stay in Derbyshire is complete without visiting Chatsworth, the best known of the stately homes, with impressive interiors and magnificent gardens and grounds, and for a contrasting step back in time go to Crich Tramway Village for a tram ride down a period street and on into the countryside.

SPINGLE BARN

Luxury Holiday Accommodation in the heart of the Peak District National Park

Sleeps 9 (additional beds by arrangement).Two ground floor bedrooms with en suite wetroom/shower facilities, both designed with both mobile and less mobile guests in mind. An additional full bathroom is situated on the ground floor. Two further en suite bedrooms on the first floor, one of which can be used as a family room if required. All the bedrooms are available as single,twin or double with flat screen LCD TV (satellite channels), DVD players and iPod docking stations. Pets are welcome with well behaved owners. Free Wifi throughout. Long weekends and midweek getaways available.

For details contact: 07971 038702 / 01629 813521
Rowson House Farm, Church Street, Monyash, Bakewell DE45 1JH
e-mail: rowsonfarm@btconnect.com • www.rowsonhousefarm.com

Wolfscote Grange
Farm Cottages
Hartington, Near Buxton, Derbyshire SK17 0AX
Tel & Fax: 01298 84342

Charming cottages nestling beside the beautiful Dove Valley in stunning scenery.

Cruck Cottage is peaceful 'with no neighbours, only sheep' and a cosy 'country living' feel.

Swallows Cottage offers comfort for the traveller and time to relax in beautiful surroundings. It sparkles with olde worlde features, yet has all modern amenities including en suite facilities and spa bathroom.

The farm trail provides walks from your doorstep to the Dales. Open all year. Dogs by arrangement only.

Weekly terms from £180 to £490 (sleeps 4)
& £180 to £600 (sleeps 6).

e-mail: wolfscote@btinternet.com
www.wolfscotegrangecottages.co.uk

Barnoldby-Le-Beck

Lincolnshire

SB

Wi-Fi

Three well appointed cottages and riding school situated in the heart of the Lincolnshire Wolds.
The tasteful conversion of a spacious, beamed Victorian barn provides stylish and roomy cottages,
one sleeping 6, and two sleeping 4 in one double and one twin bedroom, comfy sittingroom
and diningroom. Fully equipped kitchen. Bathroom with bath and shower.

You don't need to ride with us, but if you do....

The Equestrian Centre offers professional tuition, an all-weather riding surface,
stabling for guests' own horses, and an extensive network of bridle paths.

GRANGE FARM COTTAGES & RIDING SCHOOL
Waltham Road, Barnoldby-le-Beck, N.E. Lincs DN37 0AP
For Cottage Reservations Tel: 01472 822216 • mobile: 07947 627663
www.grangefarmcottages.com

symbols ⊼ ⚘ SB ♿ ♟ Wi-Fi

⊼	*Pets Welcome*	⚘	*Children Welcome*
SB	*Short Breaks*	♿	*Suitable for Disabled Guests*
♟	*Licensed*	**Wi-Fi**	*Wi-Fi available*

Louth

Brackenborough Hall
Coach House Holidays

🪀
🐕
SB

♿
Wi-Fi

Three luxury self-catering cottages in a
Listed 18th century Coach House in the
beautiful county of Lincolnshire.
Stables and Saddle Room sleep up to 4,
Granary sleeps up to 8
Short Breaks all year round.

Winner 'Best Self-Catering Holiday in England 2009/10' Silver Award
'Best Holiday for Families in East Midlands' 2009/10

Paul & Flora Bennett,
Brackenborough Hall, Louth, Lincolnshire LN11 0NS
Tel: 01507 603193 • 07974 687779
e-mail: PaulandFlora@BrackenboroughHall.com
www.BrackenboroughHall.com

Westfield Farm

🪀
🐕
SBi

Self Catering
Holiday Cottages

Situated in the small village of Stewton,
just two miles from the centre of Louth set in peaceful open countryside.
One, two and three bedroom converted cottages, sleeping 2, 4 or 6 people.
Set in peaceful open countryside. just 2 miles from Louth.The cottages were converted
from some 19th Century farm buildings and retain the names that were used during
their original use.
Open all year, any length of stay, from one night to three months,
short breaks available. We can accommodate you for any length of stay
from one night to three months. We do not have fixed arrival days.

Stewton, Louth, Lincolnshire LN11 8SD
Tel: 01507 354892 or 07885 280787
www.westfieldfarmcottages.co.uk

Church Stretton

Shropshire

If you're looking for a break from the pace of life today, but with plenty to do and see, Shropshire is the place to visit. For the active visitor the quiet countryside bordering on the Welsh Marches offers opportunities for walking, cycling, horse riding, kayaking, canoeing, and quad and mountain biking, while if the history of the region's turbulent past appeals, there are over 30 castles to visit, as well as stately homes and beautiful gardens. Visit the grass-roofed Shropshire Hills Discovery Centre at Craven Arms, where you can take a simulated balloon ride and meet the Shropshire mammoth, and Stokesay Castle, the finest 13th century fortified manor house in England. To find out about the more recent past visit the ten museums at the Ironbridge Gorge.

Newport

SB

Wi-Fi

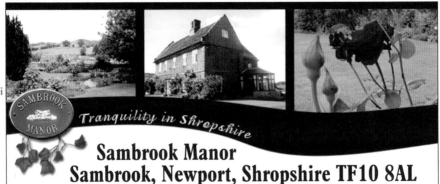

Tranquility in Shropshire

Sambrook Manor
Sambrook, Newport, Shropshire TF10 8AL

Set on the Shropshire/Staffordshire border, Sambrook Manor is the ideal place to stay to explore both counties. Our accommodation consists of **Self-Catering** in two recently converted barns, and Four Star **B&B** in the Manor farmhouse which dates back to 1702. Enjoy lovely views over fields where cattle and sheep graze; free-range hens provide eggs for B&B guests.

The Self-Catering cottages are **The Old Shippon** (sleeps 8) and **Churn Cottage** (sleeps 4 and is suitable for disabled and less able guests). They have lovely exposed beams and underfloor heating. Fully equipped with crisp white bed linen, fluffy towels, TV and DVD players and Wi-Fi.

All our Bed & Breakfast rooms are tastefully decorated, with en suite or private bathroom. Each room has colour TV, tea tray, radio alarm, hairdryer, books and magazines.

e-mail: enquiries@sambrookmanor.co.uk • www.sambrookmanor.co.uk
Tel: 01952 550256 (B&B) • 01952 551252 (S/C)

Stratford-Upon-Avon

Warwickshire

Warwickshire and Shakespeare's birthplace, Stratford-on-Avon, go hand in hand. A great way to view this interesting town of black and white, half-timbered buildings is from the tower of the newly rebuilt Royal Shakespeare Theatre next to the river. For a closer look take a guided walking tour, or for a more gentle approach to sightseeing cruise down the River Avon. Round off the day with a performance by the RSC of a favourite Shakespearian play. As well as Sir Basil Spence's Coventry Cathedral and two other churches designed by him, Coventry is home to Warwick Arts Centre, the largest in the Midlands, and of course, in the birthplace of the British motor transport industry, Coventry Transport Museum.

Bishops Frome

Worcestershire

SB

Wi-Fi

Five Bridges Cottages

Nestled in the heart of the Herefordshire cider apple and hop growing regions, the cottages are set within the owner's 4-acre garden and smallholding. Formed from part of our Grade II Listed building, the cottages have been sympathetically converted into spacious self contained cottages which sleep 2 to 3 persons. They are all on the ground floor and each has an open plan lounge and fully equipped kitchen with beamed ceilings and ceramic tiled floors, double or twin bedroom, with a bed-settee in the lounge. All fuel, power and bed linen (duvet) and towels are included. Ample parking and shared garden. The market towns of Ledbury and Bromyard are within easy reach and you can stretch your legs on the Downs at Bromyard, a National Trust woodland, and Lower Brockhampton all offering good walking with unrestricted access.

Five Bridges Cottages, Near Bishops Frome, Worcester WR6 5BX
www.fivebridgescottages.co.uk • Tel: 01531 640340

Worcestershire, stretching south-east from the fringes of Birmingham, is a county of Georgian towns, Cotswold stone villages and a Victorian spa, all centred on the cathedral city of Worcester. To the north canals were cut to satisfy the need for transport that grew with industrialisation, and now provide a wonderful opportunity for a leisurely break on a narrowboat, or take a restful look at the countryside from the Severn Valley Railway between Bromsgrove and Kidderminster. Long distance trails like the 100-mile Millenium Way cross the countryside in all directions, or follow one of the many shorter local circular walks. In the Malvern Hills choose between gentle and more strenuous exercise to appreciate the wonderful views of the surrounding countryside, or for a different kind of challenge, try mountain boarding in the hills near Malvern.

Tenbury Wells

Driffield

East Yorkshire

Raven Hill Holiday Farmhouse

With delightful views overlooking the Yorkshire Wolds, ideally situated for touring the East Coast, Bridlington, Scarborough, Moors and York, this secluded and private four-bedroom **FARMHOUSE** is set in its own acre of woodland lawns and orchard, with garden furniture, summerhouse and children's play area. Sleeps 2-8 + 2 + cot.

Clean and comfortable and very well equipped including dishwasher, microwave, automatic washing machine and dryer; TV, DVD and games room. Fully centrally heated. Beds are made up for your arrival; cot and high chair available.

Three miles to the nearest village of Kilham with Post Office, general stores, garage and public houses. Available all year.

Terms per week from £300 to £690. Brochure on request.

Mrs P. M. Savile, Raven Hill Farm, Kilham, Driffield YO25 4EG • Tel: 01377 267217

SELF CATERING

With family-friendly beaches, dramatic coastal cliffs and the gentle uplands of the Wolds inland, East Yorkshire will appeal to all age groups and interests. Following one of the many walking trails through the quiet and beautiful countryside, ramblers will discover hidden valleys and traditional villages and market towns like Beverley, with its medieval centre, 13th century Minster, and literature, jazz and folk festivals. Driffield, known as the capital of the Wolds, is an ideal centre from which to explore both countryside and coast, or for a seaside holiday with golden sands, award-winning promenades and entertainment of all kinds at the Spa, Bridlington is ideal for a family break. Take the land train up to the top of the spectacular cliffs, summer home to huge seabird colonies, try kite-flying in the North Sea breezes, or play a round of golf on the clifftop links.

Old Cobbler's Cottage

Wi-Fi

North Dalton, East Yorkshire

A delightful mid-19th century terraced beamed cottage situated in the quiet, picturesque village of North Dalton nestling in the heart of the Yorkshire Wolds.

The cottage possesses a unique view overlooking the village pond and the 11th century village church.

Ideal for walkers as The Minster Way passes through the village, with the Wolds Way close by.

The village is a short drive from Driffield and Pocklington and the historic market town of Beverley. It is only twenty miles from York and the East Coast resort of Bridlington. Also accessible for Scarborough and Whitby.

The accommodation includes a fully equipped kitchen and living room with open fire, TV with DVD/Video/CD player and iPod player.

One double and one single bedroom, Z bed to sleep a 4th person, both with attractive views. The small conservatory leads onto a patio. Off-street parking for one car. Electric central heating is fitted throughout. Wi-Fi access available.

Adjacent is an excellent, welcoming country pub serving good quality pub grub. Dogs welcome.

**Details from: Chris Wade,
2 Star Row, North Dalton,
Driffield, E Yorkshire YO25 9UX
Tel: 01377 219901/ (day) • 01377 217523
(eve) 07801 124264 (anytime)
e-mail:chris.wade@adastra-music.co.uk
www.waterfrontcottages.co.uk**

enjoyEngland.com

★★★
SELF CATERING

Hardraw

North Yorkshire

SB

Hardraw • Hawes
North Yorkshire

A delightful 18th century cottage of outstanding character. Situated in the village of Hardraw with its spectacular waterfall and Pennine Way. Market town of Hawes one mile.

This unique, traditional stone-built cottage with its beamed ceilings and open fire retains many original and unusual features. Sleeping four in comfort, in two bedrooms, it has been furnished and equipped to a high standard, using antique pine and Laura Ashley prints.

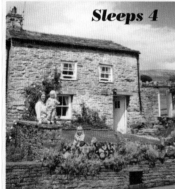

Sleeps 4

Outside, there is a south-facing garden with a "sun trap" patio and through the wall is a large paddock, blending onto the fields and fells beyond. Open all year.

Terms £150-£399 includes coal, electricity, linen and fishing rights. For more information and a brochure, contact:

**Mrs Belinda Metcalfe,
Southolme Farm, Little Smeaton,
Northallerton DL6 2HJ
Tel: 01609 881302/881052
e-mail: bm@adventuretoys.co.uk**

Dominated by the magnificent York Minster, the largest medieval Gothic cathedral in northern Europe, the city of York in North Yorkshire is full of attractions for the visitor. Have fun finding your way through the Snickelways, the maze of hidden alleyways, and enjoy a morning – or longer – in the array of independent shops and boutiques as well as all the top high street stores. Explore York's past at Jorvik, the recreation of the original Viking city from 1000 years ago or become an archaeologist for the day at Dig! and excavate for yourself items from Viking, Roman, medieval and Victorian times. Outside the city the vast open stretches of the North York Moors and Yorkshire Dales National Parks and the golden sandy beaches of the coast are perfect for an active holiday.

ABBEY HOLIDAY COTTAGES
Middlesmoor,
Near Pateley Bridge HG3 5ST

SB

Commanding unrivalled panoramic views of Nidderdale, and offering peace and tranquillity in an Area of Outstanding Natural Beauty. The cottages are an excellent base for walking, birdwatching and exploring the Dales, Brimham Rocks, Fountains Abbey, Stump Cross Caverns, Masham, Leyburn, Ripon, Harrogate, York and the North York Moors.

Our traditional stone-built cottages have been modernised, refurbished and maintained to a high standard. The cottages sleep up to 6 people, and all have oil-fired central heating. All fuel, power, bed linen and towels provided; cot and high chair available. Off-road parking.

12 Panorama Close,
Pateley Bridge,
Harrogate HG3 5NY
01423 712062
info@abbeyholidaycottages.com

www.fhgahcottages.com

Dales View Holiday Homes

SB

offers a unique selection of stone-built self catering holiday cottages and apartments situated in the market town of Leyburn, some with stunning views across the Yorkshire Dales. Excellent local attractions, the perfect base for a countryside holiday. Ideal touring and walking centre for The Dales and only 80 metres from Leyburn marketplace.

Sleeping from 2-6, the properties are comfortable and well-maintained.

Private parking and garden • Children and pets welcome • Terms from £175 low season.

Dales View Holiday Homes, Jenkins Garth, Leyburn, North Yorkshire DL8 5SP
Tel: 01969 623707/622808 • Fax: 01969 623707
e-mail: bookings@daleshols.co.uk • www.daleshols.co.uk

SB

Wi-Fi

Hill House Farm Cottages
Julie & Jim Griffith
Hill House Farm
Little Langton, Northallerton DL7 0PZ
e-mail: info@hillhousefarmcottages.com

These former farm buildings sleeping 2/4 have been converted into 4 well-equipped cottages, retaining original beams. Cosily heated for year-round appeal. Peaceful setting with magnificent views. Centrally located between Dales and Moors with York, Whitby and Scarborough all within easy driving distance. Weekly rates from £210 incl. all linen, towels, heating and electricity. Short Breaks available. Pub food 1.5m, Golf 2m, Shops 3m. Pets welcome.

For a free colour brochure please call 01609 770643 or see our website
www.hillhousefarmcottages.com

Northallerton, Skipton

Otterington Park

Situated in the Vale of York on a family-run farm, Otterington Park is a quality, purpose built 5-acre site designed to cater for up to 40 touring units. Electricity and luxury heated amenity block complete with individual bath/shower rooms, disabled facilities and laundry facilities available. Coarse fishing on site. Children and dogs welcome! There is also a brand new development, adjoining the Touring Caravan site, ready for 40 Luxury Holiday Lodges and Static Caravans. Full details on request.

This is an ideal base for visiting the moors and dales of Yorkshire including locations from TV favourites such as *Heartbeat, Brideshead Revisited* and *Emmerdale*, market towns, leisure centres, golf courses, theme parks and other tourist attractions.

Otterington Park, Station Farm,
South Otterington, Northallerton DL7 9JB
Tel: 01609 780656
www.otteringtonpark.com • info@otteringtonpark.com

SB

New Close Farm

A supa dupa cottage on New Close Farm in the heart of Craven Dales with panoramic views over the Aire Valley. Excellent area for walking, cycling, fishing, golf and touring.

- Two double and one single bedrooms; bathroom. • Colour TV and DVD.
- Full central heating and double glazing.
- Bed linen, towels and all amenities included in the price.
- Sorry, no young children, no pets.
  - Non-smokers preferred.
  - From £375-£400.
Winter Short Breaks available.

The weather can't be guaranteed but your comfort can

FHG DIPLOMA
AWARD WINNER

Kirkby Malham,
Skipton BD23 4DP
Tel: 01729 830240
Fax: 01729 830179

www.newclosefarmyorkshire.co.uk
e-mail: brendajones@newclosefarmyorkshire.co.uk

Staithes

SB

Pennysteel Cottage

An old 19th century fisherman's cottage located in the beautiful fishing village of Staithes in North Yorkshire. The oak beamed and wood panelled cottage is set in the heart of the village and retains much of its original character, and has breathtaking views over the harbour from every room and from its sun terrace.

The cottage is situated only 20 yards from a local public house, serving excellent bar meals. The village also boasts two other pubs, a range of cafés and shops, as well as the Captain Cook Museum.

Fully fitted kitchen – including electric hob and cooker, microwave, fridge freezer and dishwasher. Lounge /dining room with TV/DVD/video/CD player, books and games.

One double and one single bedroom on the first floor, with twin (attic) bedroom and bathroom on the second floor. Cot and high chair available.

All rooms and the sun terrace overlook the sea

Details from: Chris Wade, 2 Star Row, North Dalton, Driffield, E Yorkshire YO25 9UX
Tel: 01377 219901/ (day) • 01377 217523 (eve) 07801 124264 (anytime)
e-mail: chris.wade@adastra-music.co.uk
www.waterfrontcottages.co.uk

Clitherbecks Farm • Danby • Whitby

Self catering accommodation for up to seven people in this traditional hill farmhouse. Beautiful view across Eskdale. Near Danby and the National Parks Moors Centre. Own entrance. Open all year.

Wi-Fi

Mrs Catherine Harland, Clitherbecks Farm, Danby, Whitby YO21 2NT • Tel: 01287 660321
e-mail: enquiries@clitherbecks.co.uk
www.clitherbecks.co.uk

symbols ★☺SB&♀Wi-Fi

★	Pets Welcome	☺	Children Welcome
SB	Short Breaks	&	Suitable for Disabled Guests
♀	Licensed	Wi-Fi	Wi-Fi available

York Lakeside Lodges
Moor Lane, York YO24 2QU

A taste of the countryside, but with all the advantages of the City of York, just two miles away. Stroll in the parkland, relax by the lake (possibly doing a spot of fishing), catch a glimpse of the kingfisher, or go further afield to the North Yorkshire Moors, Yorkshire Dales or the coast.

York Lakeside Lodges is owned and run by the Manasir family who live in the grounds and are at hand for friendly help and advice.

The lodges are situated along one side of the 10-acre lake. Facing south, with beautiful views over the water, they are reached by a private road leading to a parking space beside each lodge.

The two adjoining brick cottages with balconies overlooking the lake have their own cottage garden. All properties are well insulated, double glazed and heated.

Throughout the grounds and in the lodges and cottages wireless internet access is available.

Tel: 01904 702346
e-mail: neil@yorklakesidelodges.co.uk
www.yorklakesidelodges.co.uk

Todmorden

West Yorkshire

SB

Shoebroad Barn
Todmorden • West Yorkshire

Shoebroad Barn is a substantial semi-detached barn conversion enjoying a superb semi-rural setting and commanding wonderful views. The property is within one mile of the town centre and railway station and is convenient for hilltop pubs and local amenities.

The spacious accommodation boasts a grand reception hall with feature staircase and four double bedrooms. Children are most welcome. Open all year. Short breaks available.

Plus adjacent twin bedded Studio Cottage.

Contact Mrs Horsfall • Tel: 01706 817015 • Mobile: 07966 158295
www.shoebroadbarn.co.uk • e-mail: lynne100@live.com

West Yorkshire is a mix of wild moorland and towns and cities with an historic industrial heritage. Spend some time in one of the many fascinating museums of past working life, then stride out over the moors, taking in the dramatic scenery, before a shopping spree or a wonderful afternoon tea. Visit the Rhubarb Triangle near Wakefield early in the year to see the crop being harvested by candlelight. At the model Victorian village for mill workers at Saltaire UNESCO World Heritage Site, Salts Mill has been transformed into the Hockney Gallery, with a restaurant and everything from musical instruments to carpets for shoppers to browse and buy. From there, wander along the banks of the Leeds-Liverpool Canal, so vital for trade in a past age, and watch the Five Rise Locks in action.

Bishop Auckland

Durham

New Cottage

SB

is a delightful little cottage in a very peaceful location. The accommodation is very cosy and comfortable and all on one level – there are no stairs. Panoramic views from the lounge are a never-ending source of delight – they are stunning, and made even more beautiful in winter when there is a light dusting of snow. The cottage is accessible for country walks and sightseeing, and being able to start walks from the cottage is a real bonus. Oil fired central heating is included in price. **And the sunsets are something else – truly magnificent.**

Rates: £250 per week, all year round. Details from Mrs Margaret Partridge.

New Cottage, 'Law One', Hollymoor Farm, Cockfield, Bishop Auckland DL13 5HF
Tel: 01388 718567/ 718260 • www.hollymoorfarm.co.uk

If you're looking for a few days' break somewhere different, why not go to the city of Durham? Set between the North Pennines and the Durham Heritage Coast, the old medieval heart with its cobbled streets is dominated by the cathedral and castle, a World Heritage Site, and a must for visitors. On the way back to the modern shopping centre, browse through individual boutiques and galleries in the alleys and vennels, then enjoy a stroll along the riverside walks. Stay for longer in County Durham, tour all the heritage sites and enjoy invigorating walks and hikes through the dramatic Pennines countryside and along the clifftop path at the coast. There are paths, trails and tracks for all standards of fitness, whether a family ramble and picnic or a hike along the Pennine Way. High Force, the highest waterfall in England, on the Raby Castle estate, is easily accessible. Include it in a long distance hike or a gentle wander from the car park.

Lanchester

Hall Hill Farm

Two country cottages, well equipped and comfortable. Situated in an ideal location for Durham City and Beamish Museum. You will have a free pass for the week to visit our own open farm. Please write or telephone for brochure.

Sleep up to four people • Children welcome. Sorry no pets.
Rates: from £180 per week.

Mrs Ann Darlington, Hall Hill Farm, Lanchester, Durham DH7 0TA
Tel: 01207 521476 • Tel & Fax: 01388 730300
e-mail: cottages@hallhillfarm.co.uk
www.hallhillfarm.co.uk1207 521476

Northumberland

Bamburgh

WAREN LEA HALL

Waren Mill, Bamburgh
Luxurious Self-Catering
Holiday Accommodation
for families, parties and friends.

LONG and SHORT BREAKS on the beautiful Northumberland coast.

Standing on the shore of beautiful Budle Bay, an Area of Outstanding Natural Beauty and a Site of Special Scientific Interest for its birdlife, lies spectacular WAREN LEA HALL. This lovely, gracious old Hall, set in 2 ½ acres of shoreline parkland and walled gardens, enjoys breathtaking views across the bay and sea to Lindisfarne. In addition to THE HALL there are two entirely self-contained apartments, GHILLIE'S VIEW and GARDEN COTTAGE.

THE HALL *(for up to 14 guests, with 6 bedrooms)*

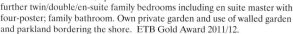

Beautifully furnished to complement its Edwardian grandeur, with high ceilings, chandeliers, sash windows, fireplaces and polished wooden floors. Breathtaking views from every room. Large drawing and dining rooms opening on to floodlit terrace; large, fully equipped kitchen/breakfast room. Ground floor twin bedroom and cloakroom/shower room; upstairs five further twin/double/en-suite family bedrooms including en suite master with four-poster; family bathroom. Own private garden and use of walled garden and parkland bordering the shore. ETB Gold Award 2011/12.

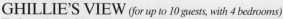

GHILLIE'S VIEW *(for up to 10 guests, with 4 bedrooms)*

The former home of the estate ghillie, accommodation is all on one level, with luxurious furnishings throughout. Fully equipped kitchen/dining room, semi-circular drawing room with balcony, and master bedroom with four-poster and en suite shower; all with fine views across the river and bay to Holy Island. Family, double and twin bedrooms, one en suite, and family bathroom. Guests have use of secluded walled garden and parkland bordering the shore. ETB Gold Award 2011/12.

GARDEN COTTAGE *(for up to 4 guests, with 2 bedrooms)*

The terrace wing of Waren Lea Hall, reached through its own entrance from the garden. All the light and sunny rooms are prettily furnished with high quality fabrics, pine furniture and polished wooden floors throughout, and face the lovely gardens with parkland bordering the shore which guests can use. The well equipped kitchen/dining room, lounge, double and twin bedrooms, one en suite, and family shower room are all on one level. ETB Gold Award 2011/12.

For further information please contact the owners:

Carolynn and David Croisdale-Appleby
Abbotsholme, Hervines Road
Amersham, Buckinghamshire HP6 5HS
Tel: 01494 725194 • Mobile: 07901 716136
e-mail: warenleahall@gmail.com
www.warenlea-hall.co.uk

enjoyEngland.com
★★★★★
SELF CATERING

Hexham

High Dalton Cottage

Cosy and comfortable cottage on a family-run working farm set in 270 acres of beautiful scenery and wildlife.

The cottage has been converted from stables and has two double rooms and one twin, each with en suite bath/shower room. The cottage is in an area of Northumberland's most picturesque and interesting countryside and has private parking and an enclosed garden with patio. The quaint Roman towns of Hexham and Corbridge are nearby.

The award-winning championship golf courses of Slaley Hall and Matfen Hall are a short distance away; other attractions include Newcastle, Kielder Water and Gateshead Metro Centre.

For details contact **Mrs J. Stobbs, High Dalton Farm, Hexham NE46 2LB • tel: 01434 673320 e-mail: stobbsjudy@aol.com**

★★★★ SELF CATERING

Quote FHG

Moorgair Cottage

★★★★ SELF CATERING

**Slaley, Hexham NE47 0AN
Tel: 01434 673473
or 07425 160446
Contact: Vicki Ridley
moorgair@btinternet.com
www.moorgair.co.uk**

This charming cottage for 4/5 people is attached to the owner's home on a small working farm in rural Northumberland, home of Moorgair Alpacas. The cottage is furnished to a high standard and has every convenience to make your holiday stress-free and enjoyable. Cot and high-chair available. Private garden and parking.

From the doorstep there are miles of forest tracks and country lanes for walkers and cyclists, and the cottage is ideally situated to explore Northumberland, Durham and the Scottish Borders. A small shop, post office and two pubs serving food (one with an excellent adventure playground) are within 1½ miles of the cottage.

Isaacs Cottage

SB

Sparty Lea, Allendale, Northumbria.

A semi-detached cottage set in the beautiful rolling countryside of Allendale, perfectly placed for exploring Northumberland, Cumbria and the Northern Dales by car. Very comfortably furnished, accommodation comprises sitting room, dining kitchen; one double, one twin and one family bedroom; bathroom and shower room. Full oil-fired central heating and log fires. **Sleeps 7**. Fishing, walking and cycling on the doorstep.

Hannah's & Rose Cottage Allenheads, Northumbria.

Two semi-detached cottages in peaceful rural surroundings within the North Pennines Area of Outstanding Natural Beauty, both traditionally furnished with panoramic views. Centrally heated with open fires; TV/DVD/video; well equipped kitchens; large shared garden. Linen provided. Off-road parking. No smoking. Abundant opportunities for walking, cycling and exploring the region. Allendale is 5 miles away with friendly pubs, tea rooms and craft shops. **Sleeps 6**

Contact:
**Mrs H. Robson • Allenheads Farm
Hexham, Northumberland NE47 9HT
Tel: 01434 685312**

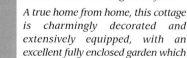

SEA WINDS
NEWTON-BY-THE-SEA

Wi-Fi

Come and enjoy the enchanting coast of Northumberland from our luxury four-star self-catering cottage which is nestled within the pretty coastal village of Low Newton-by-the-Sea.

Sleeping up to 6 people in a double, twin and two single room format, this cottage provides an excellent family base for all ages, as two bedrooms and the main bathroom are on the ground floor.

A true home from home, this cottage is charmingly decorated and extensively equipped, with an excellent fully enclosed garden which is ideal for dogs and children.

The Alnwick Garden, Cheviot Hills, Holy Island, Hadrian's Wall and a bounty of castles are but a few local treasures for you to explore.

Contact:
**Mrs Jo Leiper
Bygate,
Black Heddon,
Newcastle Upon
Tyne NE20 0JJ**
Tel: 01661 881506
or
07720 051201

**e-mail: stay@buston.co.uk
www.buston.co.uk**

Morpeth

SB

Wi-Fi

Rambling over the heather-clad Cheviot moorlands, exploring the castles and pele towers built to ward off invading Scots, watching the feast of wildlife on the coast and in the countryside, breathing in the wonderful sea air on a golden sandy beach, you'll find it all in Northumberland. On the coast, a designated Area of Outstanding Natural Beauty, keen walkers can take the Coast Path from the walled Georgian market town of Berwick-on-Tweed to Cresswell, stopping at little fishing villages on the way. Follow the section along Embleton beach from Craster, best known for its traditionally smoked kippers, to get the best views of the ruins of Dunstanburgh Castle. At the lively market town of Alnwick visit the castle, Hogwarts in the Harry Potter films, with its redeveloped gardens, magnificent water features and even a poison garden! Rare and endangered wildlife is found all along the coast and the ultimate destination for enthusiasts is the Farne Islands, with boat trips from the family resort of Seahouses to watch the grey seals and seabirds, including puffins, in the breeding seasons. Wildlife is abundant in the uplands to the west too. In the heather moorlands of the Cheviot Hills there are plenty of opportunities for birdwatching, as well as horse riding, fishing, canoeing and rock climbing, while at Kielder Water and Forest Park watch the red squirrels and ospreys, follow forest trails and mountain bike tracks or watch the stars in the dark night skies. Learn too about the Romans by watching a re-enactment of Roman life at one of the settlements along Hadrian's Wall, or walk along its length from coast to coast. Hexham and Haltwhistle are good bases for a visit, and these and other market towns and villages dotted all over the county make a stay here a very pleasant one.

Macclesfield

Cheshire

The Old Byre
Pye Ash Farm,
Leek Road, Bosley,
Macclesfield

SB

The Old Byre at Pye Ash Farm is particularly well designed to suit two families wishing to spend their holidays together in the countryside.

Set amongst the fields but only half a mile from Bosley Village, with a choice of two pubs, many walks can be taken from the farm, into the fields and woods. Bosley Minns overlooks the reservoir and forms part of the Gritstone Trail. Alton Towers is 15 miles away.

All accommodation is on the ground floor, suitable for the less able visitor. The Cow Shed and the Sheep Shed both sleep four, with well equipped kitchen and shower room; rear porch with washing and drying facilities. Ample parking.

**For further details please contact: Dorothy Gilman,
Woodcroft, Tunstall Road, Bosley, Macclesfield SK11 0PB
Tel: 01260 223293 • mobile: 07895 894116
e-mail: dotgilman@hotmail.co.uk • www.bosley-byre-stay.co.uk**

In Cheshire, just south of Manchester, combine a city break in historic Chester with a day or two at one of relaxing spas either in the city itself or in one of the luxury resorts in the rolling countryside. A round at an on-site golf course offers an alternative way of enjoying the break, and while out in the country, why not visit one of the many gardens open to the public? Chester, with its wonderful array of Roman, medieval and Georgian buildings is a fascinating place to visit. Walk round the most complete example of city walls in the whole country, past the beautiful cathedral, before browsing through the wonderful range of shops, art galleries and museums, making sure you visit The Gallery, a 700 year-old mall with two tiers of boutiques, jewellers and eateries. Explore the history of the area at the Dewa Roman Experience, with reconstructed Roman streets, and take the opportunity to see the Roman, Saxon and medieval remains on view.

Cumbria

Broughton-in-Furness, Kendal

Thornthwaite Farm

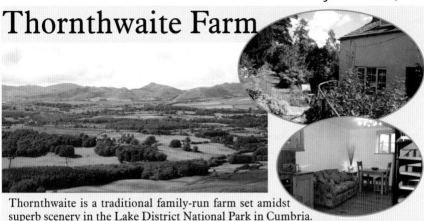

🎠
🐕
SB

Thornthwaite is a traditional family-run farm set amidst superb scenery in the Lake District National Park in Cumbria.

We offer a range of pet-friendly self-catering accommodation overlooking the beautiful Woodland Valley, a wildlife/birdwatchers paradise with private fishing lake.

Well equipped cottages sleep 2/6. All ETC ★★★/★★★★ Gold Award.
Camping Barn sleeps 12, ideal for groups • Caravan, sleeps 4, in large 2-acre orchard.
Short Breaks available.

Thornthwaite, Woodland, Broughton-in-Furness, Cumbria LA20 6DF
Tel & Fax: 01229 716340
e-mail: info@lakedistrictcottages.co.uk • www.lakedistrictcottages.co.uk

Shaw End Mansion

🎠
SB

Situated on a 200 acre estate, in a beautiful location and surrounded by fields and woodland, Shaw End Mansion's four stylish and spacious Georgian apartments with open fireplaces provide an excellent holiday base or short break destination.

Shaw End is also a popular destination for family reunions, weddings and corporate accommodation and can be booked as a whole sleeping up to 18 people.
All apartments are furnished to a high standard and incorporate many period features. There is fishing on our own river and tarn, horse riding within one mile and miles of open fell and countryside to enjoy.

Short Breaks available
most of the year from £115.

Contact Mr & Mrs Robinson,
Haveriggs Farm,
Kendal LA8 9EF
Tel: 01539 824 220
e-mail: robinson@fieldendholidays.co.uk
www.fieldendholidays.co.uk

enjoyEngland.com
★★★★
SELF CATERING

SB

Wi-Fi

LAKELAND hideaways COTTAGES

Large enough to offer choice... small enough to care

- Local, friendly agency
- Choice of more than 70 cottages in and around Hawkshead
- Pets Welcome
- Traditional and contemporary cottages
- Short breaks available
- Award winning website, online booking

'Hawkshead – The prettiest village in the Lake District'

The Square, Hawkshead, Cumbria LA22 0NZ | Tel: 015394 42435 | Fax: 015394 36178
Email: bookings@lakeland-hideaways.co.uk | www.lakeland-hideaways.co.uk

Keswick

IRTON HOUSE FARM
lake district holiday cottages

telephone joan on
017687 76380

Farm location with superb views of lake and mountains. Family accommodation (suitable for disabled guests – wheelchair accessible). Sleeps 2/6. Children welcome. Totally non-smoking. Interesting walking area and comfortable motoring. Facilities for fishing, swimming and golf nearby. Ample parking. Also 6-berth static caravan for hire. Please telephone for colour brochure.

IRTON HOUSE FARM, ISEL, COCKERMOUTH, CUMBRIA CA13 9ST
Accessible & Disabled-Friendly Holiday Cottages in the Lake District
e-mail: joan@irtonhousefarm.co.uk • www.irtonhousefarm.com

SB

Wi-Fi

Location! Location! Location!

Brook House Cottage Holidays
Near Keswick,
Cumbria CA12 4QP
Tel: 017687 76393

By a stream with ducks. Delightful cottages charmingly restored and cared for in this attractive hamlet near Keswick. Various cottages sleep 2-10. Larger cottages ideal for reunions or family get-togethers, and our cosy 'nest' for two is delightful. Excellent food at village pub. Ideally situated just two miles from Skiddaw and Bassenthwaite Lake and just six miles from Keswick and Cockermouth.

www.holidaycottageslakedistrict.co.uk
e-mail: stay@amtrafford.co.uk

Mid-week and weekend breaks from £160 to £480, available off peak.

KESWICK COTTAGES

**Lakeland View, How Lane, Portinscale
Keswick CA12 5RS**

Superb selection of 4/5 Star cottages and apartments in and around Keswick. All of our properties are well maintained and thoroughly clean. From a one bedroom cottage to a four bedroom house we have something for everyone. Children and pets welcome. Contact us for a brochure or visit us online.

Tel: 017687 80088

**e-mail: info@keswickcottages.co.uk
www.keswickcottages.co.uk**

SB

Wi-Fi

BLANDSWATH COTTAGE

In a lovely tranquil position on the banks of the River Eden, this old, well established, spacious farm cottage is comfortably furnished and well equipped. Situated on the owners' 100-acre working farm, where visitors are free to roam.

An excellent base for exploring and walking in the Lake District and Yorkshire Dales. Just two miles away is the town of Kirkby Stephen with everyday facilities, restaurants, pubs and tearooms.

- *Free fishing for one person available in season.*
- *Sorry, no pets.*
- *No smoking.*
- *Sleeps six, plus cot.*
- *Short Breaks from £200*

Contact: Mrs Sandra Watson
Blandswath Farm, Appleby Road
Kirkby Stephen, Cumbria CA17 4PG
Tel: 017683 41842
e-mail: Watson@blandswath.freeserve.co.uk
www.blandswathcottage.co.uk

SB

symbols ★🐕SB♿♍Wi-Fi

🐕	Pets Welcome	🎠	Children Welcome
SB	Short Breaks	♿	Suitable for Disabled Guests
♍	Licensed	**Wi-Fi**	Wi-Fi available

Kirkoswald

Lake District, Lamplugh

"Your own country house in the Lakes"

Two luxury holiday houses available to rent in the Lake District.

Routen House

Routen House is a beautiful old farmhouse set in 4 acres in an outstanding position with fabulous views over Ennerdale Lake. Fully modernised while retaining the character of the old farmhouse, it has been furnished to a very high standard. Sleeps 12 plus cot.

Little Parrock is an elegant Victorian Lakeland stone house a short walk from the centre of Grasmere with large rooms and a wealth of period features. Lovely private garden. Fully modernised to a very high standard; real log fires. Sleeps 10 plus cot.

Little Parrock

Both houses are non-smoking but pets are very welcome.

Please contact:

Mrs J. Green • Tel & Fax: 01604 505115

e-mail: joanne@routenhouse.co.uk

www.routenhouse.co.uk • www.littleparrock.co.uk

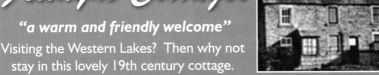

Mungrisdale, Penrith

SB

Copy Hill

Mungrisdale, Penrith

An 18th century farm cottage, overlooking the northern fells, featuring oak beams and open fireplace. Situated in the quiet and unspoilt village of Mungrisdale, eight miles from Keswick and 10 miles from Penrith. An ideal base for touring the Lakes or walking in the hills. Comprises comfortable lounge/dining room, fully equipped kitchen, downstairs cloakroom with shower, three bedrooms (two doubles and one twin), bathroom. Village inn ¼ mile.

Price from £300 to £400 per week including electricity, central heating, colour TV and bed linen. Ample parking. Sorry, no pets. Available all year. Please telephone for details.

Mrs Wilson, High Beckside, Mungrisdale, Penrith CA11 0XR • Tel: 017687 79636
www.mungrisdale.com

SB

Wi-Fi

Howscales

NATIONAL ACCESSIBILITY SCHEME: CATEGORY 2

SELF CATERING

Howscales was originally a 17th century farm. The red sandstone buildings have been converted into four self-contained cottages, retaining many original features.

Set around a cobbled courtyard, the cosy, well-equipped cottages for 2-6, are surrounded by award-winning gardens and open countryside. Shared laundry facilities.

Cared for by resident owner. Ideal base from which to explore the Eden Valley, Lakes, Pennines and Hadrian's Wall.

Please contact us or see our website for details.

- **£285 to £795 weekly • Sleep 2/6**
- **Log stoves • Open all year**
- **Short breaks available**
- **Well-behaved pets welcome by arrangement**

Liz Webster, Howscales, Kirkoswald, Penrith CA10 1JG
Tel: 01768 898666 • Fax: 01768 898710
e-mail: liz@howscales.co.uk • www.howscales.co.uk

Penrith

SB

Wi-Fi

Morland Hall and three beautifully presented self-catering houses are situated within 15 acres of ancient woods and parkland in the glorious rolling countryside of the Eden Valley in Cumbria. All have been beautifully restored and furnished.

The Hall can sleep up to 20 people in 9 bedrooms (3 en suite); within the estate are 3 very well equipped 4-bedroom cottages sleeping 8/10, 9/10 and 7/8. Each property has own garden and patio. Sleeping a total of 48 in 21 bedrooms, Morland Hall is ideal for weddings, corporate events, as well as holiday lets and short breaks. The properties can be rented individually or together.

THE MORLAND HALL ESTATE
Morland Hall, Morland, Penrith Cumbria CA10 3BB
Tel: 01931 714715 • stay@morland-hall.co.uk • www.morland-hall.co.uk

Lancashire

Generations of excited holiday-makers have visited Lancashire's coastal resorts, and amongst them Blackpool stands out as the star attraction. For seaside fun, amusements and entertainment it's difficult to beat, but the quieter resorts along the coast with traditional seaside attractions have their own appeal. For an outdoor break there are all kinds of activities from hot air ballooning to fishing on offer inland, from the lowland plain, along the winding valleys of the Ribble and the Lune, up into the Forest of Bowland and on to the moors of the western Pennines. Further north at Morecambe take part in the Catch the Wind Kite Festival held on the sands in July, just one of a number of events in the town each year. With the winds blowing in every direction conditions on this Irish Sea coast are perfect for kite-surfing, and instruction is available at Fleetwood, a family-orientated Victorian resort where the Fylde Folk Festival is held every September.

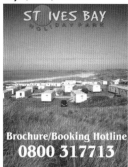

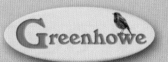

Tanglewood
Caravan Park

Tanglewood is a family-run park on the fringes of the Lake District National Park. It is tree-sheltered and situated one mile inland from the small port of Silloth on the Solway Firth, with a beautiful view of the Galloway Hills.

Large modern holiday homes are available from March to January, with car parking beside each home. Fully equipped except for bed linen, with central heating, electric lighting, hot and cold water, toilet, shower, gas fire, fridge and colour TV, all of which are included in the tariff. Touring pitches also available with electric hook-ups and water/drainage facilities, etc. Play area. Licensed lounge with adjoining children's play room. Pets welcome free but must be kept under control at all times. Full colour brochure available.

Mike Bowman
Tanglewood Caravan Park
Causewayhead
Silloth-on-Solway
Cumbria CA7 4PE
Tel: 016973 31253

e-mail: tanglewoodcaravanpark@hotmail.com
www.tanglewoodcaravanpark.co.uk

Penrith

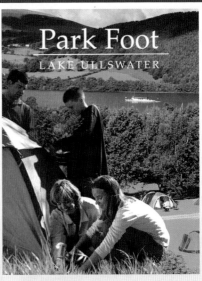
Buxton

SB
Wi-Fi

STATIC CARAVANS
TOURING SITE

Friendly, family-run touring site and static caravans situated in unspoilt countryside. Spectacular views to Dartmoor. Two modern shower blocks; electric hook-ups. Bar and restaurant with area for dogs. Large dog-walking fields. Shop, launderette and indoor/outdoor play areas. 12 miles to coast. Short Breaks available.

**HIGHER MEAD FARM,
ASHBURTON, DEVON TQ13 7LJ
Tel: 01364 654869 • Fax: 01364 654004
e-mail: parkersfarm@btconnect.com
www.parkersfarmholidays.co.uk**

SB
Wi-Fi

Alston Farm Camping & Caravan Site
Malborough, Kingsbridge TQ7 3BJ

The family-run site is set in a quiet secluded, sheltered valley adjoining the Salcombe Estuary in amongst Devon's loveliest countryside. Level pitches, ample space and conveniences. Wi-Fi available.
Dish washing and clothes washing facilities. Electric hook-ups, Calor and Gaz stockists. Shop, (high season only), payphone on site. Children and pets welcome.

From £12 per night for two adults and caravan.

Please phone for brochure:
Phil Shepherd.

Tel: 01548 561260

e-mail:
info@alstoncampsite.co.uk

www.alstoncampsite.co.uk

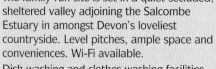

Pennymoor
Camping and Caravan Park

Modbury, Devon PL21 0SB • Tel & Fax: 01548 830542
Immaculately maintained, well-drained, peaceful rural site with panoramic views, Midway between Plymouth and Kingsbridge (A379). An ideal centre for touring moors, towns and beaches, only five miles from Bigbury-on-Sea and nine miles from Salcombe. Golf courses at Bigbury, Thurlestone and Ivybridge. Boating at Salcombe, Newton Ferrers and Kingsbridge.
Large toilet/shower block with fully tiled walls and floor, baby-change and hairdryers. Facilities for the disabled holidaymaker. Dishwashing room - FREE hot water. Laundry room. Children's equipped play area. Wi-Fi, shop, gas, public telephone. Luxury caravans for hire, all services, fully equipped, TV. Write, phone or email for colour brochure or visit our website.

e-mail: enquiries@pennymoor-camping.co.uk • www.pennymoor-camping.co.uk

SB   Wi-Fi

North Morte Farm Caravan & Camping Park

Family-run caravan park, adjoining National Trust land, only 500 yards from Rockham Beach and set in some of the most spectacular countryside in the South West. We have direct access to the South West Coast Path; only 5 minutes' walk from the village of Mortehoe with pubs, shops, Post Office and restaurants.

• Mortehoe • Woolacombe • North Devon • EX34 7EG
Tel: 01271 870381 • e-mail: info@northmortefarm.co.uk
www.northmortefarm.co.uk

Mersea Island

COSWAYS Holiday Park
Relaxed Holidays & Short Breaks 2012

Mersea Island Colchester Essex CO5 8UA
www.cosways.co.uk tel: 01206 383252
e-mail: holidays@cosways.co.uk   fax: 01206 385524

Holiday Homes for Sale & Hire
Swimming Pool • Tennis Court
Clubhouse • Play Area • Shop • Launderette
Superb Rural Setting with Private Beach
Safe & Secure

SB

5 Star Holiday Park

Cotswolds

Hayling Island

Preston

Mundesley

Hexham

SB

Greencarts is a working farm situated in Roman Wall country, ideally placed for exploring by car, bike or walking. It has magnificent views of the Tyne Valley. Campsite for 30 tents with facilities, and bunk barn with 12 beds, showers and toilet are now open from Easter until the end of October. Prices for campsite are £5 to £10 per tent, plus £1pp. Bunk barn beds from £10. Linen available. Bed and Breakfast also available from £25 to £40 .

Mr & Mrs D Maughan, Greencarts Farm,
Humshaugh, Hexham NE46 4BW
Tel/Fax: 01434 681320
e-mail: sandra@greencarts.co.uk.

GREENCARTS FARM
www.greencarts.co.uk

Tuxford

Orchard Park

Orchard Park Touring Caravan and Camping Park
Marnham Road, Tuxford NG22 0PY
Tel: 01777 870228 • Fax: 01777 870320

Situated in a quiet unspoilt location on the outskirts of the old market town of Tuxford within a mature fruit orchard, Orchard Park offers pitches for touring caravans, tents, trailer tents and small to medium sized motor homes. Ideally situated for weekend breaks, longer holidays or just an overnight stop. Within a short drive you will find the haunts of Robin Hood, acres of Sherwood Forest, Clumber Park (National Trust) and Rufford Abbey.

Amenities block with free hot showers and hairdryers. Laundry room with coin operated washing machines and tumble dryer. Separate 'access room' designed to disability standards. Electric hook-ups. Play trail for children.

A range of food essentials and Calor Gas exchange is available from reception. Brochure available on request.

www.orchardcaravanpark.co.uk

&

Wi-Fi

FREE or **REDUCED RATE** entry to Holiday Visits and Attractions –
see our **READERS' OFFER VOUCHERS** on pages 389-400

The FHG Directory of Website Addresses

on pages 381-387 is a useful quick reference guide for
holiday accommodation with e-mail and/or website details

Taunton

Quantock Orchard Caravan Park

Award-winning, family-run campsite set amidst the stunning Somerset countryside.

Quantock Orchard is situated in an idyllic setting surrounded by picturesque views of the Quantocks, in an Area of Outstanding Natural Beauty. This peaceful park is close to Exmoor, the coast and the West Somerset Railway. Relax and unwind among these beautiful surroundings whilst enjoying our Five Star facilities.

• fully heated toilet and shower block • launderette • games room • adventure playground • shop • outdoor heated pool • gym with jacuzzi, steam room and sauna • cycle hire • caravan storage

Tents, tourers and motorhomes welcome
Luxury static holiday homes for sale or hire
Open all year

Michael & Sara Barrett,
Quantock Orchard Caravan Park, Flaxpool,
Crowcombe, Near Taunton TA4 4AW
01984 618618
e-mail: qocp@flaxpool.freeserve.co.uk
www.quantock-orchard.co.uk

DE LUXE PARK

Lowestoft

Beach Farm Residential & Holiday Park Ltd

SB

I Arbor Lane, Pakefield, Lowestoft, Suffolk NR33 7BD
Tel: 01502 572794 • Mobile: 07795 001449
e-mail: beachfarmpark@aol.com • www.beachfarmpark.co.uk

Wi-Fi

A friendly, peaceful family-run park set in six acres of attractive, sheltered surroundings only 500 yards from Pakefield beach and supermarket, 2 miles from the town centre.

* De luxe caravan holiday homes with central heating
* Deluxe Country Lodges
* Luxury residential Park homes for sale
* Limited spaces for touring / camping inc. hook-ups
* Licensed bar / beer garden with children's play area
* Seasonal entertainment
* Outdoor heated swimming pool
* Launderette • Restaurant adjacent

The park is very close to many local attractions including Pleasurewood Hills Theme Park and Africa Alive.

MARSTON CAMPING AND CARAVAN PARK

KINGSBURY ROAD, MARSTON B76 0DP

NEAR SUTTON COLDFIELD AND BIRMINGHAM

Tel: 01675 470902 or 01299 400787

One mile off Junction 9 of the M42, towards Kingsbury on the left hand side. Brand new park for 120 caravans, tents and motor homes. Open all year round.

All pitches have electricity and fully hard standings. Brand new toilet/shower block, laundry room. Play area. Pets welcome.

* *Kingsbury Water Park* • *Hams Hall* • *Drayton Manor Park* •
* *Belfry Golf Course* • *National Exhibition Centre* •
* *Tamworth Ski Slope* • *Lee Manor Leisure Complex* •

Wi-Fi

You can be assured of a very friendly atmosphere at Wombleton, a small Caravan & Camping Park personally run by the Willoughby family. Wombleton Village is ideally placed just a few miles from the picturesque town of Helmsley, and the surrounding area offers an array of amenities, activities and attractions. The local pub is just one mile away. Our pitches are of a generous size – gravel or grass. Concrete bases for motorhomes. All pitches with electric hook ups. New toilet facilities with a disabled/family room. A good base to explore the North Yorkshire Moors and York and twenty miles from the east coast

Wombleton Caravan & Camping Park
Moorfield Lane, Wombleton,
Kirkbymoorside, North Yorkshire YO62 7RY
Tel/Fax: 01751 431684
e-mail: info@wombletoncaravanpark.co.uk
www.wombletoncaravanpark.co.uk

Middlewood Farm Holiday Park

SB

Small, peaceful, family park. A walkers', artists' and wildlife paradise, set amidst the beautiful North Yorkshire Moors National Park, Heritage Coast and 'Heartbeat Country'. Relax and enjoy the magnificent panoramic views of our spectacular countryside. Five minutes' walk to the village PUB and shops. Ten minutes' walk to the BEACH and picturesque Robin Hood's Bay. SUPERIOR LUXURY HOLIDAY HOMES FOR HIRE, equipped to the highest standards (Open all year). TOURERS and TENTS: level, sheltered park with electric hook-ups. Superb heated facilities, free showers and dishwashing. Laundry. Gas. Children's adventure playground. Adjacent dog walk and cycle route. Credit cards accepted. Signposted. A warm welcome awaits you.

Robin Hood's Bay, Near Whitby, Yorkshire YO22 4UF
Tel: 01947 880414
e-mail: info@middlewoodfarm.com
www.middlewoodfarm.com

Conwy, Criccieth

Anglesey & Gwynedd

Visit the FHG website
www.holidayguides.com
for all kinds of holiday accommodation in Britain

Trearddur Bay, Tywyn

Betws-y-Coed, Conwy

North Wales

The Hand at Llanarmon

Standing in the glorious and hidden Ceiriog Valley, The Hand at Llanarmon radiates charm and character. With 13 comfortable en suite bedrooms, roaring log fires, and fabulous food served with flair and generosity, this is a wonderful base for most country pursuits, or just relaxing in good company.

Tel: 01691 600666
e-mail: reception@thehandhotel.co.uk
www.TheHandHotel.co.uk

**Llanarmon DC
Ceiriog Valley
Near Llangollen
North Wales
LL20 7LD**

Ceredigion

Haverfordwest

Pembrokeshire

Pembrokeshire's entire coastline is a designated National Park, with sheltered coves and wooded estuaries, a wide choice of award-winning sandy beaches and some of the most dramatic cliffs in Britain. Enjoy the wonderful views from the clifftop golf courses, or while walking round the Pembrokeshire Coastal Path. Conditions are ideal for all kinds of water sports including surfing, scuba diving and windsurfing, or try coasteering, a combination of climbing, swimming and leaping round the rocky coast. The sea fishing is superb or just the sample the catch at the annual fish week. There are food and folk music festivals to enjoy, and Pembrokeshire's mild climate, the many delightful towns and villages, gardens, children's attractions and outdoor facilities make this a favourite holiday destination, not just for families but for everyone.

Newport

TREWERN ARMS HOTEL

Nevern, Newport, Pembrokeshire SA42 0NB
Tel: 01239 820395 • Fax: 01239 820173

Cymru
Wales

★★★★
Inn

AA

★★★★
INN

www.trewernarms.com
e-mail: info@trewern-arms-pembrokeshire.co.uk

Set deep in a forested and secluded valley on the banks of the River Nevern, this picturesque, 16th century hostelry has a warmth of welcome that is immediately apparent in the interestingly-shaped Brew House Bar with its original flagstone floors, stone walls, old settles and beams decorated with an accumulated collection of bric-a-brac. Bar meals are served here from a popular grill area. By contrast, the Lounge Bar is furnished on cottage lines and the fine restaurant has received many accolades from far and wide for its culinary delights.

The tranquil village of Nevern is ideally placed for Pembrokeshire's historic sites and uncrowded, sandy beaches and the accommodation offered at this recommended retreat is in the multi-starred class.

Powys

Powys is situated right on England's doorstep and boasts some of most spectacular scenery in Europe. It is ideal for an action-packed holiday with fishing, golf, pony trekking, climbing caving and canoeing readily available, and walkers have a choice of everything from riverside trails to mountain hikes, including The Beacons Way, crossing the beautiful Brecon Beacons National Park, the Offa's Dyke Path running for 177 miles through Border country, often following the ancient earthworks, and Glyndwr's Way which takes in some of the finest landscape features in Wales. At Machynlleth take a ride on the amazing water-balanced cliff railway at the Centre for Alternative Technology, visit the border towns with their Georgian architecture and half-timbered black and white houses to visit, or wander round the wonderful shops in the book town of Hay, famous for its Literary Festival each May.

SB

Caebetran Farm

A warm welcome...

a cup of tea and home-made cakes await you when you arrive at Caebetran Farm, a working cattle and sheep farm. Well off the beaten track, where there are breathtaking views of the Brecon Beacons and the Black Mountains, and just across a field is a 400- acre common, ideal for walking, bird-watching or just relaxing.

The rooms are all en suite and have colour TV and tea making facilities. The dining room has separate tables, there is also a comfortable lounge with colour TV, DVD and video. Caebetran is an ideal base for exploring this beautiful, unspoilt part of the country, with pony trekking, walking, birdwatching, wildlife, hang-gliding and so much more. Awaiting you are our friendly, beautiful natured collie, Lad; also Scamp the terrier will play ball, retrieve a stick and walk with you. For a brochure and terms please write, telephone, or visit our website.

The Stable - Self-catering in a 19th C stable recently renovated to a very high standard.

"Arrive as visitors and leave as our friends"
"If you are disappointed with the view - you can stay for free"
Gwyn and Hazel Davies, Caebetran Farm, Felinfach, Brecon, Powys LD3 0UL
Tel: 01874 754460 • Mob: 0789 1118594
e-mail: hazelcaebetran@aol.com • www.farmbandbinwales.co.uk

SB

Wi-Fi

Tastefully restored Tudor farmhouse on working farm in peaceful location. En suite bedrooms with breathtaking views over fields and woods, colour TV, beverage trays.

Lounge with log fire. A real taste of Wales in hospitality and cuisine. Wonderful area for wildlife, walking, cycling, near Red Kite feeding station. Safe parking. Brochure on request.

Open all year.

Holly Farm

Cymru Wales

AA
★★★★
FARMHOUSE

Bed and Breakfast
from £32 to £40 per day.

Mrs Ruth Jones, Holly Farm, Howey, Llandrindod Wells LD1 5PP
Tel & Fax: 01597 822402
ruth@hollyfarmbandb.co.uk • www.hollyfarmbandb.co.uk
Taste of Wales Tourism Award • Farm Stay UK Member

Montgomery

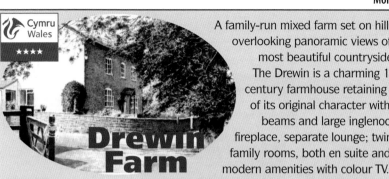

A family-run mixed farm set on hillside overlooking panoramic views of the most beautiful countryside. The Drewin is a charming 17th century farmhouse retaining much of its original character with oak beams and large inglenook fireplace, separate lounge; twin and family rooms, both en suite and all modern amenities with colour TV. Full central heating. Offa's Dyke footpath runs through the farm - a wonderful area for wildlife. Ideal base for touring the many beauty spots around. Good home cooking and a very warm welcome await our visitors.

Bed and Breakfast £30 for one night, £29 for more than one night Evening Meal by arrangement. Open March to October.

Featured in the BBC Travel Show. Holder of Essential Food Hygiene Certificate and Farmhouse Award from Wales Tourist Board, AA Best Breakfast in Wales Award.

Ceinwen Richards, The Drewin Farm, Churchstoke, Montgomery SY15 6TW • Tel & Fax: 01588 620325 drewinfarm@hotmail.com • www.offasdyke.co.uk/drewinfarm

South Wales

Bridgend

Bryngarw House

Brynmenyn, Bridgend, CF32 8UU (just off junction 36, M4)

- Set within 113 acres of magnificent country parkland.
- Award winning fine dining in our Harlequin Restaurant using the finest local produce.
- Function room for up to 120 people.
- Unique accommodation with individually decorated ensuite bedrooms.
- Conference and banqueting facilities.
- Licensed to hold weddings and civil ceremonies.

T: 01656 729009   E: bryngarw.house@bridgend.gov.uk
www.bryngarwhouse.co.uk

BRYNGARW

Cowbridge, Monmouth

symbols 🐕🐴SB♿♀Wi-Fi

🐕	Pets Welcome	🐴	Children Welcome
SB	Short Breaks	♿	Suitable for Disabled Guests
♀	Licensed	Wi-Fi	Wi-Fi available

Anglesey & Gwynedd

Treborth Leisure • Gwynedd

In a beautiful part of Wales, we believe we have everything you need to make the most of your holiday. Our leisure complex encompasses holiday cottages, a 9-hole Academy Par 3 golf course with artificial tees and greens, and a well-stocked fishing lake. Our caravanning facilities provide a sheltered, level site with hard standings, electricity and water for each plot. The site includes a toilet block and showers, a chemical toilet emptying point, a picnic area, a barbecue area, and children's amenities. There is a separate field for camping.

Treborth Leisure Ltd, The Old Barn, Treborth Hall Farm, Bangor, Gwynedd LL57 2RX
Telephone: 01248 364399 • Fax: 01248 364333
e-mail: enquiries@treborthleisure.co.uk • www.treborthleisure.co.uk

NORTH WALES HOLIDAY CHALETS

THE CHALET is set in 200 acres of parkland, 1.5 miles east of Caernarfon, at the edge of the Snowdonia National Park.
• fitted kitchen leading to lounge and dining area • bathroom
• one double bedroom, the other with one single bed and bunk bed. It can accommodate a maximum of five people .
Well behaved pets allowed (max. 2).

Amenities on the park include:
heated outdoor pool, club room, entertainment, bar meals, takeaway food, supermarket, launderette.

Enquiries/bookings:
Mr H. Arfon Jones, 12 Lon Isaf,
Menai Bridge, Anglesey LL59 5LN
Tel/Fax: 01248 712045
email: hajones@northwales-chalet.co.uk
www.northwales-chalet.co.uk

BRYN BRAS CASTLE
EXCLUSIVE CASTLE APARTMENTS

Enchanting Castle Apartments within a romantic Regency Castle of timeless charm, and a much-loved home. (Grade II* Listed Building of Architectural/Historic interest).
Centrally situated in gentle Snowdonian foothills for enjoying North Wales' magnificent mountains, beaches, resorts, heritage and history.
Many local restaurants and inns nearby.
(Details available in our Information Room).

A delightfully unique selection for 2 persons of fully self-contained, beautifully appointed, spacious, clean and peaceful accommodation, each with its own distinctive, individual character. Generously and graciously enhanced with antiques/collectables.

32 acres of truly tranquil landscaped gardens, sweeping lawns, woodland walks and panoramic hill-walk overlooking sea, Anglesey and Snowdon. The comfortable, warm and welcoming Castle in serene surroundings is open all year, including for short breaks, offering privacy and relaxation – ideal for couples. Regret children not accepted.
Fully inclusive rents, including breakfast cereals etc., and much, much more...

Please contact Mrs Marita Gray-Parry directly any time for a brochure/booking
Self catering Apartments within the Castle
e.g. 2 persons for 2 nights from £195 incl "Romantic Breaks"
Inclusive Weekly Rents from £500
Llanrug, Near Caernarfon, Gwynedd LL55 4RE
Tel & Fax: (01286) 870210
e-mail: holidays@brynbrascastle.co.uk • www.brynbrascastle.co.uk

Criccieth

SB

Wi-Fi

SB

Pwllheli

Crugeran
Gwyliau ffcrm - Farm holidays

SB

Wi-Fi

Self-catering holiday accommodation in converted barn cottages in beautiful North Wales.

NEW FOR 2012 - two large exclusive barn conversions for 10 and 14. These large luxurious cottages have the 'wow' factor, with private saunas and steam shower cabins (pets accepted in these two only).

Three cottages (sleep 4-7), very tastefully decorated in keeping with their character with antique furniture throughout, providing spacious, comfortable and well equipped accommodation. The cottages have separate patios with picnic tables, and ample parking areas in a large communal lawned garden with fruit trees, making them ideal for individual parties or a larger split party.

Abersoch, Aberdaron, Nefyn and all the beautiful sandy beaches of the peninsula are all close at hand. Walking, golf, sea fishing trips and plenty of water sport facilities are available. The market town of Pwllheli, the resorts of Criccieth and Porthmadog as well as numerous historic and scenic attractions such as the Snowdonia National Park , Ffestiniog Railway, castles and the Italianate village of Portmeirion are all easily reached from Crugeran Farm Holidays.

Cymru Wales
Hunan-ddarpar
Self-catering
★★★★:★★★★★

Mrs Rhian Parry, Crugeran, Sarn Mellteyrn, Pwllheli, Gwynedd LL53 8DT
Tel: 01758 730 375 • e-mail: post@crugeran.com
www.crugeran.com

North Wales

In North Wales there are charming towns and villages, castles, stately homes, beautiful gardens, parks, craft centres and museums waiting to be explored, as well as seaside resorts with soft, sandy beaches and rugged stretches of coastline, all with a background of hills and mountains, just the ingredients needed for an active holiday. Betws-y-Coed, North Wales' most popular inland resort, houses The Snowdonia National Visitor Centre with its craft units and thrilling video presentations – always worth a visit. For fun filled family holidays try Llandudno, where you can take the longest cable car ride in Britain, or wander along the Victorian pier. Experience the thrills of the indoor waterpark at Rhyl, meet seals, eels and sharks at the aquarium or take a traditional donkey ride along the beach.

Colwyn Bay, Conwy

SB

Wi-Fi

Aberporth

Ceredigion

Come to Ceredigion for spectacular scenery, from the cliffs and golden beaches of the coast to the uplands of the Cambrian Mountains, only some half an hour's drive the sea. This rural county, a centre for Welsh language and culture, is home to the National Library of Wales at Aberystwyth, but the books and manuscripts held there aren't the only attraction for visitors. For an active holiday break there are activity centres for all age groups, sea angling and shore fishing, walking in the mountains and along the coast, challenging mountain bike trails and quiet roads for cycling and all kinds of golf courses from parkland to coastal links. Boat trips take visitors out dolphin-spotting, and many species of bird are to be seen along the coast, including Red Kite. Tresaith, one of the locations most favoured by visitors to Ceredigion, is an almost picture-book seaside village with a wonderful sandy beach, ideal for families, with clean sands, clear waters, and rocks to climb, whilst inland lies the Teifi Valley - offering marvellous angling - and Cenarth's famous falls.

Cardigan Bay

Pembrokeshire

St Davids

SB

Ffynnon Ddofn

Ffynnon Ddofn is situated in a quiet lane between St Davids and Fishguard, with panoramic views over 18 miles of coastline.

The cottage is warm, comfortable and very well equipped, with 3 bedrooms sleeping 6, double and twin bedrooms overlooking the garden and adjoining field. Both rooms have new beds and soft furnishings. The third bedroom has pine bunk beds and sea views.

Attractive lounge/diner with exposed natural stone wall and beams, television, DVD and CD players. Bath/shower room, new fitted kitchen with dishwasher, and central heating. Washing machine, tumble dryer, freezer.

There is a large games room with table tennis and snooker, also a barbecue and pleasant, secure garden. Footpath from lane to beach and coast path. Parking beside cottage. Available all year; central heating, electricity and bed linen incl.

For details contact: **Mrs B. Rees White, Brickhouse Farm,**

Burnham Road, Woodham Mortimer, Maldon, Essex CM9 6SR

Tel: 01245 224611

www.ffynnonddofn.co.uk

Whitland

Powys

Hay-on-Wye

LANE FARM

SB

17th century farmhouse in the heart of Kilvert country, rural Radnorshire, only five miles from Hay-on-Wye the famous centre for secondhand books. You will find peace and tranquillity in this wonderful walking country. Within easy reach of the Brecon Beacons National Park, Herefordshire and even the Welsh coast. Two self-catering apartments; sleeping between two and eleven in comfort, which easily combine for a larger party. WTB ★★★

MRS E. BALLY, LANE FARM, PAINSCASTLE, BUILTH WELLS LD2 3JS
Tel & Fax: 01497 851605
e-mail: lanefarm@onetel.com　•　www.lane-farm.co.uk

Garthmyl

PENLLWYN LODGES
– MID WALES SELF CATERING HOLIDAYS –

Welcome to our Self Catering Holiday Park ...

Situated in the heart of Montgomeryshire, Mid Wales.

Penllwyn Lodges is the setting for a superb holiday for all seasons.

19 individually architect designed lodges set in 30 acres of unspoilt woodland teeming with an abundance of wildlife, offering the charming beauty of the Shropshire borders to the east and the rugged Welsh mountains and Cardigan Bay to the west.

On your arrival you will be delighted by the welcome given by Noddy the donkey, Tilley the llama, two Kune Kune pigs, Shetland ponies and Sam the parrot.

For the coarse angler we have a large pool stocked with Carp, Tench, Roach, Bream and Rudd and we also have fishing rights along the River Severn.

We have now opened a 9-hole golf course adjacent to Penllwyn Lodges with a pay and play system. The clubhouse is open all day every day serving breakfasts, lunches and evening restaurant meals.

Well behaved pets are most welcome in specified lodges.

Week and Short Breaks available.

Ideal for those seeking a peaceful and relaxing holiday.

Phillip, Daphne & Emma Jones, Penllwyn Lodges
Garthmyl, Powys SY15 6SB
Tel/Fax: 01686 640269
www.penllwynlodges.co.uk
e-mail: daphne.jones@onetel.net

Presteigne

SB

Whitehall Cottage

Cosy cottage in lovely Border countryside, two miles from Offa's Dyke, ideal centre for touring Mid Wales, its beautiful borderland, South Shropshire and Herefordshire.

- Central heating, washing machine, dishwasher, microwave, colour TV, inglenook fireplace, woodburner, linen included • Power shower over bath
- Two light and airy bedrooms – twin and double • Sleeps 4 plus cot
- Ample parking • Private secure sun-trap garden
- On working farm in peaceful hamlet • Children and pets welcome

MRS R. L. JONES, UPPER HOUSE, KINNERTON, NEAR PRESTEIGNE LD8 2PE • Tel: 01547 560207

South Wales

Gower Peninsula

Holiday Cottages

Gower's largest & most experienced holiday cottage agency

Tel +44 (0) 1792 360624
enquiries@homefromhome.com
www.homefromhome.com
101 Newton Road, Mumbles, Swansea SA3 4BN

Holyhead

Colwyn Bay

Cardigan

Aberdeen

Aberdeen, Banff & Moray

On the Victorian Heritage Trail follow in the footsteps of Queen Victoria to Royal Deeside
to reach the best-known castle of all, Balmoral, visiting many of her favourite towns and
viewpoints on the way, taking in Crathie Church, still attended by the Royal Family. Golfers
have 45 inland courses to choose from, as well as the links courses along the coast. The
countryside is ideal for mountain-biking, and there's a network of trails on the on the hills
and in the forests of the Glenlivet estate, and all kinds of snow sports are available at
Glenshee and the Lecht. Aberdeen, a university city of sparkling granite buildings, has
museums, art galleries, theatres, concerts and films, shopping from designer-wear to
Scottish crafts, as well as beaches, golf and fishing.

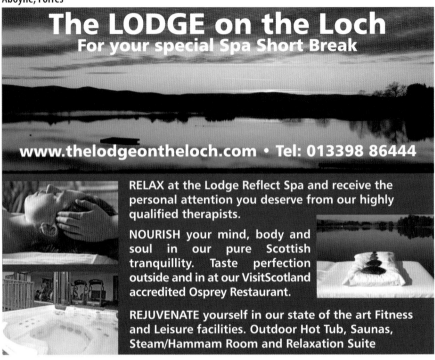

Ballachulish

Argyll & Bute

Argyll & Bute is a wonderfully unspoilt area, historically the birthplace of Scotland and home to a wealth of fascinating wildlife. Here you may be lucky enough to catch a glimpse of an eagle, a wildcat or an osprey, whales, dolphin, seals, or even a giant octopus. At every step the sea fringed landscape is steeped in history, from prehistoric sculpture at Kilmartin and Knapdale, standing stone circles and Bronze Age cup-and-ring engravings, to the elegant ducal home of the once feared Clan Campbell. On the upper reaches of Loch Caolisport can be found St Columba's Cave, and more recent times are illustrated at the Auchindrain Highland Township south of Inveraray, a friendly little town with plenty to see, including the Jail, Wildlife Park and Maritime Museum. Sample the wonderful seafood and local whiskies, walk along the Atlantic beaches or in the Arrochar Alps, and visit the many beautiful gardens.

Bunessan, Dunoon

SB

Wi-Fi

e-mail: argyllarms@isleofmull.co.uk • www.isleofmull.co.uk

The Argyll Arms Hotel, located on the waterfront of the village of Bunessan, and close to the famous Isle of Iona, provides accommodation, bar and restaurant facilities on the beautiful Isle of Mull. With spectacular sea and island views, the hotel is the perfect base from which to explore, either by car or on foot if walking is your forte, or by bike. We can arrange bike hire or why not bring your own? Secure storage is available and bikers are most welcome.The new owners invite you to enjoy their friendly and relaxed Scottish hospitality in comfortable accommodation, value-for-money bistro-style food and the unique atmosphere of the Isle of Mull. All rooms en suite.

Open all day 365 days of the year catering for residents and non residents.

West End Hotel
West Bay, Dunoon PA23 7HU
Tel: 01369 702907 • Fax: 01369 706266
e-mail: suzy@westendhotel.com • www.westendhotel.com

Scottish
TOURIST BOARD
★★
GUEST HOUSE

Wi-Fi

Enjoy the relaxed and friendly family atmosphere at the West End. Situated on the traffic-free West Bay, with private parking, the Guest House enjoys magnificent views of the Clyde Estuary, yet is only minutes' walk from the town centre and ferries. Dunoon is an ideal base from which to tour the West of Scotland.

• All families/twins/doubles have en suite facilities
• Colour TV •
• Varied menus • Licensed bar •
• Games room • Golf Breaks •

Families welcome

2 Nights D,B&B from £80
4 Nights D,B&B from £140

Isle of Gigha, Kilchrenan

SB

The community-owned Isle of Gigha (Gaelic: God's Island) is known as The Jewel of the Inner Hebrides. The Atlantic's crystal clear waters surround this six-mile long magical isle, and lap gently on to its white sandy beaches - creating an aura of peace and tranquillity.

The Gigha Hotel caters admirably for the discerning holidaymaker with comfortable accommodation and first class cuisine, including fresh local seafood. There are also holiday cottages available.
A must for any visitor is a wander around the famous sub-tropical Achamore Gardens, where palm trees and many other exotic plants flourish in Gigha's mild climatic conditions.
The Isle of Gigha Heritage Trust retails quality island-related craft products, some of which have utilised the Trust's own tartan.
Other activities on offer include organised walks, bird watching, sea fishing, a nine-hole golf course and alternative therapies.

Call us on 01583 505254 • Fax: 01583 505244
www.gigha.org.uk

TAYCHREGGAN
Kilchrenan, by Taynuilt, Argyll

This stylish hotel, once a drover's cottage, is surrounded by stunning Highland scenery, and enjoys an idyllic setting in 40 acres of wooded grounds on the shores of Loch Awe. It provides a welcoming retreat, with 18 cosy bedrooms, including luxury suites, many overlooking the loch. The award-winning restaurant features the finest Scottish produce, imaginatively prepared and presented. Children and pets welcome.

Taychreggan Hotel, Kilchrenan • by Taynuilt, Argyll PA35 1HQ
Tel: 01866 833211
e-mail: info@taychregganhotel.co.uk • www.taychregganhotel.co.uk

SB

Wi-Fi

AA
★★★
HOTEL

The Falls of Lora Hotel
Connel Ferry, By Oban PA37 1PB

Oban 5 miles, only 2½-3 hours' drive north-west of Glasgow/Edinburgh.

Overlooking Loch Etive, this fine owner-run Victorian hotel with a modern extension offers a warm welcome, good food, service and comfort. 30 bedrooms including 7 luxury rooms (one with four-poster and round bath, another with a 7' round bed and Jacuzzi bathroom), standard twins and doubles, inexpensive family rooms with bunk beds. Relax in the lochside garden across the road, or in the super Cocktail Bar with open log fire and over 100 brands of whisky to tempt you. The attractive and comfortable bistro has an extensive and varied menu. An ideal centre for touring, sailing and walking.

Tel: 01631 710483 • Fax: 01631 710694
e-mail: enquiries@fallsoflora.com • www.fallsoflora.com

Small, family-run guest house where we aim to make your stay as comfortable as possible. All rooms have central heating, colour TV and hospitality trays; some en suite. A full Scottish breakfast is served, although Continental is available if preferred. We have ample private parking at the rear of the house. Situated 10 minutes' walk from the town centre, train, boat and bus terminals. Oban boasts regular sailings to the Islands, and an excellent golf course, as well as walking, cycling, fishing, or just letting the world go by.

A warm welcome awaits you all year round.

MRS STEWART, GLENVIEW, SOROBA ROAD,
OBAN PA34 4JF • Tel: 01631 562267
e-mail: morven.stewart@hotmail.com

Rothesay

Ayrshire & Arran

Ayrshire and The Isle of Arran in Scotland's south west is flanked by Dumfries and Galloway to the south and the Central Belt to the north. Here the warm waters of the Gulf Stream meet with miles of sandy beaches and a dramatic coastline littered with rocky outcrops and caves, once a favourite with smugglers. As well as long-established seaside resorts like Ayr and Largs, the area is best known for sailing and golf, including three Open Championship courses, and of course, Robert Burns, Scotland's national poet, whose life and works are celebrated at the Burns National Heritage Park at Alloway. The Isle of Arran, as well as being one of Scotland's most accessible islands, is also arguably one of its most truly representative. From the mountainous north to the undulating south it is easy to see how the island became known as "Scotland in miniature", making it a favourite holiday destination for walking, wildlife and simply relaxing.

Borders

Dumfries & Galloway

Dumfries & Galloway combines high moorland and sheltered glens, forests, sandy beaches, crags, cliffs and rocky shores, presenting abundant opportunities for hill walking, rambling, fishing for salmon and sea trout, cycling, mountain biking, off-road driving, horse riding, pony trekking and bird watching. Catch a glimpse of a red kite soaring above, or a wild goat or red squirrel in the 300 square miles of the Galloway Forest Park or hunt for sea life in a rocky coastal pool. Golfers can choose from 30 courses, whether the challenging links at Southerness or a local course with spectacular views. Warmed by the influence of the Gulf Stream, touring in this quiet corner of south west Scotland is a pleasure, visiting the dozens of interesting castles, gardens, museums and historic sites.

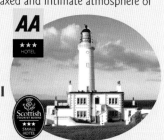

Bathgate, Edinburgh

Edinburgh & Lothians

Wi-Fi

This 17th century farmhouse is situated two miles from M8 Junction 4, which is midway between Glasgow and Edinburgh. This peaceful location overlooks panoramic views of the countryside. All rooms are on the ground floor, ideal for disabled visitors, and have central heating, colour TV and tea/coffee making facilities. We are within easy reach of golf, fishing, cycling (15-mile cycle track runs along back of property). New railway station within 5 minute walk. Edinburgh – Glasgow line.

Scottish TOURIST BOARD
★★★
B&B

Ample security parking.
Open January to December.
Children and pets by arrangement

Twin Room from £44-£55,
Family Room £60-£80

**Mrs F. Gibb, Tarrareoch Farm, Station Road, Armadale, Near Bathgate EH48 3BJ
Tel: 01501 730404**
tarrareochfarmhouse@talktalk.net

Edinburgh

INTERNATIONAL GUEST HOUSE EDINBURGH

Conveniently situated 1½ miles south of
Princes Street on the main A701,
on the main bus route. Private parking.
All bedrooms en suite, with direct-dial telephone,
colour TV and tea/coffee making facilities.
Some rooms enjoy magnificent views across to the
extinct volcano of Arthur's Seat. The full Scottish
breakfasts served on the finest bone china are a
delight. Luxury bedroom on the ground floor
suitable for the limited disabled.

AA
★★★★
Guest House

B&B from £45 to £85 single;
£70 to £150 double

37 Mayfield Gardens, Edinburgh EH9 2BX • Tel: 0131 667 2511 • Fax: 0131 667 1112
e-mail: intergh1@yahoo.co.uk • www.accommodation-edinburgh.com

---

Only 3 miles from Edinburgh Airport and 4 miles from
the city centre, this detached bungalow is in an ideal
location. There is a good bus service into the centre
of Edinburgh and we have free off-street parking
available. We are a non-smoking establishment.
We can provide single, twin, double
and multiple accommodation.
All rooms have a private entrance; en suite facilities;
television; hospitality tray; fridge; hairdryer; iron; etc.
Breakfast is served in your room (cooked or
Continental). Rates from £30 per person.

Wi-Fi

Scottish
TOURIST BOARD
★★★★
B&B

Ingleneuk

31 Drum Brae North, Edinburgh EH4 8AT
Tel: 0131 317 1743
e-mail: ingleneukbnb@btinternet.com
www.ingleneukbandb.co.uk

Linlithgow

Fife

The Kingdom of Fife - and more particularly the coastal university town of St Andrews – is renowned worldwide as the home of golf, where not only the famous links, but parkland and heathland courses number among more than 40 available for golfers to choose from. The south of this small, self-contained former county has been dominated by industry and the Forth Road and Rail Bridges, the imposing road and rail links with Edinburgh and the south, but the sandy beaches and traditional fishing villages at places like Elie, Crail, Pittenweem, and Aberdour are major attractions for holidaymakers. At North Queensferry families will love the excitement of Deep Sea World with its Underwater Safari and seal sanctuary. The historic associations of centres like Dunfermline, Scotland's former capital, the restored medieval village of Culross and the Palace of Falkland make these just some of many fascinating places to visit.

Glasgow & District

In one of Europe's most dynamic cultural centres, there's so much to see and do – from the
City of Glasgow itself, alive with heritage, architecture, entertainment and nightlife, to the
charm of the bustling towns, scenic villages and countryside of the surrounding districts.
James Watt, Adam Smith, Charles Rennie Mackintosh, Lord Kelvin and a host of others have
all played a major part in Greater Glasgow's past. Today the area has a wealth of attractions
which recall their works. Entertainment and sport feature in an exciting year round calendar
that encompasses opera and theatre, music of all kinds, Scottish ceilidhs and top sporting
events. Established as one of the UK's top shopping centres, Glasgow is home to a multitude
of shops, from boutiques and specialist stores, to the High Street favourites, and shopping
malls. Out in the easily accessible countryside, follow the famous River Clyde from New
Lanark, the site of the historic 18th century mills established by Robert Owen.

Highlands

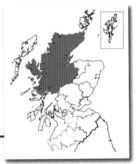

Aviemore

**A family-run Bed and Breakfast,
situated in a quiet cul-de-sac in
the centre of Aviemore**

**Pat & Alan Finlayson,
Craig-na-gower Avenue,**　　　Wi-Fi
**Aviemore,
Inverness-shire PH22 1RW**

Ideal base for a holiday, whether it is fishing, skiing, sailing, birdwatching, climbing or any other
outdoor pursuit. One double, one family and one twin, all en suite, with TV, radio, hairdryers,
controllable electric heating, and a host of other extras. Luxurious guest lounge with blazing log fire.
Purpose-built drying room and secure storage. Pick-up/drop-off service to and from the station.
Private off-road parking. Packed lunches available. Well behaved dogs by prior arrangement. Wi-Fi.
Self-catering accommodation also available.

**Tel: 01479 810717 • e-mail: enquiry@eriskay-aviemore.co.uk
www.eriskay-aviemore.co.uk**

Apart from the stunning and varied scenery, the major attraction of The Scottish Highlands
is that there is so much to see and do, whatever the season. Stretching from Fort William
in the south, to Wick in the far north, and with access links radiating out from the busy city
of Inverness, there is a wealth of visitor attractions and facilities. Perhaps the most famous
is Loch Ness, home of the legendary monster, and a good starting point for a sail down the
Caledonian Canal, through the unspoiled scenery of the Great Glen to Fort William. Just to
the south lies Ben Nevis, Glencoe and a whole range of outdoor sporting activities from
fishing and sailing to skiing. In the Cairngorm National Park it's possible to glimpse an
osprey or capercaillie while walking, climbing, skiing or cycling, or just enjoying the
stunning mountain scenery.

SB
Wi-Fi

The Clan MacDuff Hotel

Fort William, Inverness-shire PH33 6RW
Tel: (01397) 702341 • Fax: (01397) 706174
reception@clanmacduff.co.uk • www.clanmacduff.co.uk

This family-run hotel overlooks Loch Linnhe, two miles south of Fort William. Situated in its own grounds in a quiet and peaceful location with a large car park, the hotel is in an excellent location for touring and experiencing the rugged mountains and enchanting coastline of the West Highlands.

All bedrooms are en suite, have colour TV, telephone, hairdryer, hospitality tray, radio and alarm clock. This family-managed hotel with its friendly welcoming staff is dedicated to providing good quality and value hospitality.

Bed and Breakfast in an en suite room
from £33.50 per person per night.
SPRING AND AUTUMN SPECIAL OFFER
3 Nights Dinner, Bed & Breakfast
from £148.50pp.
Colour brochure on request or visit
our website.

Wi-Fi

Stronchreggan View
Achintore Road, Fort William PH33 6RW

Stronchreggan View is a family-run guest house situated on the shores of Loch Linnhe overlooking the Ardgour Hills.
An ideal base for touring the Highlands, being situated one mile south of Fort William on the A82. Fort William, also known as the Outdoor Capital of the Highlands, offers mountain biking, canoeing, walking, Ben Nevis, the highest mountain in Britain, and much more.

All bedrooms en suite/private bathroom • Children welcome
Non-smoking • Bed and Breakfast from £24 to £38
See our website for full details: www.stronchreggan.co.uk
e-mail: graeme@graememcqueen.wanadoo.co.uk
Tel: 01397 704 644

Wi-Fi

•We are a family-run guest house situated in the Highland village of Ballachulish. Set on the shores of Loch Leven and only one mile from the majesty of Glencoe, Ballachulish makes an ideal centre for exploring much of Scotland's natural beauty. Attractions in and around Glencoe, Fort William, Oban, Skye, Mull, Loch Ness, Loch Lomond and many others are easily accessible.

Imposing craggy mountains, beautiful lochs, waterfalls and forestry can all be found locally and wildlife such as seals, dolphins, otters, deer, pine-martens and eagles thrive.There are a multitude of beautiful and interesting walks, from strolls to view historic Glencoe or around the Lochan trails to mainland Britain's most challenging mountain ridge - Glencoe's Aonach Eagach (The Notched Ridge).

•All of our rooms have en suite facilities, colour TV, DVD player, hospitality tray and individually controlled room heaters.

•We have a comfortable guest lounge, snack bar, separate dining room, drying room, bike store and large car park.

•Free Wi-Fi internet access available.

•Easy to find, next door to the Tourist Information Centre.

•B&B from £20.

Mike and Christine Richardson
Strathassynt Guest House, Loanfern,
Ballachulish, Near Glencoe PH49 4JB
Tel: 01855 811261
e-mail: info@strathassynt.com
www.strathassynt.com

CRAIGARD HOUSE

Craigard House is an early Victorian House (1840) set centrally in the Scottish Highlands in picturesque Glengarry on the edge of Invergarry village. Offering bed and breakfast with an option of an evening meal, it is an ideal base for visiting the many attractions of the Highlands. The house has retained many of its original features, most of the bedrooms have their cast iron fireplaces with stone fire surround intact. The lounge and dining room still retain their original wooden shutters.

SB

Wi-Fi

There are plenty of activities available locally including hill walking, wildlife watching and fishing. There are many places of interest within easy travelling distance - Ben Nevis, Loch Ness, Isle of Skye, Urquhart Castle, Eilean Donan Castle and Inverness to name a few.

WiFi available • Packed lunches.

**Craigard Guest House,
Invergarry,
Inverness-shire PH35 4HG
Tel: 01809 501258**

andrew@craigardhouse.co.uk • www.craigard.saltire.org

Sunnyholm

♿ Wi-Fi

Situated in a large mature, secluded garden in a pleasant residential area within six or seven minutes walking distance of the town centre, tourist information office and all essential holiday amenities. The front of the house overlooks the garden, with the rear allowing easy access to guests' private parking.

All rooms are ground floor level and bedrooms are all en suite with colour TV, tea/coffee making facilities, hairdryers, central heating and double glazing. The lounge is a spacious tastefully furnished room with bay window overlooking the garden, as is the diningroom which overlooks the conservatory and garden beyond.

Double/Twin from £32pppn, single from £40pppn.

Scottish TOURIST BOARD ★★★ B&B

**Mrs A. Gordon, Sunnyholm Guest House, 12 Mayfield Road, Inverness IV2 4AE
01463 231336 • e-mail: sunnyholm@aol.com • www.invernessguesthouse.com**

This former 19th century coaching inn on the John O'Groats peninsula is set in six acres of parkland, close to the Queen Mother's former Highland home, the Castle of Mey.

Fully modernised, the hotel has eight centrally heated en suite bedrooms with colour television and tea making facilities; the spacious Pentland Suite offers a double and family room with en suite bathroom.

Locally caught salmon, crab and other fine Highland produce feature on the varied table d'hôte and grill menus available in the Garden Room, while lighter meals and snacks can be enjoyed in the cosy Pentland Lounge.

A warm Highland welcome awaits you.

www.castlearms.co.uk
Tel & Fax: 01847 851244
e-mail: castlearms.mey@btinternet.com

Scottish
TOURIST BOARD
★★
SMALL
HOTEL

THE CASTLE ARMS
HOTEL
Mey, By Thurso,
Caithness KW14 8XH

Perth & Kinross

The wonderful variety of landscape in Perthshire ensures not only that touring is a delight, but that all kinds of activities from canyoning to climbing, walking to white water rafting are available right in the centre of Scotland within easy reach of Glasgow and Edinburgh. From the southern fringes of the Cairngorm National Park and the 'gateway to the Highlands' at Pitlochry, with its Festival Theatre, through the long, narrow glens and alongside the tranquil lochs to the lowlands of the south, Perth & Kinross offers opportunities for a relaxing scenic break or action-packed adventure. Pass by Britain's tallest hedge near Blairgowrie in the fruit-growing lowlands, and explore the cluster of little resort towns including Crieff, Comrie, Dunkeld, Aberfeldy, and Pitlochry, which have grown up along the Highland Boundary Fault separating north from south.

SB

Wi-Fi

Set just outside the village of Crianlarich, Inverardran House is sited in an elevated position with views across Strathfillan to Ben Challum. This property offers excellent fishing, walking and touring prospects. We can offer you Bed and Breakfast accommodation for up to nine people in two double rooms and one twin (all en suite) and one triple room with a private bathroom. Tea/coffee making facilities in the rooms. Self-catering cottage also available.

Open all year • Prices from £25 to £28 per person per night based on two sharing, £8 surcharge for a single person. Discounts for longer stays.
Packed lunches on request.

John and Janice Christie, Inverardran House, Crianlarich FK20 8QS
Tel: 01838 300240 • e-mail: janice@inverardran.demon.co.uk
www.inverardran.demon.co.uk

Newmill Farm

Stanley PH1 4QD
Mrs Ann Guthrie •01738 828281
e-mail: guthrienewmill@sol.co.uk
www.newmillfarm.co.uk

This 330-acre farm is situated on the A9, six miles north of Perth.
Accommodation comprises twin and double en suite rooms and a family room with private bathroom; lounge, sittingroom, diningroom; bathroom, shower room and toilet.
The warm welcome and supper of excellent home baking are inclusive. Reductions and facilities for children. Pets accepted. Ample car parking area. Excellent local restaurants nearby.
The numerous castles and historic ruins around Perth are testimony to Scotland's turbulent past. Situated in

the area known as "The Gateway to the Highlands" the farm is ideally placed for those seeking some of the best unspoilt scenery in Western Europe. Many famous golf courses and trout rivers in the Perth. If walking or cycling are your interests, there are plenty of routes around the farm that are worth exploring to enjoy the views.

Double/Twin from £32pppn
Single from £45 per night

Callander

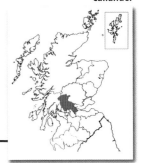

Stirling & The Trossachs

At the heart of Scotland, Stirling, Loch Lomond and the Trossachs combines history and scenic beauty, and endless opportunities for walking, cycling and boating, all within an hour of Edinburgh and Glasgow. Stirling Castle, magnificently restored to tell the story of this former seat of Scottish monarchs, provides a panoramic view from Ben Lomond across the Trossachs and over Bannockburn and other battlegrounds so important in Scotland's history. A walk through the medieval Old Town of Stirling, Scotland's newest city, is the ideal starting point for touring the area, then explore the wild glens and sparkling lochs in Loch Lomond and The Trossachs National Park, and perhaps take a steamer trip down Loch Katrine. Whatever your fitness, there are walks suitable for everyone, cycle routes, challenging mountain bike trails, golf and wildlife.

Scottish Islands

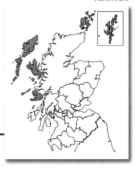

Kirkwall

So many islands are waiting to be visited off the Scottish mainland, each with a mystery and magic of its own. To the north lie the Orkney and Shetland Isles, with their strong connections to the Vikings whose influence is still seen and heard today. To the west, exposed to the Atlantic, lie the Inner and Outer Hebrides, including the islands of Skye, Islay, Mull and Tiree, Lewis, Harris and Barra, each with its own culture, traditions and heritage. Everywhere there's evidence of settlement going back to prehistoric times, including awe-inspiring standing stones and circles and chambered cairns. Some islands have mountains to climb, but most are low-lying, ideal for exploring on foot and for cycling and bird watching, while the Atlantic waves have proved a great attraction to surfers from all over the world.

Kirkwall, Loch Harray

SB
Wi-Fi

Pierowall Hotel

Accommodation in the heart of Westray

Enjoy the friendly atmosphere of a family-run hotel with views over Pierowall Bay with Papa Westray visible in the near distance. Ideally situated for visitors wishing to explore the island; we can arrange for a guided tour to pick you up from the hotel and return you for your meals here, or you could take a packed lunch with you. Why not take a flight on the plane to Papay for the world's shortest scheduled flight? We offer freshly cooked meals daily, including locally caught seafood and a variety of fresh fish. Takeaway food available. Small private parties and conferences welcome.

4 en suite rooms • 2 standard rooms • Lounge bar • Dining room

Pierowall Hotel, Pierowall, Westray, Orkney KW17 2BZ
Tel: 01857 677472 or 677208
e-mail: enquiries@pierowallhotel.co.uk
www.pierowallhotel.co.uk

The FHG Directory of Website Addresses

on pages 381-387 is a useful quick reference guide for holiday accommodation with e-mail and/or website details

FREE or **REDUCED RATE** entry to Holiday Visits and Attractions –
see our **READERS' OFFER VOUCHERS** on pages 389-400

symbols ⛺🐴SB♿♉Wi-Fi

🐕	*Pets Welcome*	🐴	*Children Welcome*
SB	*Short Breaks*	♿	*Suitable for Disabled Guests*
♉	*Licensed*	**Wi-Fi**	*Wi-Fi available*

Fraserburgh

Aberdeen, Banff & Moray

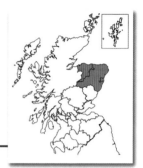

Newseat & Kirklea

both within five miles of the fishing town of Fraserburgh, are self-catering properties available from April to October. Both houses have good garden areas and ample parking in quiet surroundings.

Newseat (★) sleeps four and has four rooms and a bathroom, all situated on the one level.

Kirklea (★★★) which sleeps six, is a two-storey Victorian house set in its own grounds. The ground floor has a utility room, kitchen/diner, dining room and lounge, and three bedrooms are situated on the first floor along with the bath/ shower room.

Terms per week from £180 for Newseat and from £320 for Kirklea, both fully inclusive of gas and electricity. All bed and table linen and towels are provided.

Contact: **Mrs E.M. Pittendrigh, Kirkton, Tyrie, Fraserburgh AB43 7DQ**
Tel: 01346 541231
e-mail: pittendrigh@supanet.com

symbols

🐕	Pets Welcome	🐎	Children Welcome
SB	Short Breaks	♿	Suitable for Disabled Guests
♀	Licensed	Wi-Fi	Wi-Fi available

Glenlivet

Traditional stone cottages set amidst beautiful surroundings near rivers Avon and Livet.
All modernised and very comfortable.
Fishing available.
Ideal for exploring Highlands, Castle & Whisky Trails, walking, skiing, golf.

Edenvale Cottage

Contact:

The Post Office
Tomnavoulin
Ballindalloch
AB37 9JA
Tel: 01807 590220

www.beechgrovecottages.co.uk

Other British holiday guides from FHG Guides

SHORT BREAK HOLIDAYS in Britain

The bestselling and original **PETS WELCOME!**

The **GOLF GUIDE,** Where to Play, Where to Stay in Britain & Ireland

750 BED & BREAKFASTS in Britain

SELF-CATERING HOLIDAYS in Britain

FAMILY BREAKS in Britain

CARAVAN & CAMPING HOLIDAYS in Britain

Published annually: available in all good bookshops or direct from the publisher:

FHG Guides, Abbey Mill Business Centre, Seedhill, Paisley PA1 1TJ

Tel: 0141 887 0428 • Fax: 0141 889 7204

e-mail: admin@fhguides.co.uk • www.holidayguides.com

Johnshaven

Angus & Dundee

Brawliemuir Holiday Cottages Kincardineshire

SB

Two delightful stone-built cottages situated in a lovely country setting yet only three miles from the sea. Both cottages have central heating and are fully equipped to a high standard. Towels and bed linen included. This is a great base for exploring the Angus Glens, the Mearns countryside, the Castle Trail and the granite city of Aberdeen. Golf, fishing, horse riding, hill walking and a great beach are all nearby.

No smoking. Pets welcome. Available all year from £280 to £485 per week

Telephone Carole Duvall on **01561 362453** *or e-mail for further information.*

e-mail: carole@the-duvalls.com • www.brawliemuircottages.co.uk

The former Pictish stronghold of Angus stretches from the sand and pebble beaches and rugged cliffs of the North Sea coast inland into the deep, narrow glens at the foothills of the Cairngorm National Park, perfect countryside for walking or for climbing, with ten 'Munros' mountains over 3000 feet, to choose from. The rivers are well known for salmon and trout fishing, alternatively sea anglers can charter a boat, or simply fish from the beach. The area is a golfers' dream, with a wide choice of courses, from classic links like Carnoustie to the heathland at Edzell in the north and parkland courses nearer the lively coastal city of Dundee. Visit the ancient port of Arbroath during the Sea Fest, celebrating its maritime heritage, and taste a traditional 'smokie'. The more recent past is commemorated in Dundee at Discovery Point, now the home of the RRS Discovery, the ship that took Captain Scott on his ill-fated journey to the Antarctic.

Bridge of Awe

Argyll & Bute

tigh an daraich

SB

LUXURY LODGES

Bridge of Awe, Taynuilt PA35 1HR
Tel: 01866 822693

Five lodges set in a small exclusive woodland development of 5 acres enjoying spectacular views across the River Awe to Ben Cruachan (the hollow mountain - inside is a hydroelectric power station). Ideal base for touring the Western Isles, Oban, Fort William, Glencoe and Inveraray.

Our lodges are constructed and finished to a very high standard, and fully equipped. Strictly no smoking within the lodges.

PETS WELCOME (4 Star only). **CATEGORY 2 DISABILITY.**

e-mail: info@tighandaraich.co.uk • www.tighandaraich.co.uk

Argyll & Bute is a wonderfully unspoilt area, historically the birthplace of Scotland and home to a wealth of fascinating wildlife. Here you may be lucky enough to catch a glimpse of an eagle, a wildcat or an osprey, whales, dolphin, seals, or even a giant octopus. At every step the sea fringed landscape is steeped in history, from prehistoric sculpture at Kilmartin and Knapdale, standing stone circles and Bronze Age cup-and-ring engravings, to the elegant ducal home of the once feared Clan Campbell. On the upper reaches of Loch Caolisport can be found St Columba's Cave, and more recent times are illustrated at the Auchindrain Highland Township south of Inveraray, a friendly little town with plenty to see, including the Jail, Wildlife Park and Maritime Museum. At Rothesay on the Isle of Bute find out about the island at the Discovery Centre, explore the dungeons and grand hall of Rothesay Castle, and visit the Victorian Gothic splendour of Mount Stuart.

Dalmally, Inveraray

Situated on beautiful Seil Island with wonderful views of surrounding countryside. These lovingly restored cottages (one detached and one attached to the main croft house) retain their traditional character while incorporating all modern facilities. The cottages are near to each other and ideal for two families on holiday together. Seil is one of the most peaceful and tranquil spots in the West Highlands, with easy access to neighbouring Isles of Luing and Easdale. Oban, the hub for trips to Mull and Iona, is half an hour's drive away over the famous 18th century "Bridge Over The Atlantic". Wonderful area for hillwalking, cycling, fishing and bird watching. Short breaks from £45 per day.

SB

Wi-Fi

Kilbride Cottage

KILBRIDE CROFT

Balvicar, Isle of Seil, Argyll PA34 4RD
Contact: Mary & Brian Phillips
Tel: 01852 300475
e-mail: kilbridecroft@aol.com
www.kilbridecroft.co.uk

Croft Cottage

Duntrune Castle Holiday Cottages

Five traditional self-catering cottages set in the spacious grounds of 12th century Duntrune Castle, which guards the entrance to Loch Crinan. All have been attractively modernised and accommodate two to five persons.

The estate comprises 5000 acres and five miles of coastline. Without leaving our land, you can enjoy easy or testing walks, sea or river fishing, and watching the abundant wildlife. Nearby are several riding establishments, a bicycle-hire firm, and a number of excellent restaurants.

Prices from £300 to £550 per week. Pets are welcome.

For further details please contact:
Robin Malcolm, Duntrune Castle,
Kilmartin, Argyll PA31 8QQ
01546 510283 • www.duntrune.com

The Gardeners Cottages
Arden, Loch Lomond

Secluded in the wooded grounds of Arden House by the shores of Loch Lomond is the row of Gardeners Cottages, built as one side of a magnificent Victorian walled garden.
Linnhe and **Lomond** are ideal for families or friends (sleeping 4 to 5 each), and **Luss** is a perfect hideaway for two. Only 6 miles from the picturesque village of Luss and world famous Loch Lomond Golf Courses.

SB

Wi-Fi

The cottages are warm, comfortable and full of character, situated amidst breathtaking scenery.

The Gardeners Cottages, Loch Lomond G83 8RD
Tel/Fax 01389 850601
amacleod@gardeners-cottages.com
www.gardeners-cottages.com

SB

Wi-Fi

The Exclusive Highland Estate of

ELLARY

and lovely

CASTLE SWEEN

- *Peace* • *Seclusion*
- *Variety of interests*
- *Freedom* • *History*
- *Outstanding scenery*

This 15,000 acre Highland Estate lies in one of the most beautiful and unspoilt areas of Scotland and has a wealth of ancient historical associations within its bounds. There is St Columba's Cave, one of the first places of Christian Worship in Britain, also Castle Sween, the oldest ruined castle in Scotland, and Kilmory Chapel where there is a fascinating collection of Celtic slabs. There is a wide range of accommodation, from small groups of cottages, many of the traditional stone-built estate type, to modern holiday chalets and super luxury caravans at Castle Sween.

Most of the cottages accommodate up to six, but one will take six/eight. All units fully equipped except linen. Ellary is beautiful at all times of the year and is suitable for windsurfing, fishing, swimming, sailing and the observation of a wide variety of wildlife; there are paths and tracks throughout the estate for the visitor who prefers to explore on foot, and guests will find farmers and estate workers most helpful in their approach. For further details, brochure and booking forms, please apply to:

ELLARY ESTATE OFFICE, by LOCHGILPHEAD, ARGYLL PA31 8PA

Tel: 01880 770232/770209
or 01546 850223
info@ellary.com
www.ellary.com

Loch Lomond

Inchmurrin Island

SELF-CATERING HOLIDAYS

SB

Wi-Fi

Inchmurrin is the largest island on Loch Lomond and offers a unique experience. Three self-catering apartments, sleeping from four to six persons, and a detached cedar clad cottage sleeping eight, are available.

The well appointed apartments overlook the garden, jetties and the loch beyond. Inchmurrin is the ideal base for watersports and is situated on a working farm.

Terms from £410 to £950 per week, £285 to £600 per half week

A ferry service is provided for guests, and jetties are available for customers with their own boats. Come and stay and have the freedom to roam and explore anywhere on the island.

e-mail: scotts@inchmurrin-lochlomond.com
www.inchmurrin-lochlomond.com
Inchmurrin Island
Loch Lomond G63 0JY
Tel: 01389 850245 • Fax: 01389 850513

Kilmory, Millport

Ayrshire & Arran

Sliddery

SB

Far Horizons Holiday Cottages
Sliddery, Isle of Arran KA27 8PB
The Hayshed, Ploughman's Bothy and Blacksmith's Bothy, beautifully converted,
owner-maintained cottages in secluded coastal location on Arran's southwest corner.
Stunning views, track down to rocky shore, sunsets on Kintyre.
A great place to come home to.
Sleep 4. £350 - £525
Scottish
TOURIST BOARD
★★★
SELF CATERING
Mrs Margaret Tait. T: 01770 870295
e: wbandmg.tait@btinternet.com
www.arran-far-horizons.co.uk

Ayrshire and The Isle of Arran in Scotland's south west is flanked by Dumfries and Galloway to the south and the Central Belt to the north. Here the warm waters of the Gulf Stream meet with miles of sandy beaches and a dramatic coastline littered with rocky outcrops and caves, once a favourite with smugglers. As well as long-established seaside resorts like Ayr and Largs, the area is best known for sailing and golf, including three Open Championship courses, and of course, Robert Burns, Scotland's national poet, whose life and works are celebrated at the Burns National Heritage Park at Alloway. The Isle of Arran, as well as being one of Scotland's most accessible islands, is also arguably one of its most truly representative. From the mountainous north to the undulating south it is easy to see how the island became known as "Scotland in miniature", making it a favourite holiday destination for walking, wildlife and simply relaxing.

symbols SB Wi-Fi

	Pets Welcome		*Children Welcome*
SB	*Short Breaks*		*Suitable for Disabled Guests*
	Licensed	Wi-Fi	*Wi-Fi available*

Duns

Borders

Out of the world and into...

SB

&

Wi-Fi

Green Hope

Unsurpassed for peaceful relaxation, Green Hope lies at at the end of a private lane, a world away from the noise and rush of life.

Green Hope
Best for body and soul

The Cottage • sleeps up to 8, with extra beds and a cot available. Double room, family room upstairs. Ground floor en suite family room. Modern fully equipped kitchen. Satellite Freeview TV and DVD, video, phone.
River Suite • charming ground floor apartment sleeping two in en suite double room, sitting room, kitchen/dining room. Fully accessible to wheelchair users.
Easy access to fishing, walks and beaches. Berwick half an hour, Edinburgh one hour. Country houses near by.
Accommodation available on Self-catering or B&B basis. Pets welcome by arrangement.

Ellemford, Duns, Berwickshire TD11 3SG
Tel: 01361 890242 • Fax: 01361 890295
e-mail: guesthouse@greenhope.co.uk • www.greenhope.co.uk

Crossed by the River Tweed, which provides some of the best fishing in Scotland, the Scottish Borders stretch from the rolling hills and moorland in the west, through gentler valleys and agricultural plains, to the rocky Berwickshire coastline with its secluded coves and picturesque fishing villages. This variety of landscape has led to numerous opportunities for walking, horse riding and cycling, fishing and golf, as well as surfing, diving and birdwatching on the coast. Friendly towns, long known for their textiles, and charming villages are there to be discovered, while castles, abbeys, stately homes and museums illustrate the exciting and often bloody history of the area. It's this history which is commemorated in the Common Ridings and other local festivals, creating a colourful pageant much enjoyed by visitors and native Borderers alike.

Kelso

Castle Douglas

Dumfries & Galloway

Dumfries & Galloway combines high moorland and sheltered glens, forests, sandy beaches, crags, cliffs and rocky shores, presenting abundant opportunities for hill walking, rambling, fishing for salmon and sea trout, cycling, mountain biking, off-road driving, horse riding, pony trekking and bird watching. Catch a glimpse of a red kite soaring above, or a wild goat or red squirrel in the 300 square miles of the Galloway Forest Park or hunt for sea life in a rocky coastal pool. Golfers can choose from 30 courses, whether the challenging links at Southerness or a local course with spectacular views. Warmed by the influence of the Gulf Stream, touring in this quiet corner of south west Scotland is a pleasure, visiting the dozens of interesting castles, gardens, museums and historic sites.

Visit the FHG website
www.holidayguides.com
for all kinds of holiday
accommodation in Britain

Loch Lomond

Dunbartonshire

The Lorn Mill Cottages

Relax, unwind and recharge at The Lorn Mill - three peaceful and pretty cottages within an 18th century water mill. Tucked away in a secluded country estate overlooking Loch Lomond, the cottages provide a unique four seasons location in which to enjoy this gorgeous area of Scotland. Tennis court with stunning views. Perfect for couples.

We look forward to welcoming you.

ASSC

The Lorn Mill Cottages
Gartocharn,
Loch Lomond
Dunbartonshire G83 8LX

www.lornmill.com
e-mail: gavmac@globalnet.co.uk
Tel: 44 (0) 1389 753074

Edinburgh & Lothians

Visitors to Edinburgh, Scotland's capital, and the surrounding area, the Lothians, will find a wide range of attractions offering something for all ages and interests. Heritage is paramount, with historic and royal connections through the ages centred on Edinburgh Castle, down the Royal Mile to the Palace of Holyroodhouse, and its new neighbour, the Scottish Parliament building. Stroll through the Georgian New Town, browsing through some of the many shops on the way, or a wander through the Royal Botanic Gardens. Imagine sailing on the Royal Yacht Britannia, now berthed at Leith, or travel on a journey with our planet through time and space at Our Dynamic Earth. The Edinburgh Festival in August is part of the city's tradition and visitors flock to enjoy the performing arts, theatre, ballet, cinema and music, and of course "The Tattoo" itself. At the Festival Fringe there is a wide variety of shows and impromptu acts, and jazz and book festivals too.

Colinsburgh

Fife

Cottage to let in a conservation village in the attractive East Neuk of Fife, 3 miles from Elie and 11 from St Andrews.
Easy reach of sandy beaches, coastal walks and numerous golf courses.
Two bedrooms, lounge, kitchen/diner and a walled rear garden. Sleeps 4/5, pets welcome. Prices from £275 per week.

SB

For further details, telephone
01788 890942 or see
www.eastneukcottage.co.uk

Highlands

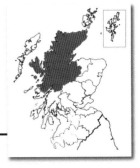

Apart from the stunning and varied scenery, the major attraction of The Scottish Highlands is that there is so much to see and do, whatever the season. Stretching from Fort William in the south, to Wick in the far north, and with access links radiating out from the busy city of Inverness, there is a wealth of visitor attractions and facilities. Perhaps the most famous is Loch Ness, home of the legendary monster, and a good starting point for a sail down the Caledonian Canal, through the unspoiled scenery of the Great Glen to Fort William. Just to the south lies Ben Nevis, Glencoe and a whole range of outdoor sporting activities from fishing and sailing to skiing. In the Cairngorm National Park it's possible to glimpse an osprey or capercaillie while walking, climbing, skiing or cycling, or just enjoying the stunning mountain scenery.

Tyndrum
Boat of Garten

Completely renovated, well furnished self-catering accommodation retaining the original pine panelling in the lounge.

Set in a rural village, Boat of Garten, in beautiful Strathspey, six miles from Aviemore, an ideal base for touring. Fishing is available locally on the River Spey, just two minutes away, with attractive riverside picnic spots. The famous Osprey nest is nearby, at Loch Garten RSPB Reserve.
Local steam train journeys, good golf and water sports; skiing at Cairngorm in season.
Shop and pub half a mile.
Large lounge, attractive dining/sitting room, spacious fully fitted dining kitchen, shower room. First floor: bathroom, one double and one twin room, both with washbasin, and one single bedroom.
Colour TV with Sky digital; dishwasher, microwave, washer/dryer and deep freeze.
Electricity, bed linen and towels inclusive. Parking. Large garden.

Contact: Mrs N.C. Clark, Dochlaggie, Boat of Garten PH24 3BU
Tel: 01479 831242 • e-mail: dochlaggie99@aol.com

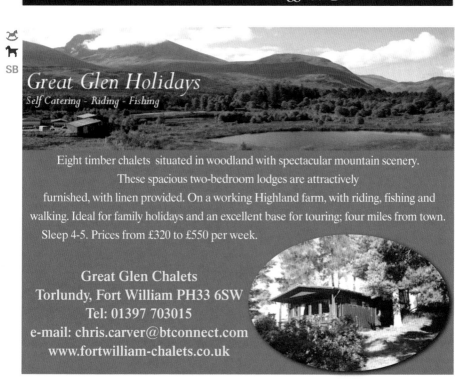

Great Glen Holidays
Self Catering - Riding - Fishing

Eight timber chalets situated in woodland with spectacular mountain scenery.
These spacious two-bedroom lodges are attractively
furnished, with linen provided. On a working Highland farm, with riding, fishing and
walking. Ideal for family holidays and an excellent base for touring; four miles from town.
Sleep 4-5. Prices from £320 to £550 per week.

Great Glen Chalets
Torlundy, Fort William PH33 6SW
Tel: 01397 703015
e-mail: chris.carver@btconnect.com
www.fortwilliam-chalets.co.uk

Invermoriston Holidays

In the heart of the Scottish Highlands by Loch Ness

Invermoriston Holidays offer a peacefully secluded yet central location in spectacular scenery only a few hundred metres from Loch Ness. Offering home-from-home comfort and privacy, all have private patio area with barbecue and garden furniture. Games room, spacious play area, aerial glide and swings. Dogs are welcome in a selection of holiday chalets. Pay telephone and launderette on site. Sleep 2-4. *Prices from £150 for a short break to £580 for a week.*

SB

Wi-Fi

**Invermoriston Holiday Chalets
Glenmoriston, By Loch Ness, Highlands IV63 7YF
Tel: 01320 351254 Fax: 01320 351343
e-mail: info@invermoriston-holidays.co.uk
www.invermoriston-holidays.co.uk**

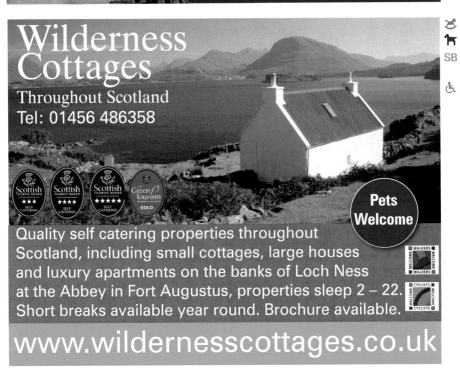

Wilderness Cottages

Throughout Scotland
Tel: 01456 486358

SB

Pets Welcome

Quality self catering properties throughout Scotland, including small cottages, large houses and luxury apartments on the banks of Loch Ness at the Abbey in Fort Augustus, properties sleep 2 – 22. Short breaks available year round. Brochure available.

www.wildernesscottages.co.uk

FREE or **REDUCED RATE** entry to Holiday Visits and Attractions –
see our **READERS' OFFER VOUCHERS** on pages 389-400

The FHG Directory of Website Addresses
on pages 381-387 is a useful quick reference guide for
holiday accommodation with e-mail and/or website details

SB

Perth & Kinross

The wonderful variety of landscape in Perthshire ensures not only that touring is a delight,
but that all kinds of activities from canyoning to climbing, walking to white water rafting
are available right in the centre of Scotland within easy reach of Glasgow and Edinburgh.
From the southern fringes of the Cairngorm National Park and the 'gateway to the
Highlands' at Pitlochry, with its Festival Theatre, through the long, narrow glens and
alongside the tranquil lochs to the lowlands of the south, Perth & Kinross offers
opportunities for a relaxing scenic break or action-packed adventure. Pass by Britain's
tallest hedge near Blairgowrie in the fruit-growing lowlands, and explore the cluster of little
resort towns including Crieff, Comrie, Dunkeld, Aberfeldy, and Pitlochry, which have grown
up along the Highland Boundary Fault separating north from south.

Carloway

Scottish Islands

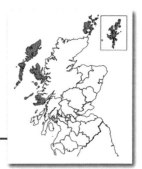

Baile Tughaidh   Blackhouse Village

*On the exposed Atlantic coast of the Isle of Lewis the blackhouse village
of Gearrannan lies steeped in history and sited in an environment
of outstanding natural beauty.*

Gearrannan Blackhouse Village offers a range of self catering thatched cottages
from ★★ group accommodation sleeping 16, to ★★★★ family cottages.
Enjoy modern comfort and complete relaxation in this beautifully restored
crofting village. Pets by arrangement. Off-season short breaks.

**Gearrannan Blackhouse Village, Carloway, Isle of Lewis HS2 9AL
tel: 01851 643416 • fax: 01851 643488
e-mail: info@gearrannan.com • www.gearrannan.com**

symbols 🐕🎠SB♿♉Wi-Fi

🐕	*Pets Welcome*		🎠	*Children Welcome*
SB	*Short Breaks*		♿	*Suitable for Disabled Guests*
♉	*Licensed*		Wi-Fi	*Wi-Fi available*

Kirkwall

SB

Wi-Fi

Sebay Mill

WORLD CLASS SELF-CATERING
HOLIDAY APARTMENTS
4-5 Star Accommodation

This former grain mill has been carefully restored to provide six luxurious self-catering apartments, with views over the Bay of Suckquoy. The apartments, which sleep one to four persons, have been completed to the highest standards and have fast gained a reputation for exellence far and wide.

**All enquiries to: Mr & Mrs W. McEwen, Oaklea Farm,
St Ola, Orkney KW15 1SX
Tel: 01856 877782 Fax: 01856 877007
Email: office@sebaymill.co.uk
www.sebaymill.co.uk**

Other British holiday guides from FHG Guides

SHORT BREAK HOLIDAYS in Britain

The bestselling and original PETS WELCOME!

The GOLF GUIDE, Where to Play, Where to Stay in Britain & Ireland

750 BED & BREAKFASTS in Britain

SELF-CATERING HOLIDAYS in Britain

FAMILY BREAKS in Britain

CARAVAN & CAMPING HOLIDAYS in Britain

Published annually: available in all good bookshops or direct from the publisher:

FHG Guides, Abbey Mill Business Centre, Seedhill, Paisley PA1 1TJ

Tel: 0141 887 0428 • Fax: 0141 889 7204

e-mail: admin@fhguides.co.uk • www.holidayguides.com

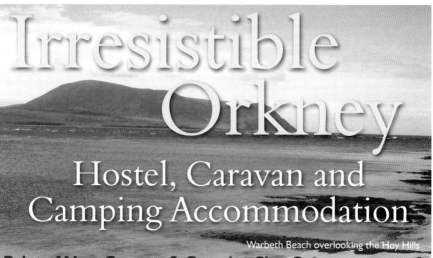

Irresistible Orkney

Hostel, Caravan and Camping Accommodation

Warbeth Beach overlooking the Hoy Hills

Point of Ness Caravan & Camping Site, Stromness

Stromness is a small picturesque town with impressive views of the hills of Hoy.
The site is one mile from the harbour in a quiet, shoreline location.
Many leisure activities are available close by, including fishing, sea angling, golf and a
swimming & fitness centre.
Contact: stromnesscashoffice@orkney.gov.uk or leisure.culture@orkney.gov.uk
www.orkney.gov.uk • Tel: 01856 850262

Birsay Outdoor Centre / Caravan & Camping Site

A new campsite located on the 3-Star hostel site in the picturesque north west of Orkney.

Hoy Centre

Four Star hostel accommodation with en suite facilities.
Ideal base for exploring Hoy's magnificent scenery and natural environment.

Rackwick Hostel

Rackwick is considered one of the most beautiful places in Orkney with towering cliffs and
steep heathery hills. This cosy hostel has spectacular views over Rackwick's cliffs and beach.
For Birsay, Hoy and Rackwick contact leisure.culture@orkney.gov.uk
Tel: 01856 873535 • www.hostelsorkney.co.uk

The Pickaquoy Centre and Camping Park, Kirkwall
Tel: 01856 879900

the pickaquoy centre

A 4-Star touring park with the latest in park amenities is situated at the Pickaquoy Centre
complex, an impressive leisure facility offering a range of activities for all the family.
Within walking distance of the St Magnus Cathedral and Kirkwall town centre.

e-mail: enquiries@pickaquoy.com
www.pickaquoy.co.uk

ORKNEY
ISLANDS COUNCIL

...ost a botanical garden, Linnhe is recognised as one of the best ...d most beautiful Lochside parks in Britain. Magnificent gardens contrast with the wild, dramatic scenery of Loch Eil and the

 mountains beyond. Superb amenities, launderette, shop & bakery, and free fishing on private shoreline with its own jetty all help give Linnhe its Five Star grading. Linnhe Lochside Holidays is ideally situated for

day trips with Oban, Skye, Mull, Inverness and the Cairngorms all within easy driving distance.

- **Holiday Caravans from £240 per week**
- **Touring pitches from £16 per night**
- **Tent pitches from £12 per night**
- **Pets welcome**
- **Tourer playground, pet exercise area**
- **Motorhome waste and water facilities**
- **Recycling on park**
- **Colour brochure sent with pleasure.**

www.linnhe-lochside-holidays.co.uk/brochure
Tel: 01397 772 376 to check availability

Wi-Fi

At end of A99 on seafront beside "last house in Scotland", caravan and camping site with showers, launderette, electric hook-ups and disabled toilet. Internet access.

John O'Groats
Caravan and Camping Site
John O'Groats KW1 4YR
Tel: 01955 611329/ 744
e-mail: info@johnogroatscampsite.co.uk
www.johnogroatscampsite.co.uk

Caravans, caravanettes and tents welcome. Booking office for day trips to Orkney Islands on site. Hotel, restaurant, cafe, harbour 150 metres.

Magnificent cliff scenery with sea birds galore including puffins, guillemots, skuas within one-and-a-half-miles. Seals are often seen swimming to and fro.

Open 1st April to 30 September.

SB

Gruinard Bay Caravan Park

Situated just a stone's throw from the beach, Gruinard Bay Caravan Park offers the perfect setting for a holiday or a stopover on the West Coast of Scotland. Family-owned and personally operated, the park boasts magnificent views across Gruinard Bay.

- Sea front touring pitches • Electric hook-ups
- Camping pitches • Free toilet and shower facilities
- Gas available on site • Laundry facilities
- Static Holiday Homes available
- Pets welcome (not in Holiday Homes)

**Tony & Ann Davis,
Gruinard Bay Caravan Park,
Laide, Wester Ross IV22 2ND
Tel/Fax: 01445 731225
www.gruinard.scotshost.co.uk**

Roy Bridge

Welcome to Bunroy Park Caravan & Camping Site

....a haven of peace in the heart of the Highlands, set in 9 acres of secluded parkland, surrounded by breathtaking scenery, and within easy reach of Ben Nevis and Fort William, an ideal base for exploring, walking, cycling, fishing or just relaxing.

• toilet/shower block • electric hook-ups
• laundry room • fridge & freezer
• short walk to two hotels, shop, Post
Office and railway station.

Also available: 8 well equipped self-catering lodges with one/two bedrooms
••••*Camping Pods now available*••••

**Alex & Flora Macdonald, Bunroy Park, Roy Bridge, Fort William
PH31 4AG • Phone: 01397 712332**
e mail : info@bunroycamping.co.uk • **www.bunroycamping.co.uk**

Abingdon

Mount View Caravan Park

Luxury holiday homes for hire on caravan park set in peaceful, unspoilt countryside with beautiful views of the Clyde valley. Good for walking, cycling, fishing, golf and touring the area. Near to Moffat, Biggar, Edinburgh, Glasgow and Scottish Borders. Fully equipped holiday home including microwave, TV/DVD and with double glazing and central heating. En suite shower room, lounge, dining area, kitchen, twin and double bedrooms. Bedding and towels can be provided at an extra cost. Easy access, just five minutes from J13 of the M74 and a short walk from the village shop.
£190 to £360 per week.

Abington, South Lanarkshire ML12 6RW   Tel: 01864 502808
e-mail: info@mountviewcaravanpark.co.uk • www.mountviewcaravanpark.co.uk

symbols 🐕🎠 SB ♿ 🍷 Wi-Fi

🐕	Pets Welcome	🎠	Children Welcome
SB	Short Breaks	♿	Suitable for Disabled Guests
🍷	Licensed	**Wi-Fi**	Wi-Fi available

Largo Leisure Parks

For Living Life to the Full

Our holiday parks are ideally suited for those seeking a tra retreat with beautiful scenery, whilst enjoying the many varied attractions of the Kingdom of Fife and Perthshire are Scotland.

Holiday homes are perfect for getting away from it all. Our parks off atmosphere to relax and enjoy the long holiday or short break.

Sauchope Links Park is situated on the shoreline, near the eastern most Fife in a beautiful, unspoilt position close to the historic town of Crail. This winning park with stunning views makes the perfect holiday destination.

Letham Feus Park is situated only 3 miles from Lundin Links with its championship course and beautiful sandy beach. The park is blessed with breathtaking views over ti Forth Estuary to the South and beautiful woodland to the north. Letham Feus is the perfect place to take that well earned break.

Braidhaugh Park is situated on the banks of the River Earn amid the scenic surroundings of Crieff. The park is an ideal base from which to explore not only the beautiful surroundings of Perthshire, but also the magnificent scenic grandeur of Central Scotland.

Loch Tay Highland Lodges Holiday Park is beautifully situated on a well established 140 acre Highland Estate nestling on the shores of Loch Tay in Perthshire. It is the perfect all year round holiday destination for those who love pure relaxation or for those energetic types who love the great outdoors.

Sauchope Links Holiday Park, Crail, Fife KY10 3XJ
Tel: 01333 450 460   info@sauchope.co.uk

Letham Feus Holiday Park, Cupar Rd by Lundin Links KY8 5NT
Tel: 01333 351 900   info@lethamfeus.co.uk

Braidhaugh Holiday Park, South Bridgend, Crieff PH7 4DH
Tel: 01764 652951   info@braidhaugh.co.uk

Loch Tay Highland Lodges, Milton Morenish Estate by Killin,
Perthshire FK21 8TY Tel: 01567 820323
info@lochtay-vacations.co.uk www.lochtay-vacations.co.uk

Largo Leisure Parks

www.largoleisure.co.uk

Ireland

Six Mile Water Caravan Park

Lough Road,
Antrim BT41 4DG

Situated at Antrim Lough Shore Park, on the tranquil and scenic shores of Lough Neagh, within easy walking distance of Antrim town and Antrim Forum Leisure Complex. The park's central location, coupled with its close proximity to Larne and Belfast harbours, make it an ideal base for touring not only the Borough of Antrim but all of Northern Ireland. The park accommodates touring caravans, motorhomes and tents.

Electric hook-up for 37 pitches. 8 camping sites. Toilet and shower block. Disabled shower room. Fully equipped laundry and dishwashing facilities. TV lounge. Games room. Recycling facilities. Licensed cafe. Dogs allowed. Group discount on request. Advance booking advisable. Open February to November.

Bookings can be made online, website or by telephone.

NITB
★★★★★

Tel: 028 9446 4963
e-mail: sixmilewater@antrim.gov.uk
www.antrim.gov.uk/caravanpark

Pubs & Inns

A selection of inns, pubs and hostelries offering food, refreshment and traditional good cheer; many also provide comfortable overnight accommodation.

 Accommodation available
Wi-Fi Wi-Fi available
 Food available
🐕 Pets welcome
P Parking
🎠 Children welcome

Marazion

The Godolphin Arms — AA ★★★★ INN

West End, Marazion, Cornwall TR17 0EN

Perched on the edge of the sand, directly opposite St Michael's Mount in historic Marazion, this family-run Inn offers ten en suite guest bedrooms, a choice of bars, beachside terrace and a varied menu. The outlook from the lounge bar and many of the bedrooms is simply stunning, with uninterrupted views to the Island and castle and across Mounts Bay towards Penzance. Perfect for exploring coast and coves.

Highly Commended in Cornwall Tourism Awards
'Pub of the Year"

01736 710202
e-mail: enquiries@godolphinarms.co.uk
www.godolphinarms.co.uk

Please note...

All the information in this book is given in good faith in the belief that it is correct. However, the publishers cannot guarantee the facts given in these pages, neither are they responsible for changes in policy, ownership or terms that may take place after the date of going to press. Readers should always satisfy themselves that the facilities they require are available and that the terms, if quoted, still apply.

TREWERN ARMS HOTEL

Nevern, Newport, Pembrokeshire SA42 0NB
Tel: 01239 820395 • Fax: 01239 820173

Inn

www.trewernarms.com
e-mail: info@trewern-arms-pembrokeshire.co.uk

Set deep in a forested and secluded valley on the banks of the River Nevern, this picturesque, 16th century hostelry has a warmth of welcome that is immediately apparent in the interestingly-shaped Brew House Bar with its original flagstone floors, stone walls, old settles and beams decorated with an accumulated collection of bric-a-brac. Bar meals are served here from a popular grill area. By contrast, the Lounge Bar is furnished on cottage lines and the fine restaurant has received many accolades from far and wide for its culinary delights.

The tranquil village of Nevern is ideally placed for Pembrokeshire's historic sites and uncrowded, sandy beaches and the accommodation offered at this recommended retreat is in the multi-starred class.

The Plough
AT EATON

Macclesfield Road, Eaton,
Near Congleton, Cheshire CW12 2NH
Tel: 01260 280207 • Fax: 01260 298458

Traditional oak beams and blazing log fires in winter reflect the warm and friendly atmosphere of this half-timbered former coaching inn which dates from the 17th century.

The heart of the 'Plough' is the kitchen where food skilfully prepared is calculated to satisfy the most discerning palate. Luncheons and dinners are served seven days a week with traditional roasts on Sundays.

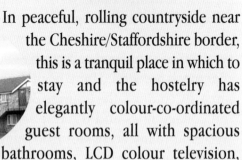

In peaceful, rolling countryside near the Cheshire/Staffordshire border, this is a tranquil place in which to stay and the hostelry has elegantly colour-co-ordinated guest rooms, all with spacious bathrooms, LCD colour television, direct-dial telephone and tea and coffee-making facilities amongst their impressive appointments. Wireless internet access available.

e-mail: theploughinn@hotmail.co.uk
www.theploughinnateaton.co.uk

THE CUMBERLAND INN
ALSTON

Deep in the heart of the North Pennines AONB,
the Cumberland Inn is within easy reach
of the Lake District, Northumberland
and the Yorkshire Dales.
The comfortable en suite rooms have TV,
hairdryer and tea/coffee making.
Bar Meals are prepared from locally sourced
ingredients where possible;
packed lunches also available.
Pets are welcome in bedrooms and in the bar.

Tel: 01434 381875
Townfoot, Alston, Cumbria CA9 3HX
stay@cumberlandinnalston.com • www.cumberlandinnalston.com

The Black Cock Inn

This 16th century Inn with its low beamed ceiling
boasts a suntrap courtyard garden during the
summer and a roaring log fire during the winter
months, giving it a wonderful traditional ambience.
There's always a selection of real ales and lagers
on offer in the bar which is open from morning 'til
night, every day. The inn has five comfortable and
very well appointed en suite guest bedrooms.
An ideal base for exploring this scenic area.

**Black Cock Inn, Princes Street,
Broughton-in-Furness, Cumbria LA20 6HQ
e-mail: theblackcockinn20@gmail.com**

Tel: 01229 716529
www.blackcockinncumbria.com

Visit the FHG website
www.holidayguides.com
for all kinds of holiday
accommodation in Britain

Brampton

Wi-Fi

Welcome to...

The Blacksmith's Arms offers all the hospitality and comforts of a traditional country inn. Enjoy tasty meals served in the bar lounges, or linger over dinner in the well appointed restaurant. The inn is personally managed by the proprietors, Anne and Donald Jackson, who guarantee the hospitality one would expect from a family concern. Guests are assured of a pleasant and comfortable stay. There are eight lovely bedrooms, all en suite.

Peacefully situated in the beautiful village of Talkin, the inn is convenient for the Borders, Hadrian's Wall and the Lake District.

There is a good golf course, walking and other country pursuits nearby.

The Blacksmiths Arms
Talkin Village, Brampton, Cumbria CA8 1LE
Tel: 016977 3452 • Fax: 016977 3396
e-mail: blacksmithsarmstalkin@yahoo.co.uk
www.blacksmithstalkin.co.uk

AA
★★★★
INN

enjoyEngland.com
★★★★
INN

Ulverston

The Stan Laurel Inn

Situated just 30 minutes from M6 (junction 36) is the bustling historic market town of Ulverston with its wonderful cobbled streets and yards. An ideal base to explore the South Lakes area, with Windermere, Kendal, Bowness, Coniston and Morecambe Bay all within easy reach of the town. The coast is only two miles away, and the area offers plenty of nice walks.

The inn is named after Stan Laurel (of Laurel and Hardy fame), who was born and lived in Ulverston before moving to America. Also situated in the town is the world famous Laurel and Hardy museum, well worth a visit while you are here.

We are located close to the town centre and offer six changing cask ales, good quality home-cooked food, and comfortable accommodation. Three bedrooms, two en suite.

Good service, good food, good beer... what more could you ask for!

Stan Laurel Inn, 31 The Ellers, Ulverston LA12 0AB
Tel: 01229 582814 • e-mail: thestanlaurel@aol.com

Further information on menus and pictures can be viewed on our website: www.thestanlaurel.co.uk

The Wild Boar
Inn, Grill & Smokehouse

Nestling in a peaceful setting in the Gilpin Valley, The Wild Boar benefits from beautiful surrounding countryside, including its own private 72 acres of woodland, and many other Lake District attractions close by.

A special venue for many an occasion, whether that be a romantic or adventurous break, family get-together, intimate business meeting or as one of our very valued frequent diners.

After undergoing a refurbishment The Wild Boar now offers individually designed bedrooms, Grill and Smokehouse with an open kitchen and chef's table.

THE WILD BOAR
INN, GRILL & SMOKEHOUSE
NEAR WINDERMERE
CUMBRIA LA23 3NF
RESERVATIONS: 08458 504 604
www.wildboarinn.co.uk

English Lakes Hotels Resorts & Venues

Dog & Partridge
Country Inn

With rooms in the grounds

Short Breaks & Offers available throughout the year

Mary and Martin Stelfox welcome you to this family-run 17th century Inn and Motel set in five acres, five miles from Alton Towers and close to Dovedale and Ashbourne. We specialise in family breaks, and special diets and vegetarians are catered for.

Children and pets welcome.

Accommodation at the Dog and Partridge is purpose-built and situated in the grounds with own parking directly outside.

Most rooms have en suite facilities and all have flat screen TV with Freeview, DVD player, tea/coffee making facilities, clock radio, direct telephone, ample heating and hot water. Family suites available.

Free Wi-Fi internet access. Hot tub and private garden.

Ideal for touring Stoke Potteries, Derbyshire Dales and Staffordshire Moorlands. Open Christmas and New Year. Restaurant open all day, non-residents welcome.

e-mail: info@dogandpartridge.co.uk
Tel: 01335 343183 • www.dogandpartridge.co.uk
Swinscoe, Ashbourne DE6 2HS

Bamford

A haven for walkers, riders, fishermen, canoeists or anyone just looking for an opportunity to enjoy the natural beauty of Dartmoor. We specialise in home-made food using local produce wherever possible. With the emphasis on Devon beers and ciders, you have the opportunity to quench your thirst after the efforts of the day with a drink at the bar or relaxing on the chesterfields in the lounge area, complete with log fire for winter evenings. Muddy paws, boots and hooves welcome.

THE FOREST INN

Hexworthy, Dartmoor
PL20 6SD
Tel: 01364 631211
Fax: 01364 631515
e-mail: info@theforestinn.co.uk
www.theforestinn.co.uk

The Red Lion

has been offering generous hospitality since 1750 when it was a Coaching House. Log fires and gleaming brass in a friendly old bar, hearty English breakfasts, terraced gardens overlooking the River Dart, and an exceptionally warm welcome all await you.

Bedrooms are individually furnished, with comfortable beds, central heating, colour TV, tea-making facilities and telephones. An extensive menu includes daily specials and features fresh produce, prime local meats, fresh fish and locally grown vegetables. Picturesque countryside and a mild climate make this a perfect holiday retreat.

THE RED LION INN
Dittisham, Near Dartmouth,
Devon TQ6 0ES
www.redliondittisham.co.uk
Tel: 01803 722235

Mark and Judy Harrison
welcome you to

THE ROYAL OAK INN
Dunsford, Devon

The Royal Oak is a traditional village pub in the heart of the beautiful Devon village of Dunsford. It's a family-run place with a warm, friendly atmosphere and something for everyone.

Real ales from all over Britain. The kitchen serves generous portions of home-cooked good food with regular well-known specials.

The Royal Oak has a walled courtyard and a large Beer Garden with beautiful views across Dunsford and the Teign Valley

Dogs on leads are welcome and there are lots of animals to visit, great for children with our own play area. Plenty of off-road parking.

Quiet newly refurbished en suite bedrooms are available in the tastefully converted 400 year old granite and cob cob barn located to the rear of the Inn. All non-smoking. Each room has its own front door which opens out onto a pretty, walled courtyard. Ideal base for touring Dartmoor, Exeter and the coast.

The Royal Oak Inn
Dunsford, Near Exeter, Devon EX6 7DA
TEL: 01647 252256 • e-mail:mark@troid.co.uk • www.royaloakd.com

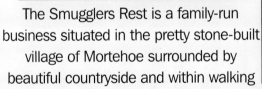

The Smugglers Rest is a family-run business situated in the pretty stone-built village of Mortehoe surrounded by beautiful countryside and within walking distance of the beaches and coves of the North Devon coast.

The luxury accommodation ranges from twin rooms through to the family suites. All rooms are en suite and have tea & coffee making facilities.

Treat yourselves and your pets to beautiful coastal walks and golden beaches, before you sample our delicious home-cooked meals, real ales and warm, year round hospitality.

The Smugglers Rest

**North Morte Road, Mortehoe,
North Devon EX34 7DR
Tel/Fax: 01271 870891
thesmugglersrest@gmail.com
www.thesmugglersrest.co.uk**

Fordingbridge

Three Lions

Stuckton, near Fordingbridge, Hampshire SP6 2HF

Tel: 01425 652489 • Fax: 01425 656144

A place to relax in a beautiful setting and come and go as you please without the formality of a hotel. All bedrooms are en suite, overlooking the gardens and beyond to the forest. Hot tub and Sauna. Ground floor accommodation with ease of access for less mobile guests.

Local attractions include the New Forest, the Dorset and Hampshire coastline with coastal walks and sandy beaches, and the cathedral cities of Salisbury and Winchester.

Family activities nearby include a leisure pool centre, Marwell Zoo, Paulton's Fun Park and Beaulieu Car Museum.

Three times Hampshire 'Restaurant of the Year', Good Food Guide.

www.thethreelionsrestaurant.co.uk

Heskin

The Farmers Arms • Heskin

Situated just two minutes from Jct 27 of the M6, The Farmers Arms is an ideal place to stay in the North West of England, for visiting family and friends, business or indeed just pleasure.

The same welcome awaits you as it did the weary travellers who used the pub and its stables back in the 1700s. In those days the Farmers Arms was aptly named *The Pleasant Retreat* and only found its new title of The Farmers in 1902.

A family-run pub, The Farmers continues to provide the very best of traditional cask ales and good hearty fayre. All rooms have been designed to retain the olde worlde charm of The Farmers Arms, yet still meet the requirements of today's discerning traveller. All are en suite with tea and coffee making facilities and TV.

Sit back, enjoy and take in the warmth of this fine country inn.

★★★ INN

Wood Lane, Heskin, Near Chorley, Lancs PR7 5NP
Tel: 01257 451276 • Fax: 01257 453958
info@farmersarms.co.uk • www.farmersarms.co.uk

Winterton-on-Sea

Happisburgh

This attractive free house on the lonely Norfolk coast at Happisburgh (pronounced 'Hazeborough') was once the

THE *Hill House*
Happisburgh NR12 0PW
Tel & Fax: 01692 650004

favourite haunt of the remarkable Sir Arthur Conan Doyle, creator of Sherlock Holmes. Clues may be found in that the coastline here is renowned for its ghosts and has been a graveyard for ships over the years which have foundered on the formidable Haisborough Sands, some seven miles off-shore. However, conviviality and good fare is provided by a visit to the inn's beamed bar and restaurant.

Excellent accommodation is available in spacious rooms and there is a large garden in which a double en suite room has been created in a converted signal box overlooking the sea. Different!

Hexham

THE BayHorse INN
NORTHUMBERLAND

West Woodburn, Hexham NE48 2RX

A delightful 18thC coaching inn, nestling by a stone bridge over the River Rede. On the A68, 6 miles from Otterburn, 20 miles from Corbridge, 24 miles from Newcastle Airport; ideally placed for Hadrian's Wall, Kielder Water, Alnwick and the Scottish Borders. • Excellent home-cooked cuisine • Lounge bar. 7 bedrooms, all en suite, all individually decorated in a delightful cottage style, with colour TV, tea and coffee making facilities, hairdryer, ironing facilities and trouser press.

Tel: 01434 270218
enquiry@bayhorseinn.org
www.bayhorseinn.org

Seahouses

Wi-Fi

Main Street, Seahouses, Northumberland NE68 7RD
Tel: 01665 720200 • Fax: 01665 721383

A former farmhouse dating from 1745, the inn stands overlooking the harbour in the village of Seahouses.

The Olde Ship, first licensed in 1812, has been in the same family for over 100 years and is now a fully residential Inn.

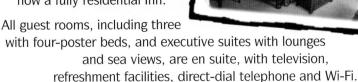

All guest rooms, including three with four-poster beds, and executive suites with lounges and sea views, are en suite, with television, refreshment facilities, direct-dial telephone and Wi-Fi.

The bars and corridors bulge at the seams with nautical memorabilia. Good home cooking features locally caught seafood, along with soups, puddings and casseroles.

www.seahouses.co.uk
e-mail: theoldeship@seahouses.co.uk

Longframlington, Wooler

The Anglers Arms
A Legend in the very Heart of Northumberland

This traditional Coaching Inn is situated only 6 miles from Morpeth, beside picturesque Weldon Bridge on the River Coquet. Bedrooms are cosy and welcoming, with a touch of olde worlde charm. Be prepared for a hearty Northumbrian breakfast! Meals can be be enjoyed in the friendly bar, or outdoors on sunny summer days; alternatively dine in style and sophistication in the à la carte Pullman Railway Carriage restaurant. Ideal for exploring both coast and country, the Inn also caters for fishermen, with its own one-mile stretch of the River Coquet available free to residents.

The Anglers Arms, Weldon Bridge, Longframlington, Northumberland NE65 8AX

Tel: 01665 570271/570655 • Fax: 01665 570041
email: info@anglersarms.com • www.anglersarms.com

The Black Bull Hotel
2 High Street, Wooler NE71 6BY
Tel & Fax: 01668 281309
e-mail: theblackbullhotel@hotmail.com
www.theblackbullhotel.co.uk

17thC coaching inn situated on the main street of Wooler, a wonderful base for walking, riding, golf and fishing.

The hotel is fully licensed and serves good home-made food each lunchtime and evening (not Sunday evenings).

All rooms en suite, with hairdryers, tea/coffee making facilities and Freeview TV. Wifi available. Gym for use of guests.

Hindon

The Lamb Inn
High Street, Hindon
Wiltshire SP3 6DP
Tel: 01747 820573 • Fax: 01747 820605
www.lambathindon.co.uk

The fascinating history of this ancient inn is related in its brochure, which reveals among other intriguing facts that it was once the headquarters of a notorious smuggler. No such unlawful goings-on today – just good old-fashioned hospitality in the finest traditions of English inn-keeping. Charmingly furnished single, double and four-poster bedrooms provide overnight guests with cosy country-style accommodation, and the needs of the inner man (or woman!) will be amply satisfied by the varied, good quality meals served in the bar and restaurant. Real ales can be enjoyed in the friendly bar, where crackling log fires bestow charm and atmosphere as well as warmth.

Clapham

New Inn
Clapham – 'As relaxed as you like'

Quality Accommodation in the Yorkshire Dales.

A comfortable hotel in the Yorkshire Dales National Park, The New Inn has a fine blend of old and new to retain the characteristics of this fine 18th Century Coaching Inn.

This traditional Village Inn has 19 en suite bedrooms, including ground floor and disabled bedrooms. Residents' lounge, Restaurant, two comfortable bars serving a selection of local ales, fine wines and a large selection of malt whiskies. Our food offers a mix of traditional and modern cooking.

New Inn, Clapham, Near Ingleton, North Yorkshire LA2 8HH
e-mail: info@newinn-clapham.co.uk
www.newinn-clapham.co.uk
Tel: 015242 51203
Fax: 015242 51824

Wi-Fi

Wi-Fi

Llanymynech

Llanymynech, Powys SY22 6EJ

Set in the historic village of Llanymynech, this former coaching inn has been renovated and upgraded to a very high standard. There are 5 superb bedrooms, all en suite, with tea/coffee making facilities and colour TV.

High quality home-cooked cuisine using local produce is served in the conservatory or more formal restaurant.

Situated in an area of outstanding natural beauty on the English/Welsh border, the hotel is an ideal base for walking on the nearby Offa's Dyke Trail and for exploring this historic area.

Tel: 01691 830582 • Fax: 01691 839009
e-mail: catelou@tesco.net • www.bradfordarmshotel.com

Ardfern

The Galley of Lorne Inn

Ardfern, Argyll ☎ 01852 500 284

THE GALLEY OF LORNE

Located 30 mins drive from Oban
on the lochside at Ardfern

Follow us online:

Restaurant ★ Accommodation ★ Beer Garden
Sundeck ★ Public & Lounge Bar ★ Free WiFi

Great Food

Treat Yourself to some home comfort
Award-winning 17th Century Inn with 6 en-suite rooms
Loch View Restaurant serving delicious locally sourced food
Cosy bars & lounges and friendly service

Great Rooms

www.galleyoflorne.co.uk

Ullapool

Sleat

ARDVASAR
HOTEL
ISLE OF SKYE
Where tranquility and pleasure meet ...

Since the 1700s this solid white-washed hotel has gazed over the Sound of Sleat to the Knoydart Mountains and the beautiful Sands of Morar, and as well as being one of the oldest coaching inns on the west coast, it is surely one of the most idyllically situated. Less than 5 minutes' drive from the ferry terminal ar Armadale, it is ideally placed for exploring this most beautiful island.

Not surprisingly, seafood features extensively on the menu here, together with local venison and other fine Scottish produce, and tasty bar lunches and suppers are offered as an alternative to the more formal cuisine served in the restaurant.

We offer a high standard of accommodation in ten comfortable bedrooms, all individually designed and recently renovated to a very high standard with new contemporary bathrooms. Amenities include tea & coffee making facilities, direct-dial telephone, colour television, and hair dryer.

The sea view rooms offer stunning views across the Sound of Sleat. For early risers the sun rising above the Knoydart mountains can be spectacular and inspiring. The garden view rooms are also popular and provide very peaceful surroundings. In addition there is a spacious Four-Poster room which is ideal for a romantic break.

Ardvasar, Sleat, Isle of Skye IV45 8RS

Tel: 01471 844223 • Fax: 01471 844495 • www.ardvasarhotel.com

e-mail: richard@ardvasar-hotel.demon.co.uk

Accommodation Standards: Star Grading Scheme

The AA, VisitBritain, VisitScotland, and the VisitWales now use a single method of assessing and rating serviced accommodation. Irrespective of which organisation inspects an establishment the rating awarded will be the same, using a common set of standards, giving a clear guide of what to expect. They have full details of the grading system on their websites.

www.enjoyEngland.com

 www.visitScotland.com

 www.visitWales.com

www.theaa.com

Using a scale of 1-5 stars the objective quality ratings give a clear indication of accommodation standard, cleanliness, ambience, hospitality, service and food.

This shows the full range of standards suitable for every budget and preference, and allows visitors to distinguish between the quality of accommodation and facilities on offer in different establishments. All types of board and self-catering accommodation are covered, including hotels, B&Bs, holiday parks, campus accommodation, hostels, caravans and camping, and boats.

Gold and Silver awards are given to Hotels and Guest Accommodation that provide exceptional quality, especially in service and hospitality.

The more stars, the higher level of quality

★
acceptable quality; simple, practical, no frills

★★
good quality, well presented and well run

★★★
very good level of quality and comfort

★★★★
excellent standard throughout

★★★★★
exceptional quality, with a degree of luxury

National Accessible Scheme Logos for mobility impaired and older people

If you have particular mobility impairment. look out for the National Accessible Scheme. You can be confident of finding accommodation or attractions that meet your needs by looking for the following symbols.

Older and less mobile guests
If you have sufficient mobility to climb a flight of steps but would benefit from fixtures and fittings to aid balance.

Part-time wheelchair users
You have restricted walking ability or may need to use a wheelchair some of the time and can negotiate a maximum of 3 steps.

Independent wheelchair users
You are a wheelchair user and travel independently. Similar to the international logo for independent wheelchair users.

Assisted wheelchair users
You're a wheelchair user and travel with a friend or family member who helps you with everyday tasks.

DIRECTORY OF WEBSITE AND E-MAIL ADDRESSES

A quick-reference guide to holiday accommodation with an e-mail address and/or website, conveniently arranged by country and county, with full contact details.

•LONDON

Hotel
Athena Hotel, 110-114 Sussex Gardens, Hyde Park, LONDON W2 1UA
Tel: 020 7706 3866
• e-mail: stay@athenahotellondon.co.uk
• website: www.athenahotel.co.uk

•BERKSHIRE

Touring Campsite
Wellington Country Park, Odiham Road, Riseley, Near READING, Berkshire RG7 1SP
Tel : 0118 932 6444
• e-mail:
info@wellington-country-park.co.uk
• website:
www.wellington-country-park.co.uk

•CHESHIRE

Farmhouse B & B
Astle Farm East, Chelford, MACCLESFIELD, Cheshire SK10 4TA
Tel: 01625 861270
• e-mail: stubg@aol.com
• website: www.astlefarmeast.co.uk

•CORNWALL

Self-Catering
Penrose Burden Holiday Cottages, St Breward, BODMIN, Cornwall PL30 4LZ
Tel : 01208 850277
• website: www.penroseburden.co.uk

Self-Catering / Caravan
Mrs A. E. Moore, Hollyvagg Farm, Lewannick, LAUNCESTON, Cornwall PL15 7QH
Tel: 01566 782309
• website: www.hollyvaggfarm.co.uk

Self- Catering
Mr Lowman, Cutkive Wood Holiday Lodges, St Ive, LISKEARD, Cornwall PL14 3ND
Tel: 01579 362216
• e-mail: holidays@cutkivewood.co.uk
• website: www.cutkivewood.co.uk

Self-Catering
Butterdon Mill Holiday Homes, Merrymeet, LISKEARD, Cornwall PL14 3LS
Tel: 01579 342636
• e-mail: butterdonmill@btconnect.com
• website: www.bmhh.co.uk

Caravan / Camping
Quarryfield Caravan & Camping Park, Crantock, NEWQUAY, Cornwall
Contact: Mrs A Winn, Tretherras, Newquay, Cornwall TR7 2RE
Tel: 01637 872792
• e-mails:
quarryfield@crantockcaravans.orangehome.co.uk
info@quarryfield.co.uk
• website: www.quarryfield.co.uk

B&B
Bolankan Cottage B & B, Crows-an-Wra, St Buryan, PENZANCE, Cornwall TR19 6HU
Tel: 01736 810168
• e-mail: bolankancottage@talktalk.net
• website: www.bolankan-cottage.co.uk

Caravan / Camping
Globe Vale Holiday Park, Radnor, REDRUTH, Cornwall TR16 4BH
Tel: 01209 891183
• e-mail: info@globevale.co.uk
• website: www.globevale.co.uk

Guest House
Mr S Hope, Dalswinton House, ST MAWGAN-IN-PYDAR, Cornwall TR8 4EZ
Tel: 01637 860385
• e-mail: dalswintonhouse@btconnect.com
• website: www.dalswinton.com

Self-Catering
Maymear Cottage, ST TUDY
Contact: Ruth Reeves, Polstraul, Trewalder,
Delabole, Cornwall PL33 9ET
Tel: 01840 213120
• e-mail: ruth.reeves@hotmail.co.uk
• website: www.maymear.co.uk

Self-Catering
The Garden House, Port Isaac, Near
WADEBRIDGE, Cornwall
Contact: Mr D Oldham, Trevella,
Treveighan, St Teath, Cornwall PL30 3JN
Tel: 01208 850529
• e-mail: david.trevella@btconnect.com
• website: www.trevellacornwall.co.uk

•CUMBRIA

Caravan Park
Greenhowe Caravan Park, Great Langdale,
AMBLESIDE, Cumbria LA22 9JU
Tel: 015394 37231
•e-mail: enquiries@greenhowe.com
•website: www.greenhowe.com

B&B
Smallwood House, Compston Road,
AMBLESIDE, Cumbria LA22 9DH
Tel: 015394 32330
• website: www.smallwoodhotel.co.uk

Self-Catering
Mrs Almond, Irton House Farm, Isel, Near
KESWICK, Cumbria CA13 9ST
Tel: 017687 76380
• e-mail: joan@irtonhousefarm.co.uk
• website: www.irtonhousefarm.com

Self-Catering
Mr D Williamson, Derwent Water Marina,
Portinscale, KESWICK, Cumbria CA12 5RF
Tel: 017687 72912
• e-mail: info@derwentwatermarina.co.uk
• website: www.derwentwatermarina.co.uk

Self-Catering
Mrs S.J. Bottom, Crossfield Cottages,
KIRKOSWALD, Penrith, Cumbria CA10 1EU
Tel: 01768 898711
• e-mail: info@crossfieldcottages.co.uk
• website: www.crossfieldcottages.co.uk

•DERBYSHIRE

Self-Catering Holiday Cottages
Mark Redfern, Paddock House Farm Holiday
Cottages, Peak District National Park,
Alstonefield, ASHBOURNE, Derbyshire
DE6 2FT
Tel: 01335 310282 / 07977 569618
• e-mail: info@paddockhousefarm.co.uk
• website: www.paddockhousefarm.co.uk

Caravan
Golden Valley Caravan Park, Coach Road,
RIPLEY, Derbyshire DE55 4ES
Tel: 01773 513881
• e-mail:
enquiries@goldenvalleycaravanpark.co.uk
• website: www.goldenvalleycaravanpark.co.uk

•DEVON

Self-Catering
Mrs A. Bell, Wooder Manor, Widercombe-in-
the-Moor, Near ASHBURTON, Devon
TQ13 7TR
Tel: 01364 621391
• website: www.woodermanor.com

Hotel
Fairwater Head Hotel, Hawkchurch, Near
AXMINSTER, Devon EX13 5TX
Tel: 01297 678349
• e-mail: stay@fairwaterheadhotel.co.uk
• website: www.fairwaterheadhotel.co.uk

Self-Catering / B&B
Lake House Cottages and B&B, Lake
Villa, BRADWORTHY, Devon EX22 7SQ
Tel : 01409 241962
• email: lesley@lakevilla.co.uk
• website: www.lakevilla.co.uk

Self-Catering
Linda & Jim Watt, Northcote Manor
Farm Holiday Cottages, Kentisbury,
COMBE MARTIN, Devon EX31 4NB
Tel: 01271 882376
• e-mail: info@northcotemanorfarm.co.uk
• website: www.northcotemanorfarm.co.uk

Self-Catering
G Davidson Richmond, Clooneavin,
Clooneavin Path, LYNMOUTH, Devon
EX35 6EE
Tel: 01598 753334
• e-mail: relax@clooneavinholidays.co.uk
• website: www.clooneavinholidays.co.uk

Guest House

Mr. & Mrs D. Fitzgerald, Beaumont, Castle Hill, SEATON, Devon EX12 2QW
Tel: 01297 20832
• e-mail: **beaumont.seaton@talktalk.net**
• **website:**
www.smoothhound.co.uk/hotels/beaumon1.html

Caravans / Camping

Salcombe Regis Camping & Caravan Park, SIDMOUTH, Devon EX10 0JH
Tel: 01395 514303
• e-mail: **contact@salcombe-regis.co.uk**
• website: **www.salcombe-regis.co.uk**

Self-Catering / Camping

Dartmoor Country Holidays, Magpie Leisure Park, Bedford Bridge, Horrabridge, Yelverton, TAVISTOCK, Devon PL20 7RY
Tel: 01822 852651
• website: **www.dartmoorcountryholidays.co.uk**

Caravan & Camping

North Morte Farm Caravan & Camping Park, Mortehoe, WOOLACOMBE, Devon EX34 7EG
Tel: 01271 870381
• e-mail: **info@northmortefarm.co.uk**
• website: **www.northmortefarm.co.uk**

•DORSET

Self-Catering

C. Hammond, Stourcliffe Court, 56 Stourcliffe Avenue, Southbourne, BOURNEMOUTH, Dorset BH6 3PX
Tel: 01202 420698
• e-mail: **rjhammond1@hotmail.co.uk**
• website: **www.stourcliffecourt.co.uk**

Self-Catering Cottage / Farmhouse B & B

Mrs S. E. Norman, Frogmore Farm, Chideock, BRIDPORT, Dorset DT6 6HT
Tel: 01308 456159
• e-mail: **bookings@frogmorefarm.com**
• website: **www.frogmorefarm.com**

B&B

Nethercroft, Winterbourne Abbas, DORCHESTER, Dorset DT2 9LU
Tel: 01305 889337
• e-mail: **val.bradbeer@btconnect.com**
• website: **www.nethercroft.com**

Farmhouse B&B / Caravan & Camping

Luckford Wood Farmhouse, Church Street, East Stoke, Wareham, Near LULWORTH, Dorset BH20 6AW
Tel: 01929 463098 / 07888 719002
• e-mail: **luckfordleisure@hotmail.co.uk**
• website: **www.luckfordleisure.co.uk**

Self-Catering

Westover Farm Cottages, Wootton Fitzpaine, Near LYME REGIS, Dorset DT6 6NE
Tel: 01297 560451/07979 265064
• e-mail: **wfcottages@aol.com**
• website: **www.westoverfarmcottages.co.uk**

Hotel

The Knoll House, STUDLAND BAY, Dorset BH19 3AH
Tel: 01929 450450
• e-mail: **info@knollhouse.co.uk**
• website: **www.knollhouse.co.uk**

Inn B&B

The White Swan, The Square, 31 High Street, SWANAGE BN19 2LJ
Tel: 01929 423804
• e-mail: **info@whiteswanswanage.co.uk**
• website: **www.whiteswanswanage.co.uk**

•GLOUCESTERSHIRE

Self-Catering

Two Springbank, 37 Hopton Road, Cam, DURSLEY, Gloucs GL11 5PD
Contact: Mrs F A Jones, 32 Everlands, Cam, Dursley, Gloucs G11 5NL
Tel: 01453 543047
• e-mail: **info@twospringbank.co.uk**
• website: **www.twospringbank.co.uk**

B & B

Mrs A Rhoton, Hyde Crest, Cirencester Road, Minchinhampton, STROUD, Gloucs GL6 8PE
Tel: 01453 731631
• e-mail: **stay@hydecrest.co.uk**
• website: **www.hydecrest.co.uk**

•HAMPSHIRE

Holiday Park

Downton Holiday Park, Shorefield Road, Milford-on-Sea, LYMINGTON, Hampshire SO41 0LH
Tel: 01425 476131 / 01590 642515
• e-mail: **info@downtonholidaypark.co.uk**
• website: **www.downtonholidaypark.co.uk**

•LANCASHIRE

Guest House

Parr Hall Farm, Parr Lane, Eccleston, Chorley, PRESTON, Lancs PR7 5SL
Tel: 01257 451917
• e-mail: **enquiries@parrhallfarm.com**
• website: **www.parrhallfarm.com**

•NORFOLK

Self-catering
Scarning Dale, Dale Road, Scarning,
DEREHAM, Norfolk NR19 2QN
Tel: 01362 687269
• e-mail: jean@scarningdale.co.uk
• website: www.scarningdale.co.uk

Holiday Park
Waveney Valley Holiday Park, Airstation
Lane, Rushall, DISS, Norfolk IP21 4QF
Tel: 01379 741228
• e-mail: waveneyvalleyhp@aol.com
• website: www.caravanparksnorfolk.co.uk

Self-Catering
Blue Riband Holidays, HEMSBY,
Great Yarmouth, Norfolk NR29 4HA
Tel: 01493 730445
• websites: www.blueribandrolidays.co.uk
    www.parklandshemsby.co.uk

Self-Catering
Winterton Valley Holidays, Edward Road,
WINTERTON-ON-SEA, Norfolk NR29 4BX
Contact:15 Kingston Avenue, Caister-on-
Sea, Norfolk NR30 5ET
Tel: 01493 377175
• e-mail: info@wintertonvalleyholidays.co.uk
• website: www.wintertonvalleyholidays.co.uk

•NOTTINGHAMSHIRE

Caravan & Camping Park
Orchard Park, Marnham Road, Tuxford,
NEWARK, Nottinghamshire NG22 0PY
Tel: 01777 870228
• e-mail: info@orchardcaravanpark.co.uk
• website: www.orchardcaravanpark.co.uk

•OXFORDSHIRE

B&B
Middle Fell, Moreton Road, Aston Upthorpe,
DIDCOT, Oxfordshire OX11 9ER
Tel: 01235 850207
• e-mail: middlefell@ic24.net
• website: www.middlefell.co.uk

B & B / Guest House
June Collier, Colliers B&B, 55 Nethercote
Road, Tackley, KIDLINGTON, Oxfordshire
OX5 3AT
Tel: 01869 331255 / 07790 338225
• e-mail: junecollier@btinternet.com
• website: www.colliersbnb.co.uk

•SHROPSHIRE

Self-Catering
Clive & Cynthia Prior, Mocktree Barns
Holiday Cottages, Leintwardine, LUDLOW,
Shropshire SY7 0LY
Tel: 01547 540441
• e-mail: mocktreebarns@care4free.net
• website: www.mocktreeholidays.co.uk

Self-Catering
Jane Cronin, Sutton Court Farm Cottages,
Sutton Court Farm, Little Sutton, LUDLOW,
Shropshire SY8 2AJ
Tel: 01584 861305
• e-mail: enquiries@suttoncourtfarm.co.uk
• website: www.suttoncourtfarm.co.uk

•SOMERSET

Farm / Guest House / Self-Catering
Jackie Bishop, Toghill House Farm, Freezing
Hill, Wick, Near BATH, Somerset BS30 5RT
Tel: 01225 891261
• e-mail:
accommodation@toghillhousefarm.co.uk
• website: www.toghillhousefarm.co.uk

Self-Catering
Westward Rise Holiday Park, South Road,
BREAN, Burnham-on-Sea, Somerset TA8 2RD
Tel: 01278 751310
• e-mail: info@westwardrise.com
• website: www.westwardrise.com

Self-Catering / Holiday Park / Touring Pitches
James Randle, St Audries Bay Holiday Club,
West Quantoxhead, MINEHEAD, Somerset
TA4 4DY
Tel: 01984 632515
• e-mail: info@staudriesbay.co.uk
• website: www.staudriesbay.co.uk

Farm / Guest House
G. Clark, Yew Tree Farm, THEALE,
Near Wedmore, Somerset BS28 4SN
Tel: 01934 712475
• e-mail: enquiries@yewtreefarmbandb.co.uk
• website: www.yewtreefarmbandb.co.uk

•SUFFOLK

Self-Catering
Kessingland Cottages, Rider Haggard Lane,
KESSINGLAND, Suffolk.
Contact: S. Mahmood, 156 Bromley Road,
Beckenham, Kent BR3 6PG
Tel: 020 8650 0539
• e-mail: jeeptrek@kjti.co.uk
• website: www.k-cottage.co.uk

Holiday Park
Broadland Holiday Village, Oulton
Broad, LOWESTOFT, Suffolk NR33 9JY
Tel: 01502 573033
• e-mail: **info@broadlandvillage.co.uk**
• website: **www.broadlandvillage.co.uk**

•EAST SUSSEX

Hotel
Grand Hotel, 1 Grand Parade, St Leonards,
HASTINGS, East Sussex TN37 6AQ
Tel: 01424 428510
• e-mail: **info@grandhotelhastings.co.uk**
• website: **www.grandhotelhastings.co.uk**

Self-Catering
"Pekes", CHIDDINGLY, East Sussex
Contact: Eva Morris, 124 Elm Park
Mansions, Park Walk, London SW10 0AR
Tel: 020 7352 8088
• e-mail: **pekes.afa@virgin.net**
• website: **www.pekesmanor.com**

Guest House / Self-Catering
Longleys Farm Cottage, Harebeating Lane,
HAILSHAM, East Sussex BN27 1ER
Tel: 01323 841227
• website: **www.longleysfarmcottage.co.uk**

• WEST SUSSEX

Guest Accommodation
St Andrews Lodge, Chichester Road,
SELSEY, West Sussex PO20 0LX
Tel: 01243 606899
• e-mail: **info@standrewslodge.co.uk**
• website: **www.standrewslodge.co.uk**

•WARWICKSHIRE

Guest House
John & Julia Downie, Holly Tree
Cottage, Pathlow, STRATFORD-UPON-
AVON, Warwickshire CV37 0ES
Tel: 01789 204461
• e-mail: **john@hollytree-cottage.co.uk**
• website: **www.hollytree-cottage.co.uk**

•NORTH YORKSHIRE

Self-Catering
Rudding Holiday Park, Follifoot,
HARROGATE, North Yorkshire HG3 1JH
Tel: 01423 870439
• e-mail: **stay@ruddingpark.com**
• website: **www.ruddingholidaypark.co.uk**

Self-Catering
Southfield Farm Holiday Cottages,
Darley, HARROGATE, North Yorkshire
HG3 2PR
Tel: 01423 780258
• e-mail: **info@southfieldcottages.co.uk**
• website: **www.southfieldcottages.co.uk**

Farmhouse B & B
Mrs Julie Clarke, Middle Farm, Woodale,
Coverdale, LEYBURN, North Yorkshire
DL8 4TY
Tel: 01969 640271
• e-mail: **j-a-clarke@hotmail.com**
• **www.yorkshirenet.co.uk/stayat/middlefarm/
index.htm**

Self-Catering
2 Hollies Cottages, Stainforth, SETTLE,
N.Yorkshire
Contact : Bridge Cottage, Stainforth,
Near Settle BD24 9PG
Tel: 01729 822649
• e-mail: **vivmills30@hotmail.com**
• website: **www.stainforth-holiday-cottage-
settle.co.uk**

Self-Catering
York Lakeside Lodges Ltd, Moor Lane,
YORK, North Yorkshire YO24 2QU
Tel: 01904 702346
• e-mail: **neil@yorklakesidelodges.co.uk**
• website: **www.yorklakesidelodges.co.uk**

WALES

•ANGLESEY & GWYNEDD

Self-Catering Chalet
Chalet at Glan Gwna Holiday Park, Caethro,
CAERNARFON, Gwynedd
Contact: Mr H A Jones, 12 Lon Isaf, Menai
Bridge, Anglesey LL59 5LN
Tel: 01248 712045
• e-mail: hajones@northwales-chalet.co.uk
• website: www.northwales-chalet.co.uk

Self-Catering
Parc Wernol, Chwilog Fawr, Chwilog,
PWLLHELI, Criccieth, Gwynedd LL53 6SW
Tel: 01766 810506
• e-mail: catherine@wernol.co.uk
• website: www.wernol.co.uk

• PEMBROKESHIRE

Self-Catering
Llanteglos Estate, Llanteg, Near
AMROTH, Pembs SA67 8PU
• e-mail: llanteglosestate@supanet.com
• website: www.llanteglos-estate.com

Self-Catering
Timberhill Farm, BROAD HAVEN,
Pembrokeshire SA62 3LZ
Contact: Mrs L Ashton, 10 St Leonards
Road, Thames Ditton, Surrey KT7 0RJ
Tel: 02083 986349
• e-mail: lejash@aol.com
• website: www.33timberhill.co

Self-Catering
Quality Cottages, Cerbid, Solva,
HAVERFORDWEST, Pembrokeshire SA62 6YE
Tel: 01348 837871
• e-mail: reserve@qualitycottages.co.uk
• website: www.qualitycottages.co.uk

Self-Catering
Ffynnon Ddofn, Llanon, Llanrhian, Near ST
DAVIDS, Pembrokeshire.
Contact: Mrs B. Rees White, Brick House
Farm, Burnham Road, Woodham Mortimer,
Maldon, Essex CM9 6SR. Tel: 01245 224611
• e-mail: daisypops@madasafish.com
• website: www.ffynnonddofn.co.uk

•POWYS

Self-Catering
Lane Farm, Paincastle, BUILTH WELLS,
Powys LD2 3JS
Tel: 01497 851 605
• e-mail: lanefarm@onetel.com
• website: www.lane-farm.co.uk

SCOTLAND

•ARGYLL & BUTE

Self-Catering
Appin House Lodges, APPIN, Argyll
PA38 4BN
Tel: 01631 730207
• e-mail: denys@appinhouse.co.uk
• website: www.appinhouse.co.uk

Self-Catering
Blarghour Farm Cottages, Blarghour Farm,
By Dalmally, INVERARAY, Argyll PA33 1BW
Tel: 01866 833246
• e-mail: blarghour@btconnect.com
• website: www.self-catering-argyll.co.uk

Hotel
Falls of Lora Hotel, Connel Ferry, By OBAN,
Argyll PA37 1PB
Tel: 01631 710483
• e-mail: enquiries@fallsoflora.com
• website: www.fallsoflora.com

•DUMFRIES & GALLOWAY

Hotel
Corsewall Lighthouse Hotel, Kirkcolm,
STRANRAER, Dumfries & Galloway
DG9 0QG Tel: 01776 853220
• e-mail info@lighthousehotel.co.uk
• website: www.lighthousehotel.co.uk

•EDINBURGH & LOTHIANS

Self-Catering
Mrs C. M. Kilpatrick, Slipperfield House,
WEST LINTON, Peeblesshire EH46 7AA
Tel: 01968 660401
• e-mail: cottages@slipperfield.com
• website: www.slipperfield.com

•HIGHLANDS

Self-Catering
Frank & Juliet Spencer-Nairn, Culligran
Cottages, Struy, Near BEAULY, Inverness-
shire IV4 7JX . Tel: 01463 761285
• e-mail: info@culligrancottages.co.uk
• website: www.culligrancottages.co.uk

FHG Guides

Caravan Park
A.J.Davis, Gruinard Bay Caravan Park,
LAIDE, Ross-shire IV22 2ND
Tel: 01445 731225
• e-mail: gruinard@ecosse.net
• website: www.gruinardbay.co.uk

•PERTH & KINROSS

Self-Catering
Atholl Cottage, Killiecrankie, PITLOCHRY,
Perthshire PH16 5LR
Contact: Mrs Joan Troup, Dalnasgadh,
Killiecrankie, Pitlochry, Perthshire PH16 5LN
Tel: 01796 470017
• e-mail: info@athollcottage.co.uk
• website: www.athollcottage.co.uk

•ORKNEY

Caravan & Camping
Point of Ness, STROMNESS, Orkney
Tel: 01856 873535
• e-mail: leisureculture@orkney.gov.uk
• websites: www.orkney.gov.uk
    www.hostelsorkney.co.uk

NORTHERN IRELAND

Caravan Park
Six Mile Water Carvan Park, Lough
Road, ANTRIM BT41 4DG
Tel: 028 9446 4963
• e-mail: sixmilewater@antrim.gov.uk
• website: www.antrim.gov.uk/caravanpark

INTERNET & Wi-Fi Access

Wi Fi™
ZONE

•OXFORDSHIRE

DIDCOT • *B&B*

Middle Fell B&B, Moreton Road, Aston Upthorpe, Didcot OX11 9ER
Tel: 01235 850207 or 07833 920678
e-mail: middlefell@ic24.net
website: www.middlefell.co.uk
Wi-Fi connection in every room free of charge.

FHG
·K·U·P·E·R·A·R·D·
READERS' OFFER 2013

BEKONSCOT MODEL VILLAGE & RAILWAY
Warwick Road, Beaconsfield,
Buckinghamshire HP9 2PL
Tel: 01494 672919
e-mail: info@bekonscot.co.uk
www.bekonscot.co.uk

*One child FREE when accompanied by two
full-paying adults. Valid February to October 2013*

NOT TO BE USED IN CONJUNCTION WITH ANY OTHER OFFER

FHG

·K·U·P·E·R·A·R·D·
READERS' OFFER 2013

NENE VALLEY RAILWAY
Wansford Station, Stibbington,
Peterborough, Cambs PE8 6LR
Tel: 01780 784444
e-mail: nvrorg@nvr.org.uk
www.nvr.org.uk

One child FREE with each full paying adult.
Valid Jan. to end Oct. 2013 (excludes galas and pre-ticketed events)

NOT TO BE USED IN CONJUNCTION WITH ANY OTHER OFFER

FHG

·K·U·P·E·R·A·R·D·
READERS' OFFER 2013

TAMAR VALLEY DONKEY PARK
St Ann's Chapel, Gunnislake,
Cornwall PL18 9HW
Tel: 01822 834072
e-mail: info@donkeypark.com
www.donkeypark.com

*£1 OFF per person, up to 6 persons
Valid from Easter until end October 2013*

NOT TO BE USED IN CONJUNCTION WITH ANY OTHER OFFER

FHG

·K·U·P·E·R·A·R·D·
READERS' OFFER 2013

LAPPA VALLEY RAILWAY
Benny Halt, St Newlyn East,
Newquay, Cornwall TR8 5LX
Tel: 0844 4535543
e-mail: info@lappavalley.co.uk
www.lappavalley.co.uk

*£1 per person OFF up to a maximum of £4. Valid Easter
to end October 2013 (not on Family Saver tickets)*

NOT TO BE USED IN CONJUNCTION WITH ANY OTHER OFFER

Be a giant in a magical miniature world of make-believe depicting rural England in the 1930s. "A little piece of history that is forever England."

Open: 10am-5pm daily mid February to end October.

Directions: Junction 16 M25, Junction 2 M40.

Take a trip back in time on the delightful Nene Valley Railway with its heritage steam and diesel locomotives, There is a 7½ mile ride from Wansford to Peterborough via Yarwell, with shop, museum and excellent cafe at Wansford Station (free parking).

Open: please phone or see website for details.

Directions: situated 4 miles north of Peterborough on the A1

Cornwall's only Donkey Sanctuary set in 14 acres overlooking the beautiful Tamar Valley. Donkey grooming, goat hill, children's playgrounds, cafe and picnic area. All-weather play barn. Well behaved dogs on leads welcome.

Open: Easter to end Oct: daily 10am to 5pm. Nov to March: weekends and all school holidays 10.30am to 4.30pm

Directions: just off A390 between Callington and Gunnislake at St Ann's Chapel.

Three miniature railways, plus leisure park with canoes, crazy golf, large children's play area with fort, brickpath maze, wooded walks (all inclusive). Dogs welcome (50p).

Open: Easter to end October

Directions: follow brown tourist signs from A30 and A3075

**READERS'
OFFER
2013**

THE BEACON
West Strand, Whitehaven,
Cumbria CA28 7LY
Tel: 01946 592302 • Fax: 01946 598150
e-mail: thebeacon@copelandbc.gov.uk
www.thebeacon-whitehaven.co.uk

*One FREE adult/concesssion when accompanied by one full paying
adult/concession. Under 16s free. Valid from Oct 2012 to end 2013.
Not valid for special events. Day tickets only.*

NOT TO BE USED IN CONJUNCTION WITH ANY OTHER OFFER

**READERS'
OFFER
2013**

DEVONSHIRE COLLECTION OF PERIOD COSTUME
Totnes Fashion & Textiles Museum,
Bogan House, 43 High Street,
Totnes, Devon TQ9 5NP
Tel: 01803 862857 • www.devonmuseums.net

*FREE child with a paying adult with voucher
Valid from Spring Bank Holiday to end of Sept 2013*

NOT TO BE USED IN CONJUNCTION WITH ANY OTHER OFFER

**READERS'
OFFER
2013**

WOODLANDS FAMILY THEME PARK
Blackawton, Dartmouth,
Devon TQ9 7DQ
Tel: 01803 712598 • Fax: 01803 712680
e-mail: fun@woodlandspark.com
www.woodlandspark.com

*15% discount off full individual admission price.
No photocopies. Valid 30 March to 1st November 2013.*

NOT TO BE USED IN CONJUNCTION WITH ANY OTHER OFFER

**READERS'
OFFER
2013**

THE MILKY WAY ADVENTURE PARK
The Milky Way, Clovelly,
Bideford, Devon EX39 5RY
Tel: 01237 431255
e-mail: info@themilkyway.co.uk
www.themilkyway.co.uk

*10% discount on entrance charge.
Valid Easter to end October (not August).*

NOT TO BE USED IN CONJUNCTION WITH ANY OTHER OFFER

The Beacon is the Copeland area's interactive museum, tracing the area's rich history, from as far back as prehistoric times to the modern day. Enjoy panoramic views of the Georgian town and harbour from the 4th floor viewing gallery. Art gallery, gift shop, restaurant. Fully accessible.

Open: open all year (excl. 24-26 Dec) Tues-Sun, plus Monday Bank Holidays. Please contact before visit to check.

Directions: enter Whitehaven from north or south on A595. Follow the town centre and brown museum signs; located on harbourside.

Themed exhibition, changed annually, based in a Tudor house. Collection contains items of dress for women, men and children from 17th century to 1990s, from high fashion to everyday wear.

Open: Open from 22 May to end September. 11am to 5pm Tuesday to Friday.

Directions: centre of town, opposite Market Square. Mini bus up High Street stops outside.

A wide variety of rides, plus zoo and farm, makes a fantastic day out for all ages. Awesome indoor adventure centres, ball blasting arenas, mirror maze and soft play ensures wet days are fun. 16 family rides including white knuckle Swing Ship, electrifying Watercoasters, terrifying Toboggan Run, Superb Falconry Centre, Zoo Farm, tractor ride, weird and wonderful creatures. An all-weather attraction.

Open: 23 March to 3 November 2013 open daily 9.30am. In winter open weekends and local school holidays.

Directions: 5 miles from Dartmouth on A3122. Follow brown tourist signs from A38.

The day in the country that's out of this world! With 5 major rides and loads of great live shows. See Merlin from 'Britain's Got Talent' 5 days a week. All rides and shows included in entrance fee.

Open: daily Easter to October. Please call or check online for full details.

Directions: on the main A39 one mile from Clovelly.

DORSET HEAVY HORSE FARM PARK
Edmondsham Road,
Near Verwood,
Dorset BH21 5RJ
Tel: 01202 824040
www.dorset-heavy-horse-centre.co.uk

READERS' OFFER 2013

£1 off adult ticket. One voucher per person.
Not valid with any other offer or family ticket/concessions

KILLHOPE - THE NORTH OF ENGLAND LEAD MINING MUSEUM
Near Cowshill, Upper Weardale,
Co Durham DL13 1AR
Tel: 01388 537505 • Fax: 01388 537617
e-mail: info@killhope.org.uk
www.killhope.org.uk

READERS' OFFER 2013

2-4-1 (cheapest free) or Like-4-Like
Valid April - October 2013

TWEDDLE CHILDREN'S ANIMAL FARM
Fillpoke Lane, Blackhall Colliery,
Co. Durham TS27 4BT
Tel: 0191 586 3311
e-mail: info@tweddlefarm.co.uk
www.tweddlefarm.co.uk

READERS' OFFER 2013

FREE bag of animal food to every paying customer.
Valid until end 2013

BARLEYLANDS FARM & CRAFT VILLAGE
Barleylands Road, Billericay,
Essex CM11 2UD
Tel: 01268 290223 • Fax: 01268 290222
e-mail: info@barleylands.co.uk
www.barleylands.co.uk

We are
barleylands

READERS' OFFER 2013

FREE entry for one child with each full paying adult. Valid
during 2013 - not with any other offer or on special events days.

Entertainment for all ages: fascinating daily shows, FREE wagon and tractor rides, straw fun barn, go-kart arena, gypsy wagons and Romany talks, blacksmith's workshop. Drive a real tractor, pony rides, 'hands-on' activities with the farm animals, over 20 rescued heavy horses. Lots undercover; cafe and gift shop + much more!

Open: 10am to 5pm Easter to end October.

Directions: On the Edmondsham Road, approx. 1½ miles from Verwood. Within easy reach of Bournemouth, Poole, Southampton, Ringwood and surrounding areas.

FHG GUIDES, ABBEY MILL BUSINESS CENTRE, PAISLEY PA1 1TJ • www.holidayguides.com

---

Killhope is a multi-award winning Victorian Lead Mining Museum, offering a grand day out. Accompany a guide on a mine tour. Our enthusiastic team ensure you have a day to remember, finding minerals, and working as a washerboy. Woodland trails, exhibitions, Killhope shop and cafe complete a great day out.

Open: April-October 10.30am-5pm

Directions: midway between Alston and Stanhope on A689

FHG GUIDES, ABBEY MILL BUSINESS CENTRE, PAISLEY PA1 1TJ • www.holidayguides.com

---

Children's farm and petting centre. Lots of hands on with bottle feeding events and bunny cuddling etc. Indoor and outdoor play areas, indoor and outdoor go-kart tracks, crazy golf, gift shop, tea room and lots more.

Open: March to Oct: 10am-5pm daily; Nov to Feb 10am to 4pm daily. Closed Christmas, Boxing Day and New Year's Day.

Directions: A181 from A19, head towards coast; signposted from there.

FHG GUIDES, ABBEY MILL BUSINESS CENTRE, PAISLEY PA1 1TJ • www.holidayguides.com

---

Set in over 700 acres of unspoilt Essex countryside, this former working farm is one of the county's most popular tourist attractions. The spectacular craft village and educational farm provide the perfect setting for a great day out.

Open: 7 days a week. March to October 10am-5pm; November to February 10am-4pm.

Directions: follow brown tourist signs from A127 and A12.

FHG GUIDES, ABBEY MILL BUSINESS CENTRE, PAISLEY PA1 1TJ • www.holidayguides.com

Learn how traditional cider and perry was made, how the fruit was harvested, milled, pressed and bottled. Walk through original champagne cider cellars, and view 18th century lead crystal cider glasses.

Open:
April to Oct: 10am-5pm Mon-Sat.
Nov to March: 11am-3pm Mon-Sat.

Directions: off A438 Hereford to Brecon road, near Sainsbury's supermarket.

Wildlife park with a variety of species including tigers, mountain lions, meerkats, monkeys and otters. Indoor attractions include Waterworld, Bug City and Ringo's Playbarn.

Open: daily 10am-6pm (until dusk Winter/Spring). November-February closed Tuesday and Wednesday.

Directions: signposted off A10 between Royston and Cambridge. Two minutes from Shepreth rail station on Cambridge - London Kings X line.

The world's largest helicopter collection - over 70 exhibits, includes two royal helicopters, Russian Gunship and Vietnam veterans plus many award-winning exhibits. Cafe, shop. Flights.

PETS MUST BE KEPT UNDER CONTROL

Open: Wednesday to Sunday 10am to 5.30pm. Daily during school Easter and Summer holidays and Bank Holiday Mondays. November to March: 10am to 4.30pm

Directions: Junction 21 off M5 then follow the propellor signs.

The Wedgwood Factory, Visitor Centre and Museum is set in 260 acres of lush parkland. Enjoy a fascinating tour of the ceramic workshops and museum, guided factory tours, and the opportunity to make your own piece of Wedgwood at the home of Britain's greatest ceramic company.

Open: weekdays 10am-5pm weekends 10am-4pm

Directions: from M1 follow A50 west; from M6 follow A34, then brown tourist signs.

FALCONRY UK BIRDS OF PREY CENTRE

Sion Hill Hall, Kirby Wiske
Near Thirsk, North Yorkshire YO7 4EU
Tel: 01845 587522
e-mail: mail@falconrycentre.co.uk
www.falconrycentre.co.uk

READERS'
OFFER
2013

*TWO for ONE on admission to Centre. Cheapest ticket
free with voucher. Valid 1st March to 31st October.*

NOT TO BE USED IN CONJUNCTION WITH ANY OTHER OFFER

MUSEUM OF RAIL TRAVEL

Ingrow Railway Centre, Near Keighley,
West Yorkshire BD21 5AX
Tel: 01535 680425
e-mail: admin@vintagecarriagestrust.org
www.vintagecarriagestrust.org

READERS'
OFFER
2013

"ONE for ONE" free admission
Valid during 2013 except during special events (ring to check)

NOT TO BE USED IN CONJUNCTION WITH ANY OTHER OFFER

RHEILFFORDD TALYLLYN RAILWAY

Gorsaf Wharf Station, Tywyn,
Gwynedd LL36 9EY
Tel: 01654 710472
e-mail: enquiries@talyllyn.co.uk
www.talyllyn.co.uk

RHEILFFORDD
TALYLLYN
RAILWAY

READERS'
OFFER
2013

20% OFF ticket price of full adult round trip
Not valid on special/excursion trains or Christmas services

NOT TO BE USED IN CONJUNCTION WITH ANY OTHER OFFER

INIGO JONES SLATEWORKS

Groeslon, Caernarfon,
Gwynedd LL54 7UE
Tel: 01286 830242
e-mail: slate@inigojones.co.uk
www.inigojones.co.uk

INIGO JONES
Established 1961

READERS'
OFFER
2013

TWO for the price of ONE on self-guided tour.
Valid during 2013

NOT TO BE USED IN CONJUNCTION WITH ANY OTHER OFFER

Birds of prey centre with over 70 birds including owls, hawks, falcons, kites, vultures and eagles. 3 flying displays daily. When possible public welcome to handle birds after each display. No dogs allowed.

Open: 1st March to 31st October 10.30am to 5pm. Flying displays 11.30am, 1.30pm and 3.30pm daily (weather permitting).

Directions: on the A167 between Northallerton and the Ripon turn off. Follow brown tourist signs.

FHG GUIDES, ABBEY MILL BUSINESS CENTRE, PAISLEY PA1 1TJ • www.holidayguides.com

---

A fascinating display of railway carriages and a wide range of railway items telling the story of rail travel over the years.

ALL PETS MUST BE KEPT ON LEADS

Open: daily 11am to 4pm

Directions: approximately one mile from Keighley on A629 Halifax road. Follow brown tourist signs

FHG GUIDES, ABBEY MILL BUSINESS CENTRE, PAISLEY PA1 1TJ • www.holidayguides.com

---

The Talyllyn Railway is a historic narrow-gauge steam railway running through the beautiful mid-Wales countryside, from Tywyn on the coast to the delightful Dolgoch Falls and wooded Nant Gwernol.

Open: daily from Easter to October and at other times of the year. See website for details of timetables.

Directions: on the A493 on the Aberdyfi side of Tywyn, 300 yards from Tywyn mainline rail station and bus stops.

FHG GUIDES, ABBEY MILL BUSINESS CENTRE, PAISLEY PA1 1TJ • www.holidayguides.com

---

A unique, thriving, fully operational slateworks. Enter the workshops for a fascinating and inspiring insight into an ongoing era of techniques and expertise. Self-guided tours including Lettercutting and Calligraphy Exhibitions.

Open: seven days a week 9am-5pm. Closed Christmas/Boxing/New Year's days

Directions: main A487 6 miles south of Caernarfon going towards Porthmadog.

FHG GUIDES, ABBEY MILL BUSINESS CENTRE, PAISLEY PA1 1TJ • www.holidayguides.com

READERS'
OFFER
2013

GWILI RAILWAY
The Railway Station,
Bronwydd Arms,
Carmarthenshire SA33 6HT
Tel: 01267 238213
www.gwili-railway.co.uk

TWO FOR ONE (lowest price ticket free). Valid March-Oct 2013 except Thomas or "Special" events and/or Christmas

---

READERS'
OFFER
2013

THE GRASSIC GIBBON CENTRE
Arbuthnott, Laurencekirk,
Aberdeenshire AB30 1PB
Tel: 01561 361668
e-mail: lgginfo@grassicgibbon.com
www.grassicgibbon.com

TWO for the price of ONE entry to exhibition (based on full adult rate only). Valid during 2013 (not groups)

READERS'
OFFER
2013

BO'NESS & KINNEIL RAILWAY
Bo'ness Station, Union Street,
Bo'ness, West Lothian EH51 9AQ
Tel: 01506 822298
e-mail: enquiries.railway@srps.org.uk
www.bkrailway.com

FREE child train fare with one paying adult/concession. Valid April-Oct 2013. Not Premier Fare events

---

READERS'
OFFER
2013

SCOTTISH DEER CENTRE
Cupar,
Fife KY15 4NQ
Tel: 01337 810391
e-mail: info@tsdc.co.uk
www.tsdc.co.uk

One child FREE with one full paying adult on production of voucher. Not valid during December.

During operating days we provide a trip back in time with a round trip on a steam-hauled locomotive in the scenic Gwili valley.
Pay once and ride all day.
Check website or phone for timetables.

Open: check website or phone for information.

Directions: just off the A484, three miles north of Carmarthen.

Visitor Centre dedicated to the much-loved Scottish writer Lewis Grassic Gibbon. Exhibition, cafe, gift shop. Outdoor children's play area. Disabled access throughout.

Open: daily March to October 10am to 4.30pm. Groups by appointment including evenings.

Directions: on the B967, accessible and signposted from both A90 and A92.

Steam and heritage diesel passenger trains from Bo'ness to Manuel. Explore the history of Scotland's railways in the Museum of Scottish Railways. Coffee shop and souvenir shop.

Open: weekends April to October, most days in July and August.
See website for dates and timetables.

Directions: in the town of Bo'ness. Leave M9 at Junction 3 or 5, then follow brown tourist signs.

55-acre park with 14 species of deer from around the world. Guided tours, trailer rides, treetop walkway, children's adventure playground and picnic area. Other animals include wolves, foxes, otters and a bird of prey centre.

Open: 10am to 5pm daily except Christmas Day and New Year's Day.

Directions: A91 south of Cupar. Take J9 M90 from the north, J8 from the south.

Index of Towns and Counties

Visit the FHG website
www.holidayguides.com
for details of the wide choice of accommodation featured in the full range of FHG titles

404 INDEX OF TOWNS AND COUNTIES

Please note...

All the information in this book is given in good faith in the belief that it is correct. However, the publishers cannot guarantee the facts given in these pages, neither are they responsible for changes in policy, ownership or terms that may take place after the date of going to press. Readers should always satisfy themselves that the facilities they require are available and that the terms, if quoted, still apply.

Accommodation Standards: Star Grading Scheme

The AA, VisitBritain, VisitScotland, and the VisitWales now use a single method of assessing and rating serviced accommodation. Irrespective of which organisation inspects an establishment the rating awarded will be the same, using a common set of standards, giving a clear guide of what to expect.   They have full details of the grading system on their websites.

www.enjoyEngland.com

www.visitScotland.com

www.visitWales.com

www.theaa.com

Using a scale of 1-5 stars the objective quality ratings give a clear indication of accommodation standard, cleanliness, ambience, hospitality, service and food.

This shows the full range of standards suitable for every budget and preference, and allows visitors to distinguish between the quality of accommodation and facilities on offer in different establishments.
All types of board and self-catering accommodation are covered, including hotels, B&Bs, holiday parks, campus accommodation, hostels, caravans and camping, and boats.

Gold and Silver awards are given to Hotels and Guest Accommodation that provide exceptional quality, especially in service and hospitality.

The more stars, the higher level of quality

★
acceptable quality; simple, practical, no frills

★★
good quality, well presented and well run

★★★
very good level of quality and comfort

★★★★
excellent standard throughout

★★★★★
exceptional quality, with a degree of luxury

National Accessible Scheme Logos for mobility impaired and older people

If you have particular mobility impairment. look out for the National Accessible Scheme. You can be confident of finding accommodation or attractions that meet your needs by looking for the following symbols.

Older and less mobile guests
If you have sufficient mobility to climb a flight of steps but would benefit from fixtures and fittings to aid balance.

Part-time wheelchair users
You have restricted walking ability or may need to use a wheelchair some of the time and can negotiate a maximum of 3 steps.

Independent wheelchair users
You are a wheelchair user and travel independently. Similar to the international logo for independent wheelchair users.

Assisted wheelchair users
You're a wheelchair user and travel with a friend or family member who helps you with everyday tasks.

© FHG Guides Ltd, 2013
ISBN 978-1-85055-455-4

Typeset by FHG Guides Ltd, Paisley.
Printed and bound in China by Imago.

Distribution. Book Trade: ORCA Book Services, Stanley House,
3 Fleets Lane, Poole, Dorset BH15 3AJ
(Tel: 01202 665432; Fax: 01202 666219)
e-mail: mail@orcabookservices.co.uk
Published by FHG Guides Ltd., Abbey Mill Business Centre,
Seedhill, Paisley PA1 ITJ (Tel: 0141-887 0428 Fax: 0141-889 7204).
e-mail: admin@fhguides.co.uk

800 Great Places to Stay in Britain is published by FHG Guides Ltd,
part of Kuperard Group.

Cover design: FHG Guides
Cover Picture: with thanks to
      Bosinver Farm Cottages, Trelowth, St Austell, Cornwall (page 166)
      Duddings Country Cottages, Dunster, Somerset (page 188)

symbols

🐕	*Pets Welcome*	🐎	*Children Welcome*
SB	*Short Breaks*	♿	*Suitable for Disabled Guests*
♀	*Licensed*	Wi-Fi	*Wi-Fi available*